SENTINEL

THE U.N. EXPOSED

Veteran newsman Eric Shawn is a senior correspondent and anchor
for the Fox News Channel. He has covered stories everywhere from
the Persian Gulf to Somalia to the White House to the O. J. Simp-
son trial. He lives in New York City with his family. His Web site is
www.ericshawnnewsman.com.

How the

United Nations

Sabotages America's Security

and Fails the World

THE
U.N.
EXPOSED

Eric Shawn

SENTINEL

SENTINEL

Published by the Penguin Group

Penguin Group (USA) Inc., 375 Hudson Street, New York, New York 10014, U.S.A.
Penguin Group (Canada), 90 Eglinton Avenue East, Suite 700, Toronto, Ontario,
Canada M4P 2Y3 (a division of Pearson Penguin Canada Inc.)
Penguin Books Ltd, 80 Strand, London WC2R 0RL, England
Penguin Ireland, 25 St Stephen's Green, Dublin 2, Ireland (a division of Penguin Books Ltd)
Penguin Group (Australia), 250 Camberwell Road, Camberwell, Victoria 3124, Australia
(a division of Pearson Australia Group Pty Ltd)
Penguin Books India Pvt Ltd, 11 Community Centre, Panchsheel Park, New Delhi–110 017,
India
Penguin Group (NZ), cnr Airborne and Rosedale Roads, Albany, Auckland 1310, New Zealand
(a division of Pearson New Zealand Ltd)
Penguin Books (South Africa) (Pty) Ltd, 24 Sturdee Avenue, Rosebank, Johannesburg 2196,
South Africa

Penguin Books Ltd, Registered Offices:
80 Strand, London WC2R 0RL, England

First published in the United States of America by Sentinel, a member of Penguin Group
(USA) Inc. 2006
Published in Penguin Books 2007

10 9 8 7 6 5 4 3 2 1

THE LIBRARY OF CONGRESS HAS CATALOGED THE HARDCOVER EDITION AS FOLLOWS:

Shawn, Eric
The U.N. exposed : how the United Nations sabotages America's security and fails the
world / Eric Shawn.
    p.   cm.
Includes index.
ISBN 1-59523-020-3 (hc.)
ISBN 978-1-59523-033-1 (pbk.)
1. United Nations—United States.   2. National Security—United States.   I. Title.

JZ49997.5.U6S43   2006
341.23'73—dc22   2005056309

Printed in the United States of America / Set in New Caoledonia / Designed by Jamie Putorti

To my great joys, Lisa and Oliver;

and to my father;

*And to those at the U.N. who approach their mission
with heartfelt dedication, dignity, and ethics*

Me: You have said you do not believe Security Council votes were "bought" by Saddam's contracts. Do you believe the billions of dollars that his regime granted to France and Russia . . . influenced their policies and stance against the resulting war? Do you think economic interests influence policies of member states?

Kofi Annan: No comment.

"There never was a time you couldn't buy the board of aldermen."

> —*William Marcy "Boss" Tweed,*
> *Tammany Hall politician,*
> *October 25, 1877*

CONTENTS

viii   Contents

PREFACE

Just four weeks after the 2006 hardcover publication of *The U.N. Exposed*, U.N. Deputy Secretary-General Mark Malloch Brown jerked forcefully on the worsening rift between the United Nations and the United States.

Malloch Brown, serving under outgoing Secretary-General Kofi Annan, who presided over perhaps the most troubled era in U.N. history, publicly blamed the negative image of the U.N. on its "loudest detractors such as Rush Limbaugh and Fox News." He alleged that the U.N.'s positive contributions to the world were kept "a secret in Middle America." Such negativity, he added, unfairly undermines the U.N. and jeopardizes its potential for success.

The United States Ambassador to the U.N., John Bolton, quickly upbraided Malloch Brown for using such a "condescending, patronizing tone about the American people." With the characteristic bluntness for which George W. Bush hired him, Bolton warned, "To have the deputy secretary-general criticize the United States in

x   Preface

such a manner can only do grave harm to the United Nations." And as a member of the media, who reports the facts as they present themselves, I might add that no greater factor has undermined the U.N. more than its own glaring deficits. If the U.N. suffers from credibility problems, then they are of the U.N.'s own making.

Congressman Thaddeus McCotter of "Middle American" Michigan replied to Malloch Brown in language a tad plainer than a career diplomat at the U.N. is probably accustomed to hearing:

> *Dear Mr. Malloch Brown:*
> *We in Middle America never reward a rude beggar. Your problem is not Middle America's ignorance of the U.N.'s virtues; your problem is Middle America's awareness of your vices.*

Vices? One wouldn't know of their existence if he or she relied on the U.N.'s self-projected image. The organization proudly points to its numerous humanitarian programs that deal with hunger, disease, and development, and boasts that its eighteen peacekeeping missions deployed around the globe are enough evidence of its good works and honorable intentions. But, within its walls, its pervasive deficiencies are often dismissed, minimized, or not even addressed.

After an April 2006 appearance at his alma mater, Macalester College in Minnesota, Mr. Annan claimed "the U.N. has received some very unfair and unjustifiable criticism" that he said was part of an "organized political campaign" against it.

"Instances of mismanagement were exaggerated to paint the organization as a den of thieves which is entirely wrong," he protested. This defense deliberately ignores the larger issue of the corruption of the U.N. system as a whole. Financial incentives showered on members of the Security Council from those it is charged with judging (witness the billions from Saddam Hussein, Iran, and Sudan's oil trade with China) have tainted and crippled its leadership. And then there is this disturbing and potentially devastating flaw in the very composition of the organization: Democratic nations that share common ethics and ideals remain in the minority, while terrorism supporting states that defend the killing of civilians as a morally justified political strategy retain their membership and influence inside the world body.

It's seldom acknowledged that Iran was given a twenty-one-year head start by the U.N., and North Korea a ten-year head start, before their nuclear ambitions—potentially aimed at the United States—were even addressed by the Security Council.

It is rarely recognized that, had the Security Council backed up its resolutions against Saddam, absent of course the bribery of some of its members, there is a more than fair chance that there would have been no Iraqi war. It is no wonder that Iran's President Mahmoud Ahmadinejad brands the Council's resolutions "meaningless." He learned well through years of observation.

When the U.N.'s hypocrisies and wrongdoings are exposed in works such as this, U.N. defenders attack those who seek to right the ship. The documented realities of the sort detailed in this book are dismissed by an embattled U.N. coterie as "unchecked U.N.-bashing and stereotyping." That slander is the international body's official defensive line.

Others, however, might view the continued revelations as somber assessments of the facts, and responsible journalistic probing into what are disturbing—and frankly dangerous—truths.

Since *The U.N. Exposed*'s hardcover edition went to press, Americans—who contribute upward of $5.3 billion to the U.N. annually—have continued to receive a dubious return on their money:

Yet another sex scandal involving U.N. peacekeepers materialized, this time involving Liberian girls as young as eight years old.

The U.N.'s Disarmament Commission elected Iran's representative as its Vice Chairman, while Iran was brazenly defying Security Council orders to stop enriching uranium.

The new Human Rights Council, which the U.N. touts as the star of its reform effort, welcomed such human rights abusers as Cuba and China as members.

An independent judicial report concluded that the U.N. "failed to put in place systems which can expose and deter crimes like fraud and sexual abuse, or harassment and discrimination."

The U.N. General Assembly's anti-American bias was starkly revealed when Venezuela's flamboyant president, Hugo Chavez, received warm, enthusiastic, and sustained applause for calling America "the biggest terrorist" and "the greatest threat . . . over our planet, placing at risk the very survival of the human species." He also branded President Bush: a devil, a fascist, an assassin, a dictator, an imperialist, and a genocidal liar.

More than five years after 9/11, nearly one-third of the nations continued to ignore demands for cooperation from the U.N.'s anti-terrorism committee on nuclear proliferation, the Al-Qaeda Committee admitted that 72% (139 out of 192) of U.N. nations failed to file mandatory reports merely detailing their actions against suspected terrorists, and the Counter-Terrorism Committee was still trying to find out what, if anything, U.N. members had done to actually counter terrorism. Even the U.N.'s own top nuclear official, Mohamed ElBaradei, conceded that when it comes to global crises, "too often the Security Council's engagement is inadequate, selective, or after the fact."

Perhaps the corruption, mismanagement, and paralysis that have characterized some of the more recent internal U.N. problems can be effectively dealt with through aggressive reform and higher standards of accountability, though the steps already taken toward these ends have so far proven less than successful. Perhaps the clean slate represented by a new Secretary-General replacing Kofi Annan will facilitate a new era at the World Body.

In these dangerous times, an ethical, fiscally responsible, and effective U.N. would surely do the world good.

Eric Shawn
September 2006

INTRODUCTION

The U.S. Central Command reported that an A-10 Thun-
derbolt II flying close air support for the Baghdad clashes
was shot down by a surface-to-air missile near the U.S.-
occupied Baghdad International Airport, about 10 miles from
the city center. The pilot, who ejected, was recovered and is
listed in good condition, according to Brig. Gen. Vincent K.
Brooks, who briefed reporters at the command's regional
headquarters in Doha, Qatar. Pentagon officials said the A-10
appeared to have been hit by a French-made Roland missile.
         —*William Branigin and Anthony Shadid,*
          The Washington Post,
          April 9, 2003

All he remembers is the jolt. Air National Guard
Major Jim Ewald from the Battle Creek, Michigan, 110th Fighter
Wing, was piloting his A-10 Warthog and had been hit. "Something

reached out and slapped the airplane like the hand of God," Ewald later recalled. His wingman was on the radio.

"Hey, Jim, do you know you were hit by a SAM [surface-to-air missile]?"

"Yeah, I think I figured that out on my own," said Ewald.

What Ewald hadn't figured out, when he told me about his harrowing struggle to keep his wounded craft in the sky, was that the United Nations was responsible for that bolt from the blue.

"I would pull the nose up, and it would pitch down. I was trying to make it go left, and it would go right. I was wrestling with it and using every muscle in my body," he remembers.

And then he thought to himself, "I'm going to leave this airplane right here."

The plane was shuddering so badly that he couldn't focus his eyes on a fixed point. He saw the reflection of flames in the instrument panel, and when he strained to look back, he could see pieces of sheet metal and engine parts falling off. Suddenly, all the oil was gone, and he lost his hydraulics. "The plane went into a flat right spin, and now it's dropping like a rock," he says. "At that point, I was literally out of airspeed, altitude, and ideas."

Ewald punched out.

He blew open the canopy and ejected out of the dying aircraft as it hurtled toward the earth. He landed, lucky to be alive, but in enemy territory. Then he heard voices getting louder as they approached. Hiding in a dry canal, he got his nine-millimeter handgun out and ready. And then he peeked out. His heart sank as he saw his huge, white-and-orange parachute spread all over a field.

"Oh my God," he thought. "They know where I'm at."

And then he heard, "Hey, pilot dude! We're Americans!"

Says Ewald, "Only one of ours would ever call me dude. That's when I knew I was safe."

The thirty-seven-year-old married bomber pilot and father of three had nearly been killed by a missile manufactured by France—America's supposed ally. The weapon, believed to be a

Roland surface-to-air missile, was likely one of many in the Iraqi inventory bought with the only revenue available to the Hussein regime while the sanctions following the first Gulf War were in place: Revenue from the oil he sold under the U.N.-supervised Oil for Food program or that he received with the permission of the Security Council. Revenue that was supposed to be used exclusively to feed his people, not to buy French-made missiles to shoot down Americans.

The manufacturer of the Roland missile, the French defense firm Thales, then called Thomson, denies that it sold weapons illegally to Iraq while U.N. sanctions were in place against Saddam's regime, pointing out that the company had ceased manufacturing the missile years before. But we do know that the Iraqis were trying to buy spare Roland missile parts just three weeks before the war started on March 19, 2003, just forty days before Major Ewald was blown out of the sky.

The CIA Iraq Survey Group report by Charles Duelfer states quite clearly that Iraq was attempting to purchase "replacement parts for the Roland II surface to air missile system, valves for Iraq's air defense system, and various other high technology items with military and battlefield applications." The report continues, "These efforts were under way with Majda Khasem Al-Khalil [a Lebanese female] who in turn met with the French Thomson Company representatives. [We] found evidence of coordination on this procurement up until 23 days before OIF [Operation Iraqi Freedom]."

There seems to be no doubt that a missile manufactured by a United Nations Security Council member and bought by a tyrant through U.N.-regulated oil revenues was fired at a brave pilot from the Midwest.

The target himself is philosophical.

"It does make me angry but doesn't surprise me," says Major Ewald now. "You can't give a foreign country the benefit of the doubt that they are on our side. If they provided material or moral support to a tyrant, they need to look at themselves and reassess what they were doing. Because if they continue on that path they will be as divided as they were in the 1930s and will meet the same fate." Ewald believes America needs the United Nations but not one that, as he puts it, is "being exploited" by its own members. "Obviously," he says, "it has a serious flaw." That flaw nearly killed him.

That a United Nations Security Council member—France—would help Saddam Hussein acquire weapons used to wage war on Americans is tough for even the most pro-U.N. observers to stomach. It is one of the most glaring illustrations of how the U.N. has jeopardized the very nation whose taxpayers fund approximately $3.5 billion for the U.N. system each year.

And then there is the indigestible fact that the reason the United States had to go to war in Iraq at all was in large part because the United Nations had failed to do its job. The U.N. permitted Saddam to stall and to ignore resolution after resolution as he anticipated the day sanctions would be dropped, the day that would allow him to resume his WMD programs unencumbered by any constraints. Immediately after the war started in March 2003, Hans Blix, the top U.N. weapons inspector, told me the world would not know the truth about Saddam's capabilities "until American soldiers reach the basements of Baghdad." This from the very man who should have been able to fully and successfully implement the Security Council's resolutions.

The United Nations is broken. That is no longer a partisan issue.

Liberals have joined conservatives to question how that noble institution, the repository of good intentions, has devolved into a global version of a crooked city hall tainted by what the chief U.N. investigator of the Oil for Food scandal branded "illicit, unethical, and corrupt behavior." U.N. complicity, profiteering, malfeasance, and ignorance granted Saddam Hussein a free pass for more than a decade. This crime has emerged as the greatest grand larceny in history, a monumental violation of trust by the majority of the permanent members of the U.N. Security Council: France, Russia, and

China. Saddam Hussein, through the Oil for Food program administered by the Security Council, was enabled to remain in power and to foster ill will against the United States at the U.N. With the exception of Great Britain, our so-called allies in the Security Council were bribed to realize Saddam's designs, until this fleecing was brought to a halt by the U.S. military-led intervention in Iraq that has incurred enormous costs to the American taxpayer and, more dearly, to the American soldier and thousands of Iraqi civilians.

The U.N. should not be forgiven for its role in the war simply because democratic elections have finally been held in Iraq. Americans deserve answers from the occupants of that rectangular building overlooking New York City's East River.

This is not the U.N. that most of us believed in when we were growing up. Like many kids, I went out trick-or-treating on Halloween, collecting money for the United Nations Children's Fund. In 1966, I had $39 in coins and dollar bills in my orange box, and I was proud to win the fourth-grade UNICEF contest. Even at that age, I understood that the U.N. was meant to embody world peace and cooperation, ideals that I believed would save the world.

A few years later, when my school held its Model U.N., I was the ambassador from Tunisia. We debated international issues such as trying to end the Cold War. Afterwards, as we toured the real U.N., I searched in vain for the Tunisian table in the General Assembly, pretending that that would have been my spot on the world stage.

The U.N. was once in vogue. It represented compassion and goodness. That is the U.N. I grew up with and supported.

Then the U.N. fell from grace, and it has been a decline of its own making. As a reporter covering the internal workings of the world body, I have witnessed how the U.N. has too often betrayed the tenets of its founding, violated its mission, sabotaged American security, and failed the world. The threats we face have not been resolved in the forum that was designed to confront them. For example:

- Terrorism is not a U.N. priority. The majority of its members are focused on "development," diplomat-speak for increasing the amount of money coming into their own nations. Terrorism—even though it should be the most pressing international issue of the twenty-first century—is simply not on most U.N. agendas.

- The United States is compromised. The United States funds a whopping 22 percent of the U.N.'s $3.6 billion budget, pays 27 percent of an additional $3.6 billion in peacekeeping operation costs, and provides billions more for U.N. agencies and related operations each year. And yet the U.N. has become the coliseum for confronting and opposing the United States. With the end of the Cold War and the rise of one lone superpower, the United States's veto-wielding rivals press their agendas at our expense and maneuver for their own advantages, not ours.

- The United Nations Security Council guaranteed insecurity for the Iraqis and an unstable and untenable environment for American and British forces attempting to enforce the council's mandates from 1991, when Saddam surrendered in the Gulf War, to the 2003 invasion made necessary by the U.N.'s malfeasance. Had the council and the U.N. held to moral principles and enforced their resolutions and requirements, the war could have been prevented. There would have been clarity, not confusion, regarding Saddam's possession of WMD. His corruption and bribery of the council created conditions of uncertainty that empowered his regime.

- The same mistakes are now being repeated elsewhere. The U.N. is incapable of effectively resolving the nuclear threats posed by Iran and North Korea, member states that have, in some cases, lied to U.N. officials, including those of the International Atomic Energy Agency, or, in other cases, ignored their requests.

- While the U.N.'s humanitarian programs are rightfully praised for providing food, shelter, and medicine to millions of the world's needy, they have now also come under questioning and criticism. The U.N.'s own independent investigation headed by former U.S. Federal Reserve Board Chairman Paul Volcker found that even the gems of the U.N. system, such as the World Food Program, the World Health Organization, and UNICEF, operated in Iraq with "little transparency and oversight" amid evidence of "gross mismanagement." (UNICEF claims 88 percent of its donations go to needy children. But a study by the American Institute of Philanthropy claims the actual amount is 54 percent. Compare this to the American Red Cross, which delivers 91 percent of its public donations to those who need it. The Red Cross earns an A from the American Institute of Philanthropy. UNICEF only made a grade of C.)

- Even the amount of U.N. spending on staff salaries, administrative costs, and expenses for its tsunami response was criticized as overly excessive. A *Financial Times* analysis in December 2005 revealed that up to one-third of the U.N.'s tsunami donations were plowed into the U.N. bureaucracy, and the paper said that several U.N. agencies refused to provide an accounting of their expenditures.

"Americans have always hoped and wanted the United Nations to play a major role in the pursuit of a better world," proclaimed former Democratic Senator George Mitchell, who chaired a task force with former Republican House Speaker Newt Gingrich that recommended an overhaul of the crippled institution that is currently incapable of fulfilling those hopes. Gingrich makes clear that the U.N.'s most pressing challenge is global security, but he has warned, "Time is on the side of the evil." He says that the threat of Islamic terrorism "is gradually and inexorably building around this planet" as the diplomats delay. "The longer we use words to disguise and to hide and to avoid, the greater the danger that regimes are going to end up using weapons of mass destruction, and then we will look back with horror at events that are radically more dangerous than

9/11. . . . I'm really worried about the Iranians. [They] are being about as clear as they can humanly be. They get nukes, they intend to wipe out Israel." The Security Council has taken, he said, "no action that has any meaning in the real world. If we lose Tel Aviv one morning, looking back on a U.N. Security Council resolution will not be very useful."

"How many meetings of the Security Council to arrange a meeting do we need?" he asks.

I join countless others in profound disillusionment that a noble ideal has morphed into a bastion of arrogance and, too often, inaction. And I am disgusted by the fact that the altruistic efforts of so many U.N. staff members are undercut by the greed, corruption, and ineptitude of the bureaucracy they serve. I am also astounded by the reaction of self-proclaimed U.N. supporters who continue to accuse those who expose the U.N.'s dysfunction of being "anti-U.N." On the contrary, I would submit that the most proactive step a journalist can take to initiate positive change is to expose truths, albeit sometimes painful ones. Indeed, it is precisely this sense of mission—to enlighten, inform, and ideally be the catalyst for change—that is at the heart of the journalist's calling.

If the U.N. is to reclaim relevance and moral authority, it must engage in self-reflection and reform of the most aggressive kind. Before it takes on the world, I suggest the diplomats start with themselves and examine what really goes on inside the building, inside U.N. World.

– 1 –

WELCOME TO U.N. WORLD

"**W**elcome." *"Bonjour." "Zdravstvyti."*

The tour guides, attractive young women for the most part, from many different countries, embody the ideal of the United Nations. Like flight attendants from the optimistic sixties, they dress in crisp blue uniforms to lead groups on a nostalgic tour of a United Nations that only exists in the imagination—particularly the imaginations of the people who work there.

"This is the Security Council, where the big, important decisions are made for world security. . . ." "This is the General Assembly, a forum for cooperation where all the nations can come together in the main organ of the United Nations. . . ."

If only they could tell you the real story: "The Security Council is usually paralyzed by dissention among its five permanent members, and the ten temporary ones serve as window dressing. . . ."

"The General Assembly is an insular echo chamber that approves many useless, unenforceable declarations; and by the way,

ladies and gentlemen, you are standing in the world legislature that
has the distinction of being so dysfunctional it has been unable to
agree on a definition of *terrorism* for three decades, let alone chart
an effective response against it. . . ."

You'll never hear the truth from the tour guides. For the $11.50
admission, they are still selling the U.N. fantasy in thirteen lan-
guages. Sam Sassounian was having none of it.

"What about all the money we send here?" he was asking. The
seventy-two-year-old retired construction manager from Pasadena,
California, was sitting with about a dozen members of his tour
group in the visitors' gallery of the General Assembly chamber, peppering the guide with queries sharper than those put to the institution by most of the diplomats themselves. The young lady stood
smiling, gently and graciously countering Sam's grilling. He was
hard to miss, this Sam, a gray-haired man dressed in a seersucker
jacket over a T-shirt emblazoned with the red-white-and-blue
American flag and the words LAND OF THE FREE, HOME OF THE
BRAVE.

"We're the biggest supporters but we don't get what we want,"
Sam complained. "We're spending so much money here when we
have our own needs."

"I understand," replied the tour guide, trying to use Sam's dissention as a talking point. "Everybody has their own point of view
and it's welcome. That is what also happens here in the General Assembly." Born in Lebanon, Sam became a naturalized American citizen when he was twenty years old in 1953. He obviously had a love
for his adopted country that drove him to give the only representative of the U.N. to whom he had access, a twenty-something beauty
from Colombia, a bit of a hard time. "I don't think the U.N. war-
rants the expense," he later told me, unconvinced.

Sam's disappointment in the U.N. is reflected in national polls.
At the end of 2004, a poll conducted by the Center for Individual
Freedom Foundation found 52.1 percent of Americans believed the
U.N. was "anti-American," while 27.3 percent did not—a margin of

nearly two to one. This view cuts across ideological lines. Perhaps predictably, conservatives were the most disappointed in the world body, with 61 percent of them saying it was anti-American, and 23 percent saying it is pro-American. But moderates were 52 percent to 27 percent on the question, and even more liberals than not believed the U.N. was anti-American, 41 percent to 36 percent.

HOW U.N. WORLD HANDLES TERRORISM

The myth of the U.N. begins before the official tour starts. As the visitors gather in the information booth area where they can snap pictures standing against tapestries depicting the Secretaries-General or, for $14.95, purchase U.N. stamps personalized with their own photographs, there is a somber reminder of the U.N.'s failings. A blue-and-white U.N. flag that flew over the Baghdad headquarters at the Canal Hotel is mounted on a wall behind Plexiglas. The white leaves and globe of the U.N. symbol are tattered by shrapnel from the terrorist attack on August 19, 2003, that took the lives of twenty-two U.N. employees—including the highly respected, beloved, and dynamic personal representative of the Secretary-General, Sergio Vieira de Mello—and wounded 150 others.

The flag honors the sacrifice of those who lost their lives on the most horrific day in the U.N.'s history, and while the uninitiated observe a monument of reverence and respect, one might more appropriately view the flag with its holes as an unintentional symbol of U.N. failure.

Those terrorists could have been prevented from striking if the U.N. weren't rife with abject incompetence. A U.N. report issued two months after that bloody day cited "dysfunctional" security, the "failure of U.N. management and staff to comply with standard security regulations and directives," and "the lack of a culture of accountability" at the U.N. A professional security assessment had never been conducted, and staff "ignored basic security instructions," the report found.

Furthermore, U.N. officials had actually ordered the American military to leave and to stop protecting their compound. The Second Armored Cavalry had been posted in the building when the U.N. retook possession but were kicked out except for an antiaircraft crew. Even the American soldiers who were posted outside were told to withdraw, out of the U.N.'s fear that insurgents would consider the U.N. complicit with an American-led invasion the Security Council had not countenanced. The five-ton U.S. military truck and other heavy equipment that protected the entrance road to the building rumbled off, the rooftop observation post was dismantled, and the obstructions and barbed wire on the access road that ran alongside the building were taken down.

That shortsightedness left the building completely vulnerable, and it enabled the terrorists to drive a heavy orange-and-brown truck right up to the side to detonate a devastating 2,200-pound mix of explosives and metal right under—not coincidentally—the windows of de Mello's office.

The U.N. failed to provide the basics for its own people. Simple, standard precautions such as installing window protection film designed to stop lethal flying glass were not taken, even though the U.N.'s World Food Program had offered to pay for it. U.N. security officials were told the week before the bombing that an attack was "imminent." Yet they did not ask the American military to return. The security update for that very morning warned of the possibility of a truck bomb.

The U.N.'s mishandling of its darkest day is typical of how it deals with threats to global security. It bungles by ignoring the warnings, fumbling the strategy, and trusting the enemy. There was wide speculation that the attack was an "inside job." Instead of providing its own security, the U.N. had simply relied on the same local Iraqi guards that had enforced Saddam's will before the war, when the building was also used as the U.N.'s Baghdad headquarters.

The truck itself turned out to be an ironically apt symbol of the U.N.'s problems. Said the report, "It is believed that it was owned by the former regime in Iraq and used by the Government in the Oil for Food program."

The leadership at the U.N., in its institutional narcissism, refused to see its own shortcomings. Though Secretary-General Kofi Annan did not directly blame the United States for the attack, he did fault Washington for not providing a safe environment in the war zone, and suggested that the ultimate responsibility for the U.N.'s protection lay not with itself but with the American military. He also said U.N. officials should not have been allowed, presumably by the Americans, to turn down U.S. protection. The day after the attack, but before the U.N.'s culpability was revealed, Annan proclaimed that "the coalition forces have the responsibility for law and order, and have the responsibility of establishing a secure environment." He said the Security Council should authorize a force that would have the responsibility of protecting the U.N. personnel. If Annan or the Security Council had seen to it that the personnel already charged with that responsibility were actually doing their jobs, the attack might have been prevented.

Perhaps pointing at America has become a routine and reflexive response whenever the organization's shortcomings are exposed. The assignment of blame, however, turned out to be entirely wrongheaded once the facts of the U.N.'s malfeasance were made public. But then there seems to be little acknowledgment of the truth when it comes to U.N. mythmaking.

The U.N. comprises the smallest international territory, an enclave of only eighteen acres with immunity from the laws and tax liabilities of the nation in which it is based, a country that provides its sustenance while also serving as its most convenient punching bag. From within the soaring green glass-and-marble landmark of U.N. headquarters comes what its founders called the hope of mankind.

In some ways the United Nations does serve that purpose. It is the arena where all governments—grand democracies and criminal dictatorships, historic republics and newly minted nations—can

gather on an equal footing. But it is more than a little odd, notes former U.S. Ambassador Richard Williamson, that the United States
has the same voting strength as each of three nations whose entire
populations could fit into the MCI Center to watch the Washington
Wizards play basketball in our nation's capital. Welcome to U.N.
World.

Even Kofi Annan, as ringleader of U.N. World, had admitted
the futility of so much diplomatic drivel. "This hall has heard
enough high sounding declarations to last us for some decades to
come," admitted the Secretary-General when he introduced his
plan to try and reform the place in March 2005 and derisively characterized the endless pabulum. "Quite frankly, as it is now, they
spend lots of time discussing issues that are of interest only to those
in the room and have no impact on most of the people outside the
General Assembly and this building." U.N. World is staffed with a
population of well-meaning humanitarians dominated by a cadre of
politically savvy diplomats secure in their individual sinecures.

U.N. World itself has been under assault lately, the result of its
inability to fulfill expectations compounded by scandal and incompetence.

On June 24, 2005, Kofi Annan reflected on the U.N.'s founding
tenets in *The Wall Street Journal*. "Idealism and aspiration for the
U.N. have always outstripped its actual performance," he said. "For
sixty years Americans—conservatives and liberals alike—have expected much from the U.N. Too often, we have failed to meet those
expectations."

In U.N. World, despots and dictators, terrorists and war lords,
criminal regimes and rogue states have been allowed to threaten
their own people and others, undermining world stability and especially endangering the interests and security of the United States
and its allies.

There is perhaps no more troubling example of how the U.N. lost
its way than its handling of Iraq after the first Persian Gulf war. During the twelve years of wrangling that led up to the 2003 invasion by

American and British troops, Saddam Hussein neutered the U.N., successfully frustrating its intentions. American troops are in Iraq because the Security Council failed its fundamental duty to enforce its own mandates. And that makes the U.N. complicit in Saddam's crimes. Saddam bribed France, Russia, and China using the billions of dollars the U.N. handed him from the Oil for Food program. He fought for years within the Security Council governing body that ran the program, the Iraq Sanctions Committee (known as the 661 Committee after the resolution that created it), to ease and remove sanctions. The diplomats continually gave Saddam a pass.

Even when there appears to be unity on the Security Council, it is illusory.

On November 8, 2002, the council unanimously passed resolution 1441, calling on Iraq to fully comply with the council's demands, but it turned out to be nothing more than smoke and mirrors. All fifteen nations, including temporary member Syria, stood together declaring that Iraq was in "material breach" of its U.N. obligations and had not accounted for its weapons of mass destruction. It warned of "serious consequences" if Saddam did not comply. The Iraqis did not. But the façade of strong U.N. determination was as thin as rice paper. "Serious consequences" meant different things to different nations. France, Russia, and China accepted the term as meaning the council would, yet another time, consider what to do next if Saddam did not behave—again. The United States and Britain took it to mean that the consequences would be military action. Even when faced with repeated violations of its own purpose, the U.N. was incapable of acting, because the member nations put their own interests first.

American taxpayers foot the largest share of the U.N.'s bill, and are asked by U.N. officials to kick in much more. But American lives have been lost because of U.N. intransigence, and the U.N.'s Oil for Food resources have been used by insurgents to kill American troops and innocent Iraqis.

The U.N. is an arena where America's interests are often of no consequence; it serves as the last venue where the world's only su-perpower can be defeated—as the United States repeatedly has been. This should be no surprise. The U.N.'s track record is replete with its demands ignored, mandates dismissed, and rulings violated.

On October 15, 1999, the Security Council unanimously ap-proved resolution 1267. It demanded that the Taliban in Afghanistan immediately turn over Osama bin Laden for prosecution, a result of Al Qaeda's deadly bombings of the U.S. embassies in Africa a year earlier. The council declaration achieved the same results as if it had been issued by the Kiwanis Club of Cleveland. It was ignored.

If U.N. resolution 1267 had actually been enforced, perhaps 9/11 would not have occurred. It was passed nearly two years before that cataclysmic day. Had the Security Council been taken seriously by its own member states, the threat posed by Al Qaeda may not have matured, or at least not to the degree that it did. True, Ameri-cans were failed by our own government as well, but the failure of the world institution with respect to Al Qaeda calls into question its very reason for being.

In fact, the U.N. seemed to bend over backwards to accommo-date Bin Laden's sponsors. The Taliban's United Nations ambassador, Abdul Hakeem Mujahid, was not recognized or allowed to be seated, largely at the behest of the United States. But many U.N. officials re-portedly disagreed with that decision and publicly sought the Tal-iban's inclusion. On September 30, 1998, *The New York Times* said, "U.N. officials . . . believe that international recognition might change the movement's distrust and hostility toward the outside world."

How naïve. In early 2001, the Taliban did throw somebody out of Afghanistan, but it wasn't Bin Laden, as the U.N. demanded. They kicked out the U.N. The move was in retaliation for Washing-ton's order to close down the Taliban's diplomatic office in New York. The U.N. argued against that Bush administration decision, and the Taliban was forced to consider renting office space inside the U.N. building itself as an alternative.

Nearly a year and a half after the Security Council demanded that the Taliban cough up Bin Laden, Kofi Annan sat down with Taliban representatives during a visit to Pakistan. He asked them to abide by the Security Council's demand to turn over the terrorist mastermind. Yet like the U.N.'s most prestigious body, Annan achieved nothing. Back at U.N. headquarters Annan didn't want to discuss his Osama talks. On March 22, 2001, less than six months before 9/11, Annan admitted, "It came up, but I don't want to go into that." So much for the U.N.'s moral authority.

The U.N. response to September 11 proved as weak as its efforts to rein in the Taliban before September 11. On September 28, 2001, more than two weeks after the attack (which could be seen from the U.N.'s own offices), the Security Council passed resolution 1374, which established the specific Counter-Terrorism Committee (CTC). The CTC requires that the nations of the U.N. do not financially support terrorist groups, do not offer safe haven for terrorists, cooperate with other nations in prosecuting terrorists, and bring terrorists to justice. The fact that some members need such reminding speaks volumes about their intentions. "We all have a stake in this struggle," declared Kofi Annan, "and we must all feel that we are a part of it."

A special U.N. Al Qaeda committee was also established to monitor Bin Laden's network. "The world expects the United Nations to exercise leadership in the global campaign against terrorism," trumpeted a 2004 Security Council resolution. If the world knew better, it wouldn't.

Despite the urgency, fewer than half of United Nations members had bothered to file the required paperwork on time, forms that merely reported what the nations were supposedly doing to fight terrorism. A U.N. committee concluded that the world body's reaction to terrorist threats had negligible accomplishments and was failing. The committee admitted that only 93 of the 191 U.N. members had even filed the basics, blaming a "lack of political will, reporting fatigue, lack of resources and technical capacity and coordination of difficulties at the national level." Although all agreed that Al Qaeda remained "a major threat to international peace and security," more nations than not seemed to care less. "We need member states to deliver appropriate information to our committee," pleaded its chairman, Chilean Ambassador Heraldo Munoz, who asked that the nations also "improve the quality of information." Bin Laden, from his cave, managed to outflank the diplomats in the carpeted Security Council chamber in New York.

The report also concluded that Al Qaeda had shown great flexibility and stayed ahead of the council's own efforts, which included the freezing of assets of suspected terrorist financiers and operatives, and that U.N. antiterrorism measures had little impact. The report concluded that the prospect of a dirty-bomb attack was of grave concern. Yet the majority of U.N. members refused to follow through on the terrorist threat. They failed to conform to minimum requirements. If U.N. members do not listen to their own institution, why should Bin Laden and his brethren? Or anybody else?

The U.N.'s Al Qaeda committee held a major briefing on the threats of Bin Laden's network and what the U.N. could do about it on February 18, 2004. Fewer than half its members even bothered to attend. Only 70 nations out of 191 sent representatives to the gathering.

But still fewer diplomats sought out private Al Qaeda briefings when offered the chance. Although the Al Qaeda committee provided the opportunity to hold meetings "for more in-depth discussion of relevant issues," no one showed up. Not one person. "Throughout 2004, no Member States availed themselves of this opportunity, despite the Chairman's frequent appeals to States to do so," said the committee's report. There was hope: one meeting with a United Nations diplomat had been set for 2005.

While the U.N. has added to the list of people and entities whose terror-related assets have supposedly been frozen, the Al Qaeda committee admitted in its 2004 report that the U.N.'s efforts at tackling the terrorist group were fairly useless. "The sanctions regime imposed by the Security Council had had a limited impact, most notably owing to the constantly evolving structure of the Al

Qaeda network," said the report. The travel ban on the list of Al Qaeda operatives or associates "appeared to have little or no effect . . . because Member States were unsure what to do when a listed individual was stopped."

Even the results of finding and freezing accounts were unknown. "It is not clear from all reports of asset freezing, for example, what those assets are, their value, or who owns them," the report went on to admit. "[It has] been hard to tell what this means."

The U.N. examination of its antiterrorism failures found that three years after the Security Council imposed a travel ban on Al Qaeda and Taliban members and associates, not one U.N. member reported a violation—an absurd conclusion considering that the U.N. admitted it was difficult to believe terrorist supporters had never crossed any border. The Counter-Terrorism Committee seemed to fare no better. It took several years to get fully up and running with its own staff. One reason, conceded the pro-U.N. United Nations Association of the United States of America (UNA-USA), was that it "was established with no funding line, and the zero growth cap on U.N. budgets makes it doubtful that it will have much staffing." It wasn't until the fall of 2005 that the CTC was fully staffed with forty-one employees, creating a backlog of reports.

Only in U.N. World would the select group of experts assembled to confront the most perilous threat facing the globe admit they have no power, can't achieve much of anything, and only serve to monitor the progress or lack of it among member nations. "The counterterrorism committee emphatically insists it is not an enforcement body. It doesn't threaten states for noncompliance and it doesn't sanction them," says the UNA–USA. The administrative office was established in a New York City landmark, the Chrysler Building, an exclusive address where the average rent is about $60 per square foot. The offices were impressively named the Counter-Terrorism Committee Executive Directorate. But the committee continued to lament the fact that seventy-one nations still hadn't handed in all their reports on time.

In December 2005, a suicide bomber from Islamic Jihad struck a mall in Netyna, Israel, killing five innocent civilians and wounding thirty-five others. The United States moved quickly in the Security Council to condemn yet another terrorist act, but was defeated. Ambassador Abduallah Baali of Algeria, the only Arab member of the council, with others refused to go along. Baali also happened at the same time to serve as a vice chairman of the CTC. He objected to a resolution telling the Syrian government to stop supporting terrorist groups. He objected to criticizing the murderous Islamic Jihad. He objected to a statement that would have denounced "all forms of terrorism." And these are the people the U.N. sees fit to run its so-called *Counter*-Terrorism Committee.

Sadly, the CTC has a better record than the U.N. terrorism body that is supposed to combat the proliferation of weapons of mass destruction. By mid-2006, the 1540 Committee, named after the Security Council resolution that created it, still hadn't even heard anything from sixty-two countries, nearly 30 percent of the U.N.'s members, or received enough information from eighty-three others.

"We really must make counterterrorism the top priority. It is not enough to pay lip service to it," pleaded an American diplomat, Nicholas Rostow, the general counsel of the U.S. Mission. While he boasted that the committee opened "an ongoing dialogue" with member states regarding terrorism, and that its efforts had led to the "freezing or seizing of more than $100 million that might have been available to Al Qaeda or the Taliban," the U.N.'s own reports clearly contradict those claims of success. And as Rostow addressed the Security Council, he conceded the U.N.'s failure to confront terrorism in other areas. "Over the past few years, the Council repeatedly has called on its counterterrorism-related committees and their respective staff bodies to coordinate, cooperate, and collaborate. These calls have yet to result in significant action and change in operations. Much more needs to be done."

When it comes to terrorism, the place just doesn't work. The U.N. terrorism agencies are dysfunctional and ineffective, and, what's worse, have ignored demands to straighten themselves out. The Security Council calls on the U.N.'s own apparatus to do something, and is ignored by the very officials charged with carrying out counterterrorism mandates. How about that for a competent counterterrorism strategy?

But it gets worse.

"There remains resistance to outlawing terrorism in all circumstances," declared Rostow. In other words, some in the U.N. still endorse terrorism. Rostow asked, "Are they going to drain the swamp in which terrorists swim by arresting and prosecuting anyone who commits a terrorist act or supports it? Are they going to do so even if it seems to impugn a cause with which they agree?"

Fat chance when Syria actually sits in on the counterterrorism meetings.

The quickest way for the diplomats to expose and stop terrorists would be to look to the guy in the suit on their right. Ask Syrian Ambassador Fayssal Mekdad, who defended terrorism while attending the Security Council gathering. "His country distinguished terrorism from the legitimate struggle of all people under occupation to liberate themselves," read the report of the meeting, a standard defense for killing people usually used by the Arab block against Israel. In Syria's case, it could also be applied to the insurgents flooding across its borders to kill our troops in Iraq as well as the network of terrorist financing and support the U.S. government claims flourishes with Syria's consent and assistance. Mekdad's pronouncements supporting violence during a U.N. Security Council meeting could also offer justifications for actions by Al Qaeda and other Islamic terrorists. Since such groups believe the infidels have occupied Muslim land, Mekdad's rationale could validate Al Qaeda's intentions.

Israeli ambassador Dan Gillerman responded by pointedly attacking what he called Syria's "selective mode" of arresting terrorists. He criticized nations such as Syria, Iran, and others "who were able, but unwilling, to confront terrorism" and used terrorism "as a way of waging their own wars by proxy."

But perhaps no one could turn the Security Council antiterrorism efforts into a farce better than Venezuelan ambassador Fermin Toro Jimenez. He said that while "Venezuela had condemned terrorism . . . it recognized those that were fighting for sovereignty, liberation and respect for human rights," saying the victims had entered into a rebellion against such "tragedies" as "capitalism."

Turning the fight against terrorism from the terrorists to the targets seems to be a U.N. specialty. When the U.N. announced its investigation of terrorism and human rights in the fall of 2005, the discredited Human Rights Committee chose at first not to investigate Iran, Syria, North Korea, or even the terrorist networks in Iraq and Al Qaeda—but rather the United States and Britain.

The General Assembly passed its Declaration on Measures to Eliminate International Terrorism on December 9, 1994, a resolution endorsed by some of the same states that took daily measures to support international terrorism. Yet the U.N. had been unable to accept or endorse a comprehensive treaty on terrorism, a stark and glaring failure that defies its mandate to secure international peace and security.

The separate attempt to draft a "comprehensive convention on international terrorism" had been stalled since 1996 because of the inability to clarify what actually constitutes a terrorist act. Some nations argued that the definition could apply to the American-led invasion of Iraq. During the summit in September 2005, President Bush challenged the delegates to "put every nation on record—the targeting and deliberate killing of civilians and non-combatants by terrorists cannot be justified or legitimized by any cause or grievance." Although the U.N. took what—for it—was the brave step of condemning terrorism in all forms, some nations, specifically the Arab block, sought to exempt terrorists who kill in the name of "colonial domination and foreign occupation," a barb often aimed at Israel, but one that can also be interpreted as condoning attacks on American forces in Iraq. Only in U.N. World would the diplomats wrangle over who is and who is not appropriate to incinerate.

Ultimately, U.N. action on terrorism has amounted to more talk than anything else. The U.N. has passed thirteen conventions against terrorism, including the International Convention on Suppression of Acts of Nuclear Terrorism, which makes it illegal to possess a nuclear device or radioactive material for a dirty bomb. Surely terrorists will think twice now that the U.N. has decreed their activities against the law.

Talk is cheap in most circumstances, but when it comes from the U.N. on the topic of terrorism, its value dips a little more. The U.N. tries to talk tough about terrorism now, but it has actually spawned a culture of sympathy and support for terrorism since 1974, when Yassar Arafat, pistol in his holster, took the podium of the peace-loving General Assembly and spoke of diplomacy as "enhancements of armed struggle." He was praised as if he were a legitimately elected leader of a nation and not a terrorist mastermind whose Black September group had just one year before murdered an American diplomat, Cleo Noel (who was attending a party at the Saudi Embassy in the Sudan), as well as being responsible for countless other terrorist acts both already committed and still to come.

The U.N. granted the PLO "observer status" on a par with the Vatican's Holy See. Arafat had installed his nephew, Dr. Nasser Al-Kidwa, as the representative. It seems almost remarkable that, considering the U.N.'s coziness with the late Arafat, the pronouncements of Bin Laden haven't received similar reverence.

The General Assembly, after all, had endorsed violence by giving freedom fighters a forum from which to spread their philosophy. The Palestinian refugee camps run by the United Nations Relief Works Agency (UNRWA) have been breeding grounds for terrorists, with many reports of UNRWA workers supporting Hamas and Islamic Jihad. In the Jenin camp, diplomats infamously alleged that the Israeli troops engaged in a massacre of innocent Palestinian refugees, a claim the U.N. investigated and eventually dismissed in one of its own reports.

While the Security Council would routinely condemn terrorism, the actual resolutions and pronouncements emanating from Muslim and sympathetic Arab quarters inside the U.N. could serve to reinforce it. The General Assembly endorsed violence through the 1980s when it urged people to use "all available means, including armed struggle," to oppose "colonial and foreign domination."

"The Arab group and the nonaligned movement keep insisting on refighting this battle about national liberation movements," says a senior Bush administration official, voicing frustration that a definition specifically denouncing terrorist acts that kill civilians remains unpassed. The U.N., he says, is "not focusing on what to do about terrorism. It's still trying to define good terrorism versus bad terrorism, and it's just not acceptable."

In April 2002, the U.N.'s Organization of the Islamic Conference declared, "We reject any attempt to associate Islamic states or Palestinian and Lebanese resistance with terrorism," thereby giving implicit approval to terrorist acts from groups such as Hamas and Hezbollah. Notorious Syria, listed by the U.S. Department of State as one of the nations supporting terrorism, sat on the Security Council during the Iraq war debate and serves as a major support structure for the insurgency.

"Syrians are increasing assistance to foreign fighters preparing to enter Iraq and kill civilians and U.S. troops," reported the *Washington Times*'s Rowan Scarborough in July 2005. "Syrians are also providing barracks-like housing as the recruits from Saudi Arabia, Yemen, Morocco, and other Muslim countries prepare for a jihad or holy war. The fighters also receive weapons, training, and money in Syria."

In U.N. World, terrorists are given the benefit of the doubt.

Hezbollah is "a force in society that one will have to factor in as we implement the resolution" on Syria, proclaimed Kofi Annan, recognizing and granting legitimacy to a group the Department of State has blamed for killing hundreds of innocents in Israel, including nearly three hundred American citizens. Hezbollah has American blood on its hands—and Annan shakes them.

Annan and U.N. officials have met with Sheikh Sayyed Hassan Nasrallah regarding the Syrian occupation of and pullout from Lebanon and Hezbollah-held seats in the Lebanese Parliament. Yet Hezbollah, which means the Party of God and is known as the Islamic Jihad, has been blamed for the 1983 suicide truck bombing of the Marine barracks in Beirut that killed 241 of our soldiers, another truck bombing in 1984 of the U.S. Embassy in Beirut, the kidnapping and killing of U.S. Army Colonel William Higgins and CIA station chief William Buckley, the bombing of the Israeli Embassy in Buenos Aires, an attack on a Jewish community center in Argentina that killed ninety-five people, and sending waves of suicide bombers into Israel—all while being funded by Syria and Iran. The U.S. government also says its hundreds of terrorist operatives include cells in Europe, Africa, South America, North America, and Asia.

It's a wonder this doesn't faze the recalcitrant diplomats who work at the U.N., a building that looks out over the New York City borough of Queens. It was in Queens in 1993 that the FBI videotaped followers of Islamic Sheikh Abdul Rachman in a garage mixing the chemicals for truck bombs that were to be deployed at several New York City landmarks on July 4th of that year. The United Nations headquarters building was the first intended target of one of the truck bombs.

This plot was the second phase of attack, after the bombing of the World Trade Center five months earlier that claimed six lives and injured one thousand people.

Yet more than a decade after its own home was targeted, the U.N. could still not provide an accounting of Islamic terrorist activities within its member states. And the Security Council found that of those nations that did respond to the antiterrorism efforts, a third did nothing with lists of terrorist names, and fully half admitted to not passing potential terrorist identities on to their border agents for action. Perhaps even more preposterous was the presence on the council of Syria, a haven for anti-American fighters in Iraq; Syria, a nation that the U.S. government said helped to finance and support terrorism, including the assassinations of anti-Syrian politicians in neighboring Lebanon.

U.N. World can resemble the looking glass in *Alice in Wonderland*.

Daniel Gillerman, Israel's forthright ambassador, says he and his nation have experienced this upside-down world often. He cites the repeated instances of his inability to get the Security Council to meet after dreadful terrorist attacks, contrasting those with the times he's seen it gather at the drop of a hat to condemn Israel. "I remember when Syria asked for an emergency meeting of the Security Council on a Sunday afternoon, on the eve of Yom Kippur, after a homicidé bomber blew up twenty-two people at a restaurant in Haifa," he recalls. It turned out that Syria did not wish to protest the carnage of the innocent but, instead, the Israeli government's reaction. "The next day Israel in retaliation bombed an empty training camp in Syria, and the Security Council met Sunday afternoon. John Negroponte, who was then the American ambassador, was visiting his son in Vermont and had to drive back 450 miles or so in five hours in order to make that debate."

Says Ambassador Gillerman, "The mere fact that Syria, which everybody recognizes is one of the main perpetrators of terror in the world, can get fourteen other members of the Security Council to disrupt their holiday, to hold a meeting on the holiest of the Jewish holidays, is another manifestation of the terrible hypocrisy at the U.N."

The U.N. has long turned a blind eye to the terrorist threat. Perhaps the diplomats would have been swayed, however, by a ragtag group of protesters that gathered in their shadow on a fine spring day in 2001. It was noon on April 28, with September 11 just five months in the future, when supporters of Osama bin Laden gathered across the street from the U.N. building in the traditional rallying location of Dag Hammarskjöld Park, named after the beloved Swedish Secretary-General who died in a plane crash in 1961. On that afternoon his memory and all he stood for were defiled by a group of

Islamic extremists who denounced the U.N. and the United States and called for a jihad against the West.

It was highly unlikely that any of the diplomats actually heard the chants, for the demonstration was held on a Saturday when U.N. World was empty. Had they passed by, they would have been confronted by the followers of Al-Muhajiroun, a radical British group with followers in Queens, New York, demanding an Islamic takeover of the United States. "One day you will see the flag of Islam over the White House! Allah Akhabar!" they shouted, a declaration that would be echoed in four airline cockpits in the fall. The group also chanted, "Hezbollah, Hezbollah!" and "We support Bin Laden! Bin Laden!" They promised to produce "one hundred Bin Ladens," and after the 9/11 attacks Al-Muhajiroun went on to celebrate and praise the terrorist strikes. The group has since been banned in Britain following the July 2005 subway and bus bombings in London.

The United Nations, by permitting itself to be used as a platform by terrorists and terrorist-supporting states—inadvertently—tacitly condones their goals while officially condemning their methods. "It sends the world a very negative message," one foreign ambassador told me, when nations such as Syria, Saddam's Iraq, Iran, Algeria, and Libya attain positions of influence within the U.N. by being members of either the Security Council or the Human Rights or Disarmament committees.

"The standards are such that that not only condones terrorism but even encourages terrorism, because if there is no penalty, no naming and shaming of the countries which are guilty of some of the worst terror the world has ever seen, the countries are rewarded at the U.N. There is no crime and no punishment. And the result is that these countries feel they have a free ticket to continue to support terrorism and still be recognized and sit in very important positions in this body which was founded for totally different reasons."

Only in U.N. World would the nations responsible for state-sponsored terrorism, nations that support Islamic Jihad, sit side by side with their targets.

KEEPING US UN-SAFE FROM NUKES

In U.N. World, Iran can race to achieve nuclear capability while blatantly lying to the Security Council and deceiving U.N. nuclear inspectors with few serious consequences. For years Iran hid its underground uranium enrichment program from the eyes of U.N. inspectors, barred U.N. inspectors from sensitive sites, and even went so far as to remove U.N. seals on nuclear equipment of those the U.N. did inspect, in defiance of orders—all the while thumbing its nose at U.N. demands to fully declare and halt its nuclear programs. In 1994, present U.N. Ambassador John Bolton warned, "If we permit Iran's deception to go on much longer, it will be too late. Iran will have nuclear weapons." While the CIA's National Intelligence Estimate report predicted in 2005 that it may take up to a decade for Iran to achieve that goal, *Newsweek* quoted an unnamed diplomat as saying that Iranians are "simply lying in front of everyone."

And why not? What would the U.N. really do about it? Threaten military strikes to destroy Iranian nuclear facilities? After all, the U.N. had condemned Israel's prescient air strikes on Saddam's Osirak nuclear reactor in 1981, a bold and necessary move credited with denying Saddam a nuclear bomb. Ali Larijani, the chief Iranian nuclear envoy in charge of the U.N. talks, sounded like Alfred E. Neuman. "With the power it enjoys in the region, there is no way that Iran can be worried about the threat of the Security Council," he said.

So much for security.

When the International Atomic Energy Agency (IAEA) finally got around to referring Iran's blatant defiance for possible Security Council action in the fall of 2005, everyone knew nothing would happen because Russia and China would veto meaningful measures. The IAEA vote was split. Twenty-two out of thirty-five nations lined up with the United States, including France and India. But with the likelihood of serious sanctions or a naval blockade of Iran doomed by the looming pair of vetoes and the opposition of the nonaligned and Muslim nations assured, Iran could buy more time. It branded the U.N. action "political, illegal and illogical." The government of President Mahmoud Ahmadinejad appeared intent on continuing the quest he articulated in his speech to the General Assembly on September 17, 2005, wherein he accused the West of engaging in "nuclear apartheid" and stated his nation's intention of pursuing nuclear technology for peaceful purposes.

"Mr. Ahmadinejad delivered a crude and provocative speech at the United Nations," declared *The Washington Post*, citing his "absurd anti-American conspiracy theories."

Despite that, too many U.N. delegates continued to side with Iran, repeating the drama that bitterly split the Security Council on Iraq two years earlier. The specter of Security Council failure could be repeated with Iran, since financial interests motivate its members' foreign policies. Just as the billions in Saddam's contracts softened opposition against him, so too could Iran's $100 billion liquefied natural gas pipeline to China sway the Chinese vote. Likewise the $1 billion Russian-built reactor in Bushehr and a separate $1 billion missile deal signed in December 2005 could create Russian resistance to holding Iran accountable. Russia and China abstained from the vote that was held to merely *consider* having the Security Council deal with Iran's long history of violations of U.N. mandates. France and India actually joined the United States, but in the end that support was largely symbolic since determined Security Council action was not forthcoming. In U.N. World, "What's in it for me?" too often trumps principle. "Most of their countries buy oil from Iran, and economic sanctions that led to a boycott of Iranian oil would drive record-high oil prices even higher—as Iran has pointedly noted," wrote Joel Brinkley in *The New York Times*. Again, as in Iraq, the Bush administration pursued its own coalition of the willing to hold Iran responsible, since the U.N. can't even enforce its own dictates. It is a dilemma Kofi Annan recognizes. During the 2005 summit, he admitted, "We need to look at issues in much broader terms rather than narrow national interest," admonishing the diplomats for "a tendency to sort of look inward at their national requirements, instead of looking at the broader picture."

Even if the diplomats take Annan's advice, some predict Iranian nuclear scientists would have very little to worry about from the U.N. anyway. "If the Security Council ever did actually impose sanctions, Iran could not only easily survive them but would also continue its race to develop a nuclear bomb," warns Iranian exile Alireza Jafarzadeh. In August 2002, as the then U.S. representative of the National Council of Resistance of Iran, he revealed the existence of hidden Iranian nuclear sites, a disclosure that helped trigger the new IAEA inspections. Jafarzadeh says only that "threatening the reign of the Ayatollahs" would give Iran pause, making the chances of the U.N.'s resolving Iran's nuclear ambitions about as high as Ahmadinejad's vacationing in Israel.

The broader picture of U.N. acquiescence on Iran's nuclear programs is chilling.

The U.N.'s failure to effectively respond raises the possibility of Islamic Shabab nukes capable of taking out Paris, London, Berlin, Tel Aviv, and American forces in the Persian Gulf. As far back as 1998, Congress's Commission to Assess the Ballistic Missile Threat to the United States predicted that an "Iranian missile could hold the U.S. at risk in an arc extending northeast of a line from Philadelphia, Pennsylvania, to St. Paul, Minnesota."

Going a step further than Iran, North Korea claims it is developing its own nuclear weapons program, and the impotent powers in U.N. World remain unable to stop it. The missile commission predicted North Korean No Dong missiles could have the potential of reaching western U.S. territory in an arc extending northwest from Phoenix, Arizona, to Madison, Wisconsin.

The Senate Foreign Relations Committee predicts that the world faces a 70 percent chance of a biological, chemical, or nuclear attack by 2015. Yet the U.N.'s own vaunted nuclear proliferation efforts, undertaken to stop the spread of nuclear material that could be used in weapons from intercontinental missiles to dirty bombs, have been toothless.

It was not the U.N.'s efforts that exposed the extensive global black market in nuclear technology peddled by Pakistan's Dr. A. Q. Khan. No U.N. committee ordered Muammar Qaddafi to surrender his weapons of mass destruction programs. Those successes are among the achievements of the Proliferation Security Initiative (PSI), the brainchild of John Bolton under the Bush administration. Created by President Bush in 2003, the PSI is a consortium of more than seventy nations intent on stopping the spread of nuclear, chemical, and biological weapons. Noticeably absent among the founding participants were our Security Council partners China and Russia. (One year later, Russia did climb on board.)

PSI efforts are also credited with stopping shipments of equipment for Iran's nuclear as well as ballistic missile programs. Compare the PSI's actual achievements with the U.N.'s failures on the nuclear weapons front. PSI works because it is not encumbered by U.N. bureaucrats and anti-American diplomats second-guessing every move.

"We think that's a success, that we don't have diplomats issuing communiqués," one senior Bush administration official told me. "That's a huge difference between PSI and the U.N. One of the reasons we think it's a success is it doesn't have a headquarters, it doesn't have a budget, it doesn't have a secretary-general. We have all but dispensed with diplomatic meetings. What does that tell you when compared to [the U.N.]?"

The terrorism and nuclear treaties the United Nations does manage to pass are, in some cases, not worth the paper they are printed on. In U.N. World you can pledge to abide by international covenants and not really mean it.

"A lot of countries sign them and say, for example, they are parties to the biological weapons convention," a senior administration official told me. "They have biological weapons programs in violation of their treaty obligations, and nothing happens to them. Everybody is going to sign these treaties because it's politically easy to do so. When we [the United States] sign treaties we actually comply with them, as opposed to a lot of other countries."

The month-long 2005 conference on the Nuclear Non-Proliferation Treaty at U.N. headquarters was marked by bitter accusations aimed at America for not exceeding Washington's agreement to cut current nuclear arsenals by two-thirds. And as most of the other nations criticized the United States, they failed to thoroughly address the threats of Iran, North Korea, or terrorist pipelines.

A full three weeks were wasted by internal dissension over procedural rules and definitions, prompting even the U.N.-boosting *New York Times* to declare the result a "failure . . . very little has been accomplished."

The conference's chairman, Sergie Durate of Brazil, was asked "what the fundamental cause of the failure was, [and] he said, 'I think you can write several books on that.'"

The U.N.'s own *Disarmament Times* newspaper termed it a fiasco, and questioned what, if anything, the next nuclear gathering, set for 2010, could achieve. Kofi Annan himself wrote in a May 2005 *Wall Street Journal* op-ed that the conference's failure "seems breathtakingly irresponsible," and admitted in *The International Herald Tribune* that the U.N. conference "could not furnish the world with any solutions to the grave nuclear threats we all face [and was] unable to advance security against any of the dangers we face."

Annan was more pointed during the 2005 summit four months later. "This is a real disgrace," he lamented. "We have failed twice this year: we failed at the NPT [Non-Proliferation Treaty Conference], and we failed now." Perhaps this suggests a pattern of repeated failures at the U.N. when it comes to the most pressing security threats.

Iran is able to flout the International Atomic Energy Agency. It can violate U.N. efforts to rein in its nuclear development program because its major benefactors are either permanent members of the Security Council or among the ten countries that rotate as temporary members of the Security Council.

Iran took a cue from the I.A.E.A.'s fecklessness and in January 2006 announced it would resume its attempt to enrich uranium, which it did successfully by April. Russia and China finally agreed to report Iran to the Security Council, but the result was a weak and not even legally binding "Presidential Statement" asking Iran to please, pretty please, stop. No wonder Tehran ignored the Council's empty demands. After all, China and Russia had publicly announced their adamant opposition to sanctions, let alone military action, which effectively neutered unified Security Council action. On July 31, 2006, the Council finally passed resolution 1696 making its demand legally binding, but the result was weaker than what the United States, Britain and France had wanted. Iran immediately rejected it.

The Russians and Chinese continued to resist the tougher option in a variety of international crises. North Korea continues its nuclear bluster while its criminal masters imprison, enslave, and starve its people—without a peep about sanctions from the Security Council.

China, say diplomatic sources, refuses to seriously consider the North Korean issue in the Security Council because that could threaten its estimated $1.2 billion in trade with that nation, which only grows with each passing year.

Perhaps few officials understand the U.N.'s flawed dynamics regarding Iran and North Korea better than Ambassador Bolton. The Yale-educated diplomat has served as the under secretary of state for arms control and international security and has had extensive experience tracking the Iranians' deceptions. He was already respected in U.N. World for his accomplishments as President George H. W. Bush's assistant secretary of state for international organizations. But in the public's mind he perhaps was best known for uttering several memorable phrases about what turned out to be his posting. In 1994 he told one audience that if the U.N. headquarters "lost ten stories, it wouldn't make a bit of difference." He followed that up with "There is no United Nations. There is an international community that occasionally can be led by the only real power left in the world . . . the United

States." He advocated U.N. membership for Taiwan, which had long been blocked by China. His tough stewardship of the North Korean negotiations earned him their enmity. They branded him "human scum," "an ugly fellow," and a "bloodthirsty fiendish bloodsucker."

Bolton's contentious nomination, condemned by Senate Democrats and several Republicans, languished for an agonizing four months until President Bush exercised his recess appointment powers to give him the job in August 2005. Critics howled in outrage, claiming a man of his fearsome reputation would destroy whatever comity remained toward America in the halls of the world body. Without the seal of Senate approval he would be, in the words of Connecticut Democratic Senator Christopher Dodd, "damaged goods" who "lacks credibility."

Quite the opposite.

"The personal reception has been very warm," Bolton told me in an interview for this book when I asked about his experience as a newcomer. "Since what was said about me was a complete distortion of the way I actually operate, I'm pleased that people are happily surprised that I don't live up to my press clippings!"

His office in the U.S. Mission has bare gray walls, reserved and understated like the man himself. The bushy white mustache for which he is known caused him to be caricatured by one political cartoonist as a ferocious Yosemite Sam, angrily stomping on the Security Council table. But in person the ambassador presents a thoughtful and deliberate manner. It also turned out that the fears of his congressional critics were unfounded. After all, as one U.N. official told me, the lack of Senate confirmation didn't matter to the diplomats one bit. "Half these guys here are also appointed by only one man—their dictators!" he laughed.

Welcome to U.N. World.

"The main thing is to try and advance American interests and values. And I think the way you do that is by being candid and by not being defensive about what America's priorities are, and I think people respect that," Bolton says.

Bolton is particularly concerned about what has become Iran's Oil for Nukes program. "I think Iran has unquestionably tried to use its oil and natural gas assets to leverage its diplomatic ability and they have been very successful at it. That's why this struggle against the Iranians' effort to develop nuclear weapons capability is so important. Because if we are not able to stop Iran it sends a very bad message around the world," says Bolton. "Iran does not need a civil nuclear power program, which is its big cover story for what it's doing in pursuit of nuclear weapons. A country that floats on a sea of oil and natural gas doesn't need civil nuclear power. . . . The question is what form of international diplomatic pressure will be sufficient to convince Iran to make the strategic decision that Libya did to give up the pursuit of nuclear weapons? So far we haven't achieved that."

Based on the U.N.'s record, don't hold your breath.

A senior administration official was far more blunt in questioning the Security Council's very purpose, observing that for a period of eight years "the Chinese hadn't wanted the council to be involved in North Korea, and until 2006 the Europeans kept Iran out. So if the Security Council can't deal with the threat of a nuclear North Korea, if the Security Council can't deal with the threat of a nuclear Iran, what exactly is the council supposed to be dealing with? The question now is, can the Security Council deal with WMD proliferation and terrorism? And if it can't, then you have the prospect of a council that is just as ineffective in the age of global terrorism dealing with that problem as the council was in dealing with the program of aggressive communist states."

FAILING THE REST OF THE WORLD, TOO

In the Sudan, genocide raged on while China imported increasing amounts of oil from the troubled African nation and expanded its economic ties, calculated in 2004 to be more than $2.5 billion combined. "China is the number one economic partner of the Sudan so far, and it is our pleasure to see investment from China," boasted Sudanese Minister of External Affairs Mustafa Othman Ismail. "We hope cooperation will extend to a larger extent," he told China's Xinhua News Agency. This is why full condemnation of the Sudanese government and sanction resolutions do not reach the Security Council floor. China would veto to protect its Sudanese oil.

In the Congo and elsewhere, sexual abuse by U.N. peacekeepers was hardly checked. U.N. personnel allegedly bribed girls as young as twelve with bananas, milk, or a dollar in exchange for sex. The blue-helmeted soldiers sent to protect the innocent turned into their tormentors. More than 150 separate allegations were filed within an eighteen-month period accusing several different peacekeeping missions of sexual abuse. One French U.N. official was charged with sexually abusing young girls and allegedly taking their pictures as part of an Internet sex ring.

Allegations covered territory from Africa to Haiti, the Far East to eastern Europe, and while U.N. officials denounced the behavior and declared a zero-tolerance policy on sexual abuse, new cases have become nearly a routine part of the Secretary-General's spokesman's daily noon briefing in New York.

But even U.N. members who abuse each other suffer few consequences.

The government of one member nation can assassinate the prime minister of another member nation. For example, a U.N. investigation found high-ranking Syrian officials complicit in the car bombing of the popular reform prime minister of Lebanon, Rafik Hariri. The U.N. report was edited at the last moment before it reached the Security Council, with names of such Syrian suspects as President al-Assad's brother and brother-in-law mysteriously omitted. While the United States was joined by France in condemning the killing and singling out the alleged culprits individually, Russia proved to be Syria's Security Council lineman by blocking any resolution instituting sanctions against Syria, a state sponsor of terrorism.

Unfortunately, similar examples are not hard to find. In U.N.

World, a member can call for a fellow member to be wiped off the map and still have its flag flown at full staff outside U.N. headquarters. This is what happened when Iranian President Mahmoud Ahmadinejad called for the destruction of Israel. While Kofi Annan expressed "dismay" at the remarks and meted out the stinging punishment of canceling a visit to Tehran, Israel called for the expulsion of Iran from the world body.

The Charter of the United Nations, Chapter II, Article 6, states, "A member of the United Nations which has persistently violated the principles contained in the present Charter may be expelled from the Organization by the General Assembly upon recommendation of the Security Council."

No one has ever rated badly enough to be booted.

If the U.N. doesn't hold its own accountable, who will? Ideally, an aggressive and conscientious press corps objectively asking the tough questions of U.N. officials. But on First Avenue, journalists can be citizens of U.N. World, too . . . and as a result, for too long the institution received carte blanche from an American public kept in the dark.

– 2 –

THE U.N. PRESS CORPS COVER-UP

There is a club in the United Nations that even the diplomats cannot join.

Its headquarters is around the hallway from the balcony entrance to the Security Council. Lines of U.N. tourists snake past the discreet wood-paneled door that prevents the uninitiated from venturing into the restricted area. A large brass plaque offers the only hint of what lies inside. It reads, "UNCA."

Most people would no doubt assume that the reference is to yet another United Nations agency that dispatches personnel to trouble spots around the world. And they would be almost right, except that this is an unofficial U.N. agency that collects people from around the world. Should outsiders get through the door and into the sanctum sanctorum, they will be stopped short by a sign: "FOR UNCA MEMBERS ONLY." These elite are well protected from the eyes of the masses in what looks like a private club for harried ambassadors.

On the immediate left is a large wooden bar. The rest of the room is taken up by round tables and chairs that make the room look like an executive airport lounge or small café. The refrigerator is stocked with bottles of white wine and spirits, but there are no wait-ers milling about offering to seat you. Another part of the L-shaped room contains a large meeting area with rows of chairs, obviously prepared for presentations, but one has the odd sense that this area, larger than many Manhattan apartments, is strangely unused.

The room is empty much of the time, save the ghosts of diplo-mats past. Only the walls reveal UNCA's function. They are adorned with dozens and dozens of framed black-and-white photographs that evoke an era long past. Most date to the 1950s and 1960s and recall what appears to be a simpler and more innocent time. There are smiling men in white shirts and narrow ties, women with bouf-fant hairdos and dresses accessorized with matching purses and pearls. Many hold a highball glass in one hand and a cigarette in the other. Rob Roys and Pall Malls. Martinis and Marlboros. Cutty Sark and unfiltered Camels. The images portray a journalistic anachro-nism, an esoteric piece of United Nations history, the UNCA club, the rendezvous for the members of the media who cover the goings-on: the United Nations Correspondents Association.

One photo shows a group of reporters touring "The New Head-quarters" on July 19, 1951, standing together in the still unchanged Security Council chamber. Other photos document famous faces of international diplomacy—reporters welcoming Dean Acheson, sit-ting with Eleanor Roosevelt, chatting with John Foster Dulles. Some were taken at long-ago UNCA lunches with the newsmakers held at the since-departed midtown Manhattan restaurant, Danny's Hideaway. The reporters were hiding away with Golda Meir, Henry Cabot Lodge, and U Thant amid the white tablecloths and leather banquettes. The photos depict a camaraderie that has disap-peared, dissolved now into an annual black-tie affair often held in the U.N. diplomatic dining room. It is occasionally attended by the Secretary-General and his wife, who sit at a front row table, while assorted ambassadors, diplomats, and U.N. officials can be found at other tables, rubbing shoulders with journalists and their significant others.

UNCA was founded in 1948, and its members still rub shoulders with the international newsmakers, but the collegial liquid lunch has largely vanished. Reporters and their sources continue to dine, attend each others' parties, and share the backdoor gossip, but it took the Oil for Food scandal to finally pry the in-house press away from its close identification with the institution.

You can't really fault their sense of entitlement. I have covered the White House, Congress, New York City Hall, and several state legislatures, and almost nowhere is the access to the power players as open as at the U.N. During the run-up to the Iraqi war, if the diplomats didn't give us the answers we expected, a pack of reporters would literally chase the fleeing prey down the carpeted hallway, past the tapestry of Picasso's *Guernica,* until the hapless subject offered terms of surrender. It was like pouncing on city council members after a committee meeting. You learn that the Russian will be stern but charming, the German engaging and cooperative, the Frenchman dour and defensive, the American bland but specific, and the Chinese ambassador invisible. Reporters can stroll nearly everywhere, though showing up unannounced in a bigwig's office is considered in poor taste. If the doors are unlocked to the General Assembly chamber, you can hang around; the gathering point for peppering the members of the Security Council with questions is right outside the lounge. There is only one way out— past us. We even share the Security Council bathrooms.

Most of the diplomats are, well, diplomatic. They will honor your requests to chat with them and seem to fancy our attention. The officials who are trotted out to brief the media on agency projects or U.N. studies are visibly enthusiastic despite the often sparsely attended sessions that resemble small postgraduate tutorials. The Secretary-General is usually available. In 2004 Annan held seven solo press conferences; President Bush, three. Annan also subjected himself to our inquisitions at what are called "informal comments," stopping by the microphone at the first-floor elevators for three-minute bouts. At the U.N. headquarters alone he held seventy-eight of those encounters in 2004, plus those on his foreign trips. In all, from 2001 to mid-2005, Annan has held twenty-seven solo press conferences to President Bush's seventeen. But for a diplomat, a friendly press corps represents something close to free advertising.

In his message at the 2004 UNCA dinner, Kofi Annan wrote of the media, "If there is anything worse than being the constant critical scrutiny of journalists, it is being ignored by them. The United Nations needs and wants the attention of the media. Otherwise, our work would not only be unknown; it would be ineffective."

There are some occasions, though, when he likely wished no one knew about their work. And perhaps the organization itself wants nothing more than a mouthpiece. After all, when the explosive charges of U.N. corruption first broke, some of the scribes thought it wasn't even a story. They called it the "alleged" U.N. Oil for Food scandal.

One reason I believe the reporting on U.N. scandals met such initial resistance from the established U.N. correspondents is that they are largely a sympathetic press corps. It is not an American press corps. Most members report for the newspapers and radio stations of their home countries, where U.N. news is defined by what the Secretary-General says, what their ambassador does, and what the Security Council and General Assembly debate. Oil for Food, sex allegations against U.N. peacekeepers and officials, and stories of corruption and misbehavior just did not fit into that template. It took time for the sharp questioning to arise because that meant challenging the institution of which many reporters took pride in feeling they were almost a member.

"They tend to be enamored of the Secretary-General and the entire U.N. system. They are part of the culture. They have been there so long and believe in the system so much that they consider themselves international civil servants just merely by reporting on the U.N.," one member of the American diplomatic delegation told me.

But as coverage of Oil for Food progressed to the front pages, the embarrassing scandals spilled forth until they could no longer be conveniently dismissed inside the building or among the reporters who cover it.

"By taking on the U.N. problems, they believe they are destroying an institution in which they believe, and therefore are more apt to build it up and chastise member states [the United States] than help shed light on the problem areas of the U.N.," says the diplomat. The United States becomes a bull's-eye. "Certain reporters love to bash the U.S.," notes the envoy, saying that U.N. reporters "absolutely" side with the U.N. because of their political and philosophical views, usually a product of their being raised elsewhere. "It is very adversarial with the U.S."

Only in U.N. World do correspondents publicly offer support to the officials they are supposed to be monitoring objectively by occasionally offering their "congratulations" on the very news events they cover.

"First of all, congratulations . . ." was how one reporter prefaced a question to Kofi Annan about what actually turned out to be the dubious results of Annan's 2005 summit agenda during a September 13, 2005, news conference.

Or this, which is actually not a speech by the Cuban ambassador but part of a question to Annan from an actual U.N. correspondent: "You are confronted with an administration that has sought more frequently to stress militarism and unilateralism. In recent weeks, we have seen the appointment of an unreconstructed militarist and unilateralist as ambassador to the United Nations and now an unreconstructed militarist and unilateralist to be the head of the World Bank."

One jaded member, who has covered the goings-on since the Cuban Missile Crisis, summed up nearly fifty years of observing the U.N. up close. "Yak, yak yak," he told me, "and in the end, nothing."

The brickbats and arrows aimed at America were largely left to the U.S. mission spokesman, Richard Grenell, to answer. A Harvard-educated, Jack Armstrong all-American type, he should have earned a purple heart for parrying all the incoming rounds from the largely hostile press corps as he valiantly tried to defend his nation's diplomatic positions. He strongly defended U.S. policy and patiently tried to explain the nuances that were often lost in the headlines amid the reportorial mortar fire. He was often surrounded by a scrum of correspondents, and provided instant analysis and explanations during the Security Council's maneuvering, much like baseball commentators dissecting developments on the field during a game.

"By definition it's a sympathetic press corps," admits one of its deans, Ian Williams, a charming and irascible Welsh rogue who writes for *The Nation* and other left-leaning publications. "But this is not . . . pro-U.N. or anti-U.N. as an institution. When I go down and criticize George W. Bush, I'm not being pro–U.S. Constitution or anti–U.S. Constitution, I'm being pro the activities of one particular administration. When I'm rude about Tony Blair, just as I was rude about John Major and the others before, I was not attacking Britain as a nation or as a people or as an institution. I was saying these particular political manifestations were wrong. So, yes, I would say with very few exceptions . . . [the U.N. reporters] are sympathetic to the U.N. as an organization, as an institution, as an ideal, but I think you'll find all of them are not starry eyed about it, [are] aware of its failings, and [are] quite prepared to point them out and denounce them."

Williams has accepted a token U.N. payment, by the way, for appearing on a U.N.-produced television program—a transaction that violated no particular rule but would be frowned on in a U.S. media organization. One of the most basic tenets of American journalism is to avoid even the slightest appearance of conflict of interest.

"It's clear to me that most of the reporters covering the U.N. are in love with it," declares Cliff Kincaid, editor of Accuracy in Media (AIM), the conservative media group. "That's certainly a sharp contrast to how reporters, say in the White House press corps, treat the Bush administration."

Kincaid says the U.N. press corps is riddled with hypocrisy. "It's rare to find members of the U.N. Correspondents Association who want to even be critical of the U.N.," he says. He calls payments to U.N. reporters "an obvious conflict of interest." Says Kincaid, "Journalists shouldn't be taking money from an organization they are supposed to be covering objectively."

AIM e-mailed all members of UNCA, including myself, a questionnaire asking:

> Do you believe journalists covering the U.N. should receive payments from the U.N.?
> Do you know of any other U.N. correspondents getting paid by the world body?
> Should journalists covering the U.N. accept money from organizations, such as Ted Turner's U.N. Foundation, which promote the U.N.?

That reference was to Linda Fasulo, the reporter who covers the U.N. for the cable network, MSNBC, and who also serves as the U.N. correspondent for *NBC News*. AIM reported that she had been paid $15,000 by the U.N. Foundation, which actively supports the U.N. In its Web site AIM challenged the objectivity of Ms. Fasulo's reporting because she accepted U.N. Foundation Money for her book, *An Insider's Guide to the U.N.*, in 2004. AIM also said she received another $11,000 from the Rockefeller Foundation.

Fasulo's book, published by the Yale University Press, was a scholarly work written before Oil for Food burst open, a time when some saw the U.N. in a more positive light. She told me, "I've been criticized by people on the far left who think the book is too pro-U.S. and I've been criticized by people on the far right for the book being too pro-U.N. I'm very comfortable that I'm doing something right." The book disclosed the foundation's grants, and NBC issued a statement in early 2005 saying there was no problem. "We were not concerned when the book was published, and are not concerned now. *NBC News'* reporting on the United Nations has always been, and will continue to be, thorough, fair and factual."

A broader issue is the fact that only a handful of American news organizations bother to post full-time correspondents at the U.N. at all. That perhaps is a reflection on what some editors see as the institution's irrelevance, as many of the broadcast booths dating from the 1950s are long-abandoned relics of faded glory. There's a question of whether the journalists themselves are being watched as closely as their peers covering other beats.

Still, all Ian Williams got was dinner money in a Manhattan restaurant. "I earned $150 last year from the U.N. for one *World Chronicle*," a U.N.-produced television program about international affairs, says Williams, laughing. He calls AIM "deranged." He says, referring to AIM, "Just look at my record. I have criticized the U.N. far more substantially for far more substantial things than what they are doing. They can't point to a single point of view, which I have expressed, that they can trace a check to. One of the reasons the U.N. has never tried to employ me is because they know I'm a loose cannon. I speak my mind."

But in the eyes of Accuracy in Media, the U.N. journalists might as well be on the payroll of what Kincaid brands the pro-U.N. lobby. UNCA journalism prizes have been partly underwritten by the U.N. Foundation and George Soros's Open Society Institute to the tune of $20,000.

"We thought that was a possible conflict of interest, too, because both of those foundations are very much pro-U.N. and have a vested interest in the U.N. scandals," says Kincaid. UNCA denies any conflict, its president Jim Wurst told AIM. "We are a proud, feisty, and independent association of journalists." UNCA had 180 members in 2005, and although the days of martini lunches at Manhattan venues have passed, the organization, like others in Washington, D.C., and elsewhere, holds background breakfast briefings with ambassadors. Journalism prizes also honor UNCA members who have been killed while covering the world's trouble spots, including Iraq.

UNCA branded AIM's survey a "far-right attack on U.N. correspondents" by Kincaid, whom they termed a "veteran U.N. basher."
Williams and Wurst, along with another U.N. veteran, Tony Jenkins
of *Expresso,* cautioned the members that Kincaid was trying to suggest that their work had been tainted by pro-U.N. money.

They wrote Kincaid, saying, "We have no doubt that such an al-
legation would cause general merriment amongst the senior officials
at the U.N." They cited the fact that one prize went to *The Wall
Street Journal* for its coverage of the Oil for Food scandal. "It is
probable that a majority of our members are sympathetic to the institution we cover," UNCA continued. "That does not mean that we
pull back on criticizing whoever the incumbent is. We refuse to be
politically categorized."

Yet when the more aggressive members of the press corps took
on the U.N. powers, they were met with the typical defensive
blame-the-messenger attacks, even being accused of being desperate in their attempts to get answers to their many questions. Benny
Avni of the *New York Sun* reported on the strange fact that Annan's
then chief of staff, Mark Malloch Brown, rented his house from
George Soros, the billionaire Bush critic, who called, as Avni's story
pointed out, "defeating President Bush the central focus of my
life . . . a matter of life and death." Soros spent millions during the
2004 election in an attempt to defeat the incumbent president. Avni
reported that Malloch Brown, the top official next to Annan, paid a
staggering $120,000 a year to his landlord Soros.

Malloch Brown, no slouch when it comes to the spin department, denied any improprieties and launched a bitter broadside
against James Bone of the (London) *Times,* who questioned him
about the Soros deal. "Who gave you this story?" Malloch Brown angrily demanded. "What was their motive? What is it that now gives
free rein to any amount of bile, unproven but still publishable, with
no questioning of the motives of those who provided it?"

The possibility of a financial conflict of interest between Soros
and a top U.N. official was a legitimate story—except to the U.N.

officials who have at last found themselves under the microscope of independent, aggressive reporting. "As I've frequently told all of you in this room," Malloch Brown said, addressing the correspondents, "you have been a critical part of exposing terrible things that have gone on in this organization. But do not let your standards of journalism decline as you do that. Stick to the proper issues and evidence. . . . Get back to the plenty of real stories that are around here. I see enough nodding heads in this room to know that I'm not alone in saying that there are enough real stories for you to pursue that you can stop dragging down everyone you touch, particularly yourself, by the way you're behaving." In other words, don't question us about potential conflicts of interest.

As indicated by the nodding heads, many of the supposedly impartial reporters sided with the U.N. official over journalistic principle. Perhaps one reason could be the award Soros partly paid for that was handed out at the correspondents' dinner, with Soros himself proudly in attendance. "Stockholm syndrome," explains ABC radio's John Batchelor, whose weeknight program the *John Batchelor Show* has always asked the tough questions and demanded answers from the U.N. Batchelor is among the handful of journalists who attempt to hold the organization to an appropriate, responsible standard, and he accuses the in-house press corps of dereliction of duty.

"It's a plush post and they don't want to give it up. They also get a lot of status back home, especially the foreigners. They get to live in New York and get to claim they are working with the U.N. It's heaven for them," says Batchelor. The press corps's mission is to "cover its ass," he says. "CYA. They are deaf to the problems, and because they come from such a hodgepodge of governments they are nonjudgmental. It's the worst of the Clinton years, total nonjudgmental, passive-aggressive CYA." He notes that when the *Financial Times* interviewed President Clinton in June 2005, as allegations about Annan continued to hit the front pages, they allowed Clinton to "spin on about how Kofi made him Mr. Tsunami, and they didn't ask him about Kofi. They asked him about Abu

Ghraib, they asked him about Gitmo, but they didn't ask him about Kofi."

This on the day *The New York Times* referred to the corruption of the Oil for Food program as merely "allegations of irregularities." They think it's an accounting problem. The *Times* was the only major paper that did not report my Fox News interview with Paul Volcker in April 2005, in which he said that his investigation had not "exonerated" Annan, as the Secretary-General had so triumphantly claimed. Perhaps its editors reasoned that Volcker, a respected figure in the halls of power, criticizing Annan, a beloved leader, was not "all the news that's fit to print." Batchelor characterizes the ostriches in the media ranks as being in denial.

The hard news of corruption, duplicity, betrayal, and bribes simply did not fit the portfolio that U.N. reporters see as their prescribed venue. They have until lately seemed uncomfortable with holding the U.N. itself accountable, uneasy about reporting on anything that exposes wrongdoing or embarrassment. They choose instead to focus on the international maneuvering. They sat on the biggest crime beat and did not know it. They should be traded for the scribes in "the police shack," the home of the New York City Police Department press corps down at One Police Plaza. Switch them for a day, and at least you'll get the right questions. The U.N. may not answer, the spokespeople may deflect queries as best they can, but the world would learn what should be asked.

Perhaps the level of affinity could be judged by the fact that several reporters have been said to have applied for U.N. jobs at the very same time they were covering the institution. Who would dare ask uncomfortable questions of the very U.N. spokespeople who determine your hiring? You go from a job interview where they ask the questions of you to a press conference where you ask the questions of them. It's like a White House correspondent raising a hand at the daily briefing while angling for an administration public affairs job, a conflict of interest in American journalism. Journalists in Washington are known to jump from the media camp to government service, but usually not at the same time they are covering their prospective employer.

"We tend to think of reporters as outsiders. When they become insiders they tend to be a lot more sympathetic," notes Richard Wald, professor of journalism at Columbia School of Journalism. A former president of NBC News, Wald specializes in ethics. He agrees that the U.N. press corps seems a bit incestuous, but notes it is "not covered by American rules." American journalistic standards prohibit reporters from receiving any remuneration from the subjects or institutions they cover. At most, an appearance fee for a television interview program where a reporter can spout off as a "talking head" is acceptable, but not much beyond that. The U.N. press corps, Wald notes, should not necessarily be held to our rules, because it is a foreign press corps. "The reason you don't take money from the sources that you cover is that in America there is a general assumption that money carries influence and the influence will change the way you report." But then again, the U.N. is technically and figuratively not in America, and that can apply to the people who carry the press cards too.

"The best example was the Iranian ambassador," recalls Wald. "When you went to his house you got served huge amounts of caviar, and he used to send out Reza's [the Shah of Iran's] Christmas presents. A lot of [reporters] who got Christmas presents returned them, and some kept them. The American sense of journalistic ethics is you don't accept presents."

Those days are over, except in U.N. World, where reporters are still wined and dined by the people they cover. It is similar to the Georgetown dinner-party circuit in Washington, D.C., where newsmakers and newspeople socialize around the rack of lamb and the Bordeaux. Yet at the U.N., the get-togethers are not presented as private social engagements, but rather as business-related entertainment. It can be hard to ask the tough question of the U.N. official or diplomat who's hosted you the previous evening.

That is why the scandals of the U.N.—the confirmed bribes,

sexual harassment allegations, conflict of interest accusations, and misconduct revelations—were treated, for the most part, in a cursory manner by often somnolent inquisitors. It is also why the U.N., which has largely kept its inner workings secret from prying eyes, has gotten away with them all these years. It took outside pressure due to the twin debacles of the Security Council's Iraq failure and the accumulating U.N. scandals for many of the reporters to finally question the world body's relevance and hold it to account.

Recently there has been discernable change in the U.N. press corps's coverage of its subject. Since the release of the Volcker Commission's reports detailing the numerous ways in which the U.N. is corrupt and inept, the journalists covering the institution have largely risen to the occasion, and have given officials a proper drumming. In December 2005 the harsh questioning of the U.N. and its scandals proved to be too much for Kofi Annan. His normally unruffled veneer dissolved rather undiplomatically when he angrily lashed out at the press corps, claiming that it "badgered, mistreated, and insulated" his spokesmen and "missed a story"—oil smuggling—in its Oil for Food coverage. He went on to attack reporter James Bone as "an overgrown school boy" when he tried to ask an Oil for Food scandal-related question regarding Annan's son, Kojo. It is treatment to which the diplomats are not accustomed. Never before have they had to pass muster with reporters, columnists, editorial boards, or any constituency beyond their governments.

But the problems in U.N. World go far beyond the press corps. Thankfully, those covering the U.N. are finally asking some tough questions, and the organization is being held, in some manner, accountable for its actions or inactions. However, don't expect sweeping change at the U.N. just yet. Accountability is a rare commodity there, and the lack of it is a consequence of basic U.N. hierarchy.

The dignitaries and people of power are not elected, save one. The Secretary-General serves at the acclamation of the General Assembly. The position is traditionally shared by a rotating formula involving Europe, Africa, South America, and Asia. This means that the U.N. culture does not have to be responsive to an electorate, as any state legislator or member of Congress must be. U.N. officials do not have to be accountable to any popular constituency. Insular mind-sets at odds with the organization's purpose abound. The appointed diplomats run the show while the staff of the Secretariat—the hired help with international civil service protection who are overseen by the Secretary-General—carry out the General Assembly's and Security Council's wishes.

The diplomatic world is one of compromise and consensus. From the Secretary-General to the lowliest delegation member, there is an incentive to protect and preserve the status quo and to avoid any radical change. The ruling class has a desire to keep things going the way they have always gone; and with the Americans taking the lead at pushing for reform, challenging or criticizing U.S. positions has become a natural reaction to American power. Until the culture within the diplomatic corps and its leadership change in significant ways, America will be banging its head against a wall.

– 3 –

THE PINSTRIPE POSSE
AND THE SULTAN OF
SUTTON PLACE

Some wear French cuffs and gold watches. Others arrive for work in what's known as native dress. Others are in off-the-rack suits from a discounter. One individual, I noticed, wore the same tie nearly every day. His was a small country.

There are 192 member nations of the United Nations, and each country sends an ambassador to represent its interests. Some live in lavish residences, others in rented apartments, but they all share the distinction of being protected by diplomatic immunity from the laws of the United States. No matter how down-to-earth these people are—and I know a few—there is no escaping the sense of self-importance that comes with the appointment.

"Yes, Ambassador." Imagine hearing that five hundred times a day. It can really go to your head. You mingle with like-minded colleagues from around the globe; you receive countless gold-embossed cocktail and dinner party invitations from other missions and those seeking to curry your favor. You only really have to show up for the rare important votes and, in most cases, can send a deputy in your stead. You are coddled and catered to by professional and domestic staffs all day—assistants, secretaries, butlers, cooks, housekeepers. Your black, tinted-windowed limousine with those special DPL State Department–issued license plates remains purring outside Sparks, 21, or Le Grenouille, tended by the obligatory chauffeur. Until recently, you have not really had to pay your parking tickets if you didn't want to, except to avoid landing on the *New York Post's* annual list of offenders. You glide through the halls of the international body, confident and respected, just as long as you stay inside the building. The perks and privileges of diplomatic membership soften the barbs of those U.N. critics—Americans who you think are right-wing, xenophobic nut jobs anyway, and who, if you hail from some countries, would be swiftly jailed and executed back home. You don't have to run for election to get the job, raise money, or hold fundraisers. Just be nice to the right people and keep your head down.

The American ambassador is not exempt from the pampering. He, too, is chauffeured around in a bullet- and bomb-proof Cadillac and driven home each night to a luxurious government-supplied spread in the ultraexclusive Waldorf Astoria Hotel Towers. The five-bedroom apartment serves as the official residence of the United States ambassador to the United Nations. No American not on the Forbes Richest 500 list will ever see it or be able to afford it, but we all still chip in for it. It serves as an elegant reminder of American supremacy, if that makes you feel better.

Two brass plaques at the entrance remind you that the towers were once the home of former president Herbert Hoover and General Douglas MacArthur. Just inside the revolving door is another plaque, honoring Madeleine Albright for having been "in residence" as the U.N. ambassador.

The white-gloved doormen whisk you high up to an apartment that overshadows even the most sophisticated residences of Manhattan's multimillionaires—they lack the uniformed, white-shirted officers of the United States standing guard outside. The long living

room stretches for a good sixty feet, the red-lacquered dining room
offers a hushed evening of intelligent conversation under the elegant chandelier. If you wish to retire by the fireplace in the library
to read or watch TV, you may do so sitting under an original Roy
Lichtenstein print donated by the artist through a fund that provides art for U.S. embassies. With its beige walls and colonial-style
columns, our ambassador can seek an exclusive refuge from being
pounded all day at the office.

In U.N. World, the largest communist country on earth houses its
representative in the black-and-glass-shrouded Trump World
Tower, a behemoth that soars over the landmark U.N. headquarters
a block away. The Chinese ambassador enjoys a bird's-eye view of
Manhattan from this condo where his neighbors pay as much as $14
million for their own pieds-à-terre.

The destitute nations don't skimp in U.N. World either.

Yemen is listed as the fourteenth poorest nation on Earth, with
an average gross national income of $465 and, according to the U.S.
Agency for International Development, "a high infant and child
mortality rate [and] a high maternal mortality rate." Yemen also re-
lies extensively on international humanitarian aid. U.N. agencies
provide more than $50 million a year for health, education, and
agricultural projects. Yet Yemen wouldn't think of renting an apartment for its ambassador or stashing him somewhere in Brooklyn. In
U.N. World, even the nations on life support go first class. In July
2005, the Yemenis snapped up an 1879 neo-Greek five-story Upper
East Side Manhattan townhouse between Park and Madison avenues as the new residence for its ambassador, Abdallah al-Saidi.
The Wall Street Journal reported the sales price: $6.8 million.

Many of the 192 nations have multimillion-dollar Manhattan
townhouses that serve as either offices or residences for the ambassador and, in some cases, other diplomatic staff as well. Saddam's
Iraq owned two: one between Fifth and Madison avenues on
Seventy-ninth Street for the offices; the other, a classic redbrick

townhouse eerily resembling the British prime minister's residence at 10 Downing Street, on East Eightieth Street between Park and Lexington avenues. The week Saddam fell, the official acknowledgment of his fate came when Ambassador Mohammed Al Douri stormed past the media at the consulate declaring "game over," which was followed by the removal of Saddam's official portrait in the front lobby. Regime change also brought the new Iraqi government new wheels. The battered early 1990s-era Lincoln town car was supplemented by a shiny new black current Cartier model after Saddam's statue fell.

All this for diplomats who are deadbeats.

Their employers still owe nearly $19 million in unpaid parking tickets to New York City, and only started to pay up after Mayor Michael Bloomberg teamed up with the Department of State to deduct 110 percent of the amount of outstanding parking violations from American foreign aid. Russia, the biggest offender in the 1990s with about thirty thousand unpaid tickets amounting to millions of dollars, bought parking lots for its vehicles and now owes less than $100,000. China's tab is $372,000, and France owes about $250,000. But some of America's closest allies owe a lot more: Egypt, $1.9 million; Kuwait, $1.3 million; Nigeria, $1 million; Indonesia, $700,000. Even Sudan continues to rack up a half million dollars in unpaid tickets.

For most, especially those who represent third world nations, New York represents a luxurious getaway and cherished respite from the difficulties of their home country, even if they belong to their nation's ruling class. After all, in the past forty years the electricity has suddenly gone out in Manhattan only three times.

The only certainties outside the building may be death and taxes, but in U.N. World you only have to count on death. Under the U.S. government's "Privileges and Immunities" benefits, members of the diplomatic corps are exempt from being taxed. On anything, whether it's a laptop or a Jaguar. The Department of State provides all foreign envoys with a convenient plastic blue-and-gray card like a credit card that enables the bearer to skip out on paying taxes. I have seen diplomats present their convenient little tax-avoider to save 60 cents in New York City sales tax on their $6.85 cheeseburger deluxe at the Friar's coffee shop up the block from the U.N.

You are even automatically qualified for a "diplomatic discount" on a variety of luxuries. Kofi Annan's son, Kojo, claimed such a savings on a $39,056 Mercedes-Benz he bought for himself, nabbing a 14.3 percent discount by falsely claiming the car was for his father. The investigators for Paul Volcker's independent probe of the Oil for Food program found that Kojo also avoided paying the car's customs fees under diplomatic immunity, slicing "approximately $20,644" off the price of his new wheels.

In U.N. World, ethics rules can be as liberal as the vodka in the tonics.

American congressmen are barred by federal law from receiving gifts worth more than $50. The president and vice president of the United States must declare all gifts valued above $285 under government ethics rules. U.N. staff members enjoy a more generous allowance. They have seen nothing wrong with setting the gift limit at $10,000. A pair of diamond Tiffany earrings for a spouse or a Patek Phillip watch for yourself or a paid trip to the French Riviera are perfectly acceptable, thank you. After all, U.N. World thrives on polite and solicitous social relations where gifts can serve as a symbol of international friendship and comity, not crass or vulgar gratuities. It took until the winter of 2005 for the United Nations to be shamed into proposing to change this ethical indulgence by restricting the gift limit to $250.

What does all of this amount to when viewed from the inside, I wonder. Is it as good a deal as it seems? I asked a man whom I shall call Wallace O. Woodward. He is an erudite veteran of the United States delegation, an internationalist and foreign affairs scholar who has seen his share of bitter and frustrating disappointments along with some satisfying victories from his seat inside the Security Council chamber.

Woodward has known many foreign colleagues who come to the United States, live on the Upper East Side of New York, and realize they don't want to go back to their home countries, because their standard of living here is so much higher. "The opportunities here are completely different, so while you hear them [criticizing] the United States publicly, behind the scenes they are scrambling to get a visa or permanent green card, or a job at the U.N.," he says. "That's the other dirty little secret, how many ambassadors want jobs at the U.N. because they don't want to go back to their home country."

After all, hooking up with the U.N. payroll *usually* means you will never be fired. During his first eight years on the job, the U.N. says Secretary General Kofi Annan only summarily dismissed forty people out of twenty-three thousand. If you come from certain countries, those are pretty good odds—especially considering that a sudden coup d'état can lead to your supervisor's arrest or assassination and suddenly plunk you out on First Avenue waiting for the M15 bus with everyone else.

So what does one actually *do* at the U.N.? One *can* learn who throws the best parties. Diplomatic receptions are notorious for their catered spreads, with even the poorest nations hosting well-lubricated receptions stocked with top-brand wines, spirits, and food. The Russian mission is known for serving a brand of vodka only available to the elite in Moscow and not stocked on any American liquor store shelf. If the French call, run. The buffets can be extensive, with rows of lobsters, roast beef, caviar, cold cuts, fresh fish, native delicacies, and freshly baked desserts, all served by tuxedoed waiters quietly refilling the emptying champagne flutes.

To be fair, ambassadorial life is not always about glamour and prestige. Diplomatic service at the United Nations can also feel like an appointment to servitude, far from the free-wheeling martini and finger-food gatherings that do occur.

"I get home at 10 P.M. every night," one Security Council member complained to me. "I barely have time to see my wife and kids." He is stuck in meetings all day, darting out to take cell phone calls from his capital—a puppet on a string that runs thousands of miles. Your life is dictated by telephone appointments. At 12:30 P.M., your foreign minister or the commerce minister or the deputy commerce minister or the assistant to the deputy commerce minister is scheduled to call, so you dash back to the office and wolf down a tuna sandwich from a coffee shop while you wait for his call, which doesn't come.

Or the time difference can kill you. How would you like the home office to be six, or eight, or twelve hours ahead—or behind—with various government officials dismissing the difference, which means your bedside phone ringing at 2:00 A.M. is not an unusual occurrence? They always think what they have to tell you can't wait for the sun to peek over Forty-seventh Street. You go back to sleep, if you can, while they step out for a long lunch. Or the ministry conference call is scheduled for when everyone else can make it, which usually is 4:00 A.M. New York time, so you groggily conduct world affairs in your pajamas, struggling not to nod off on the phone in case someone on the other end suddenly pipes up and asks, "What do you think?"

"What these guys are, are largely spokesmen," says Professor Charles Hill, a professor of international relations and diplomat-in-residence at Yale University, who served as the special adviser to Secretary General Boutros Boutros-Ghali. "People are impressed by ambassadorial titles," he says, but their power is hollow. "They have a line and stay with it. They complain a lot and don't offer very much. Taken as a whole, they don't do the U.N. organization much good." He distinguishes the diplomats from the staff workers, the civil servants in the Secretariat and U.N. agencies who carry out the diplomats' decisions. "It's an unhappy life," an envoy admitted to me. He has served both in and out of the U.N. system across the globe and has represented his country in foreign capitals. "A life of meetings, of a lot of paperwork, writing reports back to your home country on everything that happens, reports that are shelved once they arrive in your country of origin because no one pays attention to them unless it's something of consequence."

He considered his diplomatic duty "very monotonous," tethered to the constraints of his distant superiors. The reports that were digested would return to him with a decision, the "yes" or "no" usually out of his hands, and sometimes not an endorsement or rejection with which he would personally agree. "The countries usually follow a certain line," he said. "You send back your memo on various items, and then within a day or so you receive instructions from your minister of foreign relations telling you how to vote on each and every one." He sees the U.N. structure as "a way to absorb the professional elite," and although he had made friends, ambassadorial life was "tiresome," he said. "It's extremely shallow, [with] a lot of back-stabbing. You have to be a professional hypocrite twenty-four hours a day because you're talking to people, to ambassadors that you know don't like your country and couldn't [care] about you. You still have to be nice to them. That's why you find so many alcoholics. My God—ninety percent of them!" Excluding the representatives of the Muslim missions, he presumes. "Unless you are an ambassador from a major country, or in a major capital, or in a medium-size country, or from a European country or the United States, you are just there to enjoy yourself. You really have no role." Because of the nature of the envoy's geographic origins, but not education and experience, he falls into the latter category of enjoying himself. This leaves most of the diplomatic corps "holding fancy titles but scant responsibility," he says.

He also found the U.N. system a lethargic obstacle. "It's frustrating and extremely bureaucratic," he says, noting an overwhelming amount of paper shuffling. "The inefficiency is mind boggling, and these are the worst bureaucrats in the world. They can be petty, vicious, and incompetent. And there are quotas of how many you can hire!" he says, laughing. The practice, he says, is to divvy out positions to separate continental or country blocks so everyone can get a piece of the pie. "These people are selected not because of their professional or moral qualities," he avers. "They're selected because of how well connected they are in the government, and how much pressure their home governments can put on the U.N. structure to hire them. [It has] absolutely nothing to do with merit. It's extremely inefficient."

As with any organization skilled in the bureaucratic arts, the U.N. has also made it really hard to lose a job. The diplomats get the glory, and their staffs get job security. At the U.N., it's not necessarily what you know but who you know and where you're from. While the U.N. Secretariat employs roughly twenty-three thousand people, those who work for associated or semiautonomous U.N. agencies bring the numbers to roughly forty-five thousand worldwide.

"Once you're in, you're in," an employee told me. The U.N. is known among the professional class to offer generous benefits and relaxed working conditions. Employment is based on an international civil service commission, similar to the U.S. government civil service corps, but the difference is that no U.S. employment law maintains jurisdiction over the U.N. system and, in reality, the positions are divided among the countries.

The organization that preaches tolerance and inclusiveness practices a subtle reverse employment practice by mandating a certain number of jobs to each nation, a quota system worthy of the worst political machine. You see the broad range of humanity walking the halls, which at first is inspiring as a tribute to the organization's diversity. Flowing African robes give way to Arab dish-dashas; Saville Row suits give way to Indian Nehru jackets. Then you realize chances are they couldn't have been hired without "a hook." In Chicago politics that person is known as your "chinaman," in New York's City Hall it's your "rabbi," and in the corporate suites on Park Avenue it's your "mentor." It's still political patronage—U.N. style.

The system can reward incompetence or plain somnolence. Stand at the front door of the Secretariat Building at 9:00 A.M. and you will have the sidewalk practically to yourself. An hour later, you'll start being mowed down by everyone showing up for work. The exodus starts at about 4:30.

One person I talked with admitted to covering up for a lazy colleague. Another told me he carried the responsibilities of two jobs because he didn't want a foreign workmate to lose his job and end up on the street. "So I just ignore it and do two jobs," he says. "It's just part of normal life in the international civil service."

It took fifty-nine years for the U.N. to finally attempt to bring its employment practices in line with the private sector. In July 2004, a human resources pilot program introduced the revolutionary concept of pay for performance, which would actually set standards based on competence and achievement. The proposal conceded that the U.N. suffers from a culture of entitlement and the experiment's goal was to try and move the lumbering bureaucracy to a culture of performance.

"Sure it's a bloated bureaucracy," admitted one inside person. "But will it hurt America? No!" But Woodward laughs at this point, because he thinks hiring should be based on merit and principle, not mediocrity or geography. "It's an absurd system," he says. "The U.N. is big on bureaucracy and formality, so they make it up as they go. There are no rules and the ones they have are all unwritten. He who is in charge makes the rules."

He says countries dole out positions as if they were playing Monopoly, trading and collecting chits to cash in on a lot of jobs or one big one. "Some countries put all their eggs in one basket for a really big position, like a director of a peacekeeping mission, while others save their chits to trade up."

Woodward also says countries "play games to get more jobs." If an official position becomes available and is slotted for a European nation, "Greece can say we should be in the running because we're in the EU. If the job is slated for a third world nation, Greece can go and stake its claim, saying, 'We should get it because we have such a low GDP.' The Arabs can have it both ways. They can be

Arab . . . or African!" In the quest for U.N. reform, America and Annan tried to strike back.

The Secretary-General's reform plan calls for a massive buyout for U.N. employees to shrink the workforce. The Newt Gingrich–George Mitchell-chaired congressional commission that found poor management and "dismal" staff morale declared that "for too many of the member states the United Nations is seen as a job placement bureau." They and many others describe a slow, unwieldy bureaucracy hampered by red tape and redundant protocols. "This place brings out the worst in people," another U.N. veteran told me.

The poisonous atmosphere was confirmed by none other than Annan's then chief of staff, who was later named Deputy Secretary-General, Mark Malloch Brown. In June 2005, as Annan was pressing his reform proposals, Malloch Brown told London's *Sunday Times,* "This place is like revolutionary France, where the level of backstabbing and betrayal would make Shakespeare wince." He said Annan's efforts to clean up the place were met by "a level of resistance by those who don't want change, frankly." What no one wants to discuss, however, is why this vacuum of leadership in the U.N. can manage only to comment on, not to change, the institutional inertia.

The U.N. staff union would undoubtedly disagree that there is need for reform on behalf of the many caring, highly motivated, and hardworking professionals attracted to international public service. I know they are there, because I have met some. But when you work within the system, it can sometimes crush you.

"You go in idealistic to try and get all kinds of projects for your country," related one envoy, and you find out your requests "have to be channeled from the U.N. office" in your country. "But if the representative in that office does not want to help you, he will not. You can write a letter and everything, and he just picks up the phone afterwards and says, 'No, forget it.' Probably a minister had called him up and told him, 'Listen, don't bring all those donated medicines into the country because my family represents those medicines, and you're going to drive us out of business!' And all the equipment for projects, you know? They get a kickback. When I opened an office [in my country] we could only buy from this company in [another country], because that company had close ties to the U.N. representative, instead of buying it locally, which is a way of helping [my nation]. You start to wonder, 'What's going on?' Slowly I found out why things were the way they were. It's because [the U.N. official] gets a kickback."

My diplomatic source found retelling his experiences depressing and disappointing. "I really hate to be like this," he apologized. "Ambassadors were originally used for dynastic purposes for alliances or to impose terms of surrender."

He points out that the modern art of the diplomatic service has its roots in 1487, when Ferdinand, the King of Spain, appointed the first permanent representative to the Court of England. It was a noble calling of importance. Being the farsighted couple that they were, five years later Ferdinand's wife, Isabella, bankrolled an Italian sailor named Christopher Columbus to go look for the new world. Judging from the U.N., Ferdinand's idea didn't pan out as well.

Five hundred years later, our disaffected diplomat considers his colleagues salesmen. "You try to get the most for your country," he says, in business, grants, and U.N. projects. He says embassies have largely turned into economic offices, and the U.N.'s ambassadorial role is to try and smooth the process while issuing pronouncements, trading votes, and filing all those dreaded reports. Still, you hope you can do some good. Leave the world a better place. And when you go home and have a drink and watch the issues play out on TV, you are never quite sure if anyone is listening.

Is anyone listening? Perhaps that question should weigh most heavily on the mind of the Secretary-General. The U.N. seems to have fostered a culture of dithering diplomats, bare-minimum bureaucrats, and frustrated idealists. There is no one more responsible than the Secretary-General, the Sultan of Sutton Place, for making the world body relevant today. Kofi Annan began his second term trying to achieve that, by pushing his agenda of U.N. reform. But as Americans pump more money into the U.N., we have to ask ourselves if the house is in any kind of order to face the challenges it is supposed to confront. The question for many Americans is, "Can the Secretary-General do the job?" Are we, and the world, getting the executive we pay for?

*   *   *

The life of a Secretary-General is so far removed from those lives with which he is entrusted that it is hard to know how anyone in the position can keep to the spirit of the work. For all the just causes for which the U.N. proudly takes credit, perhaps it should be noted that a humanitarian can wear nothing worse than excess. And in the SG's case, one needn't go any further than the front door of the official residence to see the dichotomy.

The majestic redbrick Georgian mansion has one of the most exclusive of Manhattan addresses: Sutton Place. The double-wide townhouse of four stories and more than twenty rooms faces out onto the secluded cul-de-sac. But the neighborhood's most coveted feature is hidden in the rear. In a city where light and space and privacy are commodities so rare, the dozen or so townhouses of Sutton Place have their own garden. Pruned trees, blossoming flower beds, and a lush lawn fill a full city block that extends to the very verge of the East River, creating a private sanctuary for the wealthy homeowners who are lucky enough to be able to afford to live on top of this oasis. The Secretary-General awakens to that view every day.

Each morning, when he is in New York, the SG heads downstairs and is served breakfast by the staff supplied by his nonprofit organization. As he peruses the morning newspapers for any mentions and the latest crises, he can be easily lulled into the comforting and reassuring self-satisfaction that comes with his station. He is Secretary-General of the United Nations.

For the recently retired S.G., the position was the pinnacle of a more than four-decade career in the world body's bureaucracy, during

which he rose from a lowly professional position as a budget officer with the World Health Organization to the top of the organization responsible for a sprawling empire with an annual $3.6
billion budget.

For Kofi Annan, life had been a leap of untold luxury from what it
used to be, when he lived in a modest rented apartment on Roosevelt Island just across the river. Perhaps it is a journey the SG occasionally contemplates on tranquil evenings during strolls down to the
river's edge. As he stood above the muffled rumble of the traffic
passing beneath him on the FDR Drive, he could look in the dark-
ness beyond the pearl string of white dotted lights on the Fifty-ninth
Street Bridge to the apartment complex he shared with other striv-
ing, upper-middle-class New York executives trapped in small rooms
with washing machines in the basement. That chasm was only
crossed by his appointment on December 13, 1996, by the Security
Council and approval by the General Assembly four days later, to
serve as the U.N.'s seventh chief executive. The distance is as
great as that from the Ghana of his youth to the spacious wood-
and-window-paneled office on the thirty-eighth floor of the glass-
and-marble Secretariat where some considered him "President of
the World."

He is respected and praised around the globe, lauded as the
calming voice of reason and reassurance, the discreet confidant of
presidents and prime ministers. His noble bearing presents a public
figure of quiet elegance and compassionate caring, who is revered
by millions for challenging the forces that exploit the unfortunate.
His aura of sanctity is complemented by his lawyer-and-artist wife
Nane, a striking blond woman of grace and dignity. Her international credentials are further enhanced by being a niece of the resistance hero Raoul Wallenberg, the Swedish diplomat who rescued
thousands of Jews during World War II only to vanish, presumably
kidnapped and murdered for his courageous acts. The Secretary-
General should represent all that is good in the world. But something's wrong in his house. Something doesn't fit.

It turns out that the home of the United Nations Secretary-General was commissioned in 1921 by Anne Morgan, the socially prominent and extremely wealthy daughter of Wall Street banker and robber baron J. P. Morgan. She was a trailblazing philanthropist and women's rights advocate, an activist who challenged her upper-crust peers to dedicate themselves to others. She was headstrong, defiant, different. At the outbreak of World War I, Ms. Morgan and her aristocratic friends founded a charitable effort aimed at feeding and clothing the French people who were suffering as a result of the war. The organization, the American Fund for Devastated France, had, by the war's end in 1918, collected and distributed more than $5 million worth of food, medicine, and other supplies to the belea-guered French people. That would be more than $80 million worth of food and medicine today.

She was a woman who didn't have to but did. The SG is a man who has to but can't. The house seems to have spoiled its guest.

So sell it. Why is he there, anyway?

Move the SG to the South Bronx.

He would live among people of many tongues, like himself, who are not restricted to speaking only Upper East Side or French. It's a quick trip. His office is already next to the FDR Drive. Just get on it after work and head north, to 344 East 146 Street. The cinderblock and chain-link–fenced building is the New York headquarters of Missionaries of Charity, Mother Teresa's order, which was where she would stay during her New York visits. As a professional human-itarian himself, the SG should move there. The big shots would still come for canapés and Lilet.

The New York City tax assessor values the U.N. mansion at $4,800,000, but in Manhattan's real estate market it would surely garner ten times as much. Because the owner of record is the United Nations, the building is not subject to real estate taxes. Not one dime is paid on one of the most expensive and grand residential properties in New York. If it were put on the block and put back on the tax rolls where it belongs, the house would generate an annual tax payment of $461,947.15 for the New York City treasury—enough to pay the annual salaries of four cops or five firefighters, or to feed 283,402 public school children lunch. Give up the house, and the world body can really accomplish something tangible. A purse snatcher can be caught, a fire extinguished, young American minds will have full tummies for the school day—nearly anything justifies the expenditures more.

If the U.N. sold the mansion for a likely $48,000,000, that money could be plowed right back into its own agencies to comfort the people who really need it. UNICEF says a donation "of $1 can immunize a child against polio for life, protecting him or her against the disease and preventing its spread to nearby communities." Let's see: immunize 48,000,000 children or keep the house. "Three dollars and seventy-five cents can provide educational materials for a child for one year, including a portion of the cost of teachers' supplies. Materials include books, pencils, a school bag, slate board, chalk, posters, rulers, safety scissors, and notebooks," claims UNICEF. Send 12,800,000 kids to school or keep the house. "Ten dollars provides enough high-protein biscuits to feed three hungry children for one month." Feed 1,440,000 kids or keep the house. "Two hundred and fifty dollars can provide a tent for a family whose home has been destroyed during an emergency, such as an earthquake or civil war." Put a tent over the heads of 192,000 desperate families or keep a very expensive roof over one head.

As is so typical of life at the world body, the joint's on the arm, as the New York City cop in his little corner guard booth would refer to a free meal. The lavish lifestyle ambassadors are privy to is far removed from the tangible problems the U.N. is charged with solving.

No wonder a diplomatic appointment holds such allure for so many—and no wonder the country trying hardest to focus the institution on its purpose rather than its perks is meeting overwhelming resistance.

– 4 –

THE INTERNATIONAL
ANTHEM: BLAME AMERICA!

There's probably nothing more dreaded in the U.N. than the sight of an American with a determined walk and a fixed gaze. Nothing worse than that abrasive and blunt accent demanding results and action. How vulgar that directness must seem. Much how the cautionary refrain in an everyday bureaucracy is "Don't rock the boat," the cautionary refrain inside the U.N. is "Don't let the giant roam free."

The U.N. is a place defined by the preservation of the status quo. Understanding that status quo is key to understanding the culture of the organization, key to understanding the policies it undertakes. And the status quo right now is to handcuff the world's superpower before we actually make some changes in the world. Unfortunately for the United States, if there's an international anthem at the U.N., it's got an anti-American theme.

"There's a lot of anti-Americanism at the U.N." That judgment comes from the inside, from Woodward. The charge is a familiar one from U.N. bashers, but it's rarely heard from U.N. diplomats themselves, a privileged class in the temple of world affairs. "They are definitely in their own world. There is a lot of hypocrisy. There also are a lot of people who don't like leadership, who don't like those who lead. It's like high school.

"There are times when other diplomats get up and read their anti-American statements and then they come rushing up to the United States delegation and say, 'You know I just had to read that,' and they slap you on the back, give you a handshake, and say, 'When are we going to lunch?' "

"It's stab you in the back, and then let's have lunch!" agrees another ambassador. "Some of the ambassadors I encounter who give the most venomous, poisonous speeches have lunch with me an hour later, and we have the most intellectual, cultured, and friendly conversations. Is this hypocrisy? Or is it part of the theatrics, or the rules of the game in this building?"

What Woodward particularly abhors is what he encounters from the foreign diplomats who "constantly think of themselves as the [brakes on] the United States, and yet they're begging us for a green card for their sons!" Yes, some of the top U.N. officials who criticize our country in the U.N. forum privately take advantage of their juice inside by asking for personal favors from the government they seem to spend their lives lambasting.

Woodward says despite this environment, "You have to remember, you walk into the room and you will immediately walk behind the sign that says 'UNITED STATES.' It's a simple sign, and it represents a great sense of working for your country and representing the ideals of your country." Pulling the chair to the edge of the desk, he shows his faith is restored despite the uphill nature of the battle. "When an American sits behind that sign, they are representing everything that America strives to be, the Constitution, George Washington. You hear the national anthem in your mind. For Americans that means we are going to evaluate the issues on the basis of what's right, on liberty and freedom, and not on whose hand is being greased and whose pocket is being filled."

But remember, we're in U.N. World, a location physically on the planet Earth but so often far removed from the reality beyond the organization's walls. Representing the United States can be a Sisyphean ordeal where small victories are relished in the pursuit of unattainable larger triumphs. The members of foreign delegations who speak with candor admit that the looming presence of the United States makes us a bigger target.

"There is widespread anti-Americanism" in the diplomatic corps, admits another respected member, a representative of a foreign nation who is willing to break the taboo as long as he is not identified. He speaks from experience, having served his capital in a variety of far-flung postings, ending with the prestigious plum of ambassador to the United Nations. He does not always agree with American foreign policy, but is bothered by the knee-jerk condemnation of the United States and Washington he regularly hears from his colleagues, sur-prisingly even from those who represent some of the "friendliest" countries with "long-standing historic ties" to the United States.

"I'm shocked every time I see it," he says. "I have heard it very often from many ambassadors, and it's incredible. I remember very well a discussion I had with a colleague on the Security Council," he recounts, shaking his head in disgust as he recalls one representa-tive of a large Latin American nation that is assumed to be a major U.S. ally. The specific "Excellency" in question is actually widely known to be quite vicious in his frequent private condemnations of the United States, yet he has been appointed to serve the interests of a country that earns billions in aid and trade annually from the ogre he so despises.

"America alienates the world by being better, by being moral, by trying to help, by giving aid," says one diplomat. "Hosni Mubarak [president of Egypt] once told me that his definition of foreign aid is taking money from poor people in the rich country and giving it to the rich people in the poor country!"

He agrees that while America can be respected inside the U.N. hallways, our country is also deeply resented. "It's a mixture of envy and guilt, of us looking in the mirror and not liking what we see and knowing the U.S. is probably holding us up to standards which we fail to achieve. There are obviously many other factors that make the world hate the U.S.," he says, but America simply trying to hold other nations to higher moral standards is a sore point. He recalled one world leader not so jokingly saying that what American diplomats in the U.N. system "call corruption, we call family values."

The words *bully, arrogant, resentment,* and much worse, usually associated with the word *Bush,* crop up commonly in international diplomatic circles. The most serious offenders used to be the historic anti-American Marxist hard-line communist states or dictatorships such as Cuba, Libya, North Korea, Iran, and Saddam's Iraq. The private barbs and public opposition now come from the distinguished diplomats of some U.S. allies and a new list of what some U.N. observers have taken to calling "the usual suspects," namely France and Russia . . . the duo of duplicity. "The way individual ambassadors see America actually does count in the everyday diplomatic world" to a far stronger degree than most believe, says one foreign ambassador. Many capitals rely on their United Nations representative to quickly gauge a sampling of official world opinion, and, among those who retire to the sedate delegate's lounge, complaining about American foreign policy seems to be second nature. Their attitudes no doubt affect and reflect their nations' policies to some extent.

As a reporter posted at the U.N., I can't say how frequently the U.N. employees who were American citizens would seek me out to privately complain about the anti-American attitudes of their fellow employees. Longtime staff members told me that hostility toward U.S. efforts in Iraq had further soured their working conditions.

"If you suffer from idealism when you come to this organization, you are cured," said one American U.N. employee. Granted, their perceptions were anecdotal and perhaps isolated, and their private views would certainly be denied or dismissed by U.N. officials. But a completely unscientific sampling of more than a dozen concerned citizens who, unsolicited and separately, expressed their shared disillusionment and frustrations about their fellow employees exposes a hidden bias that thrives at the core of the U.N. bureaucracy. I would ask them why, if the mood had turned so ugly and unwelcoming, they didn't quit. The response would uniformly be that the United Nations benefits are just too good, far superior to what is offered for comparable management and administrative white-collar jobs at American corporations. "They hate America. They hate Bush, they hate holding other nations responsible. It's unbelievable," one twenty-seven-year U.N. veteran told me about her colleagues. "It's getting worse, and it's really sickening."

"That is the sad part," another diplomat told me. He is a jovial, intelligent, and perceptive veteran who has represented his nation in other world capitals as well as at the U.N. complex in Geneva. "They hate the United States, they hate the hand that feeds them," he told me with regretful resignation. "I don't agree with all the decisions undertaken by the United States, but I do admire the fact that the United States has tried to clean up what is happening at the U.N. But if it were left up [to many of the member states] and they were not held accountable for that vote, they would vote against the United States."

It should not be surprising. "Of course, anyone working anywhere in the U.N. system is probably a multilateralist, is probably quietly anti-American," says another. "America makes our life extremely difficult. If you have American friends, or Western European friends, or Canadian friends working at the U.N., you have to assume they are fairly liberal minded, with few exceptions. You just can't have a United Nations with a superpower."

"It's payback time for the U.S.," admits one foreign ambassador. "At the U.N. you can say anything, vote anyway you want, and, at the end of the day, it doesn't really matter that much. It's easy to grind your ax, it's words and resolutions. Countries that either do not have the guts or ability to stand up to the U.S. at other international forums or in the international arena find the U.N. a convenient place."

"The United Nations cannot be considered anti-American, anymore than it could be considered anti-Brazilian, anti-Ukrainian or anything else like that," claimed Secretary General Kofi Annan for this book.

He is wrong.

Anti-Americanism at the U.N. does not necessarily come in the form of an overt, hate-filled, public harangue. Rather, it remains a more subtle and insidious hostility that lines up the votes against American efforts. After the summit in September 2005 achieved few U.N. reforms, *The New York Times* recognized that our country has been "rebutted by crucial partners and also by a coalition of poor countries increasingly resentful of American power" on issues ranging from Washington's attempts to rein in Iranian defiance of U.N. nuclear requirements to its efforts to clean up the U.N. bureaucracy.

The taint of anti-American sentiment has not just infected members of the diplomatic and civil service staff but also seems to have reached into the highest echelons of the world body and influenced its perspective. Michael Soussan, the former Oil for Food program coordinator, unmasked the anti-American bias of U.N. policy makers and found their prejudices mystifying and inexplicable. He claims some U.N. officials were shockingly more suspicious of American and British motives than those of a mass-murdering dictator.

"For reasons I have yet to fully understand," observed Soussan, "several U.N. leaders approached the implementation of the Oil for Food program with more distrust toward the United Kingdom and the United States than toward the regime of Saddam Hussein. In the hierarchy of hurdles we faced as we tried to make the program work, this, in my view, was problem number one."

While the member states reign in the General Assembly, the Secretariat is the bureaucracy that carries out the member nations' commands. There, confusing and conflicting agendas swamp achievement.

"I'm pretty cynical about the whole thing," observes Michael Scharf, director of the International Law Center at Case Western Reserve University School of Law. Having served as a U.S. representative at the U.N. on the Sanctions committee, he says that sanctions committees "have the no-objection procedure, which means every country gets a veto and not just the five permanent members [of the Security Council]. . . . Two things happen. You get a lot of horse trading, the 'I won't object to this if you don't object to my project,' which is not in the best interest of the whole world. The other thing that happens is that you get a least common denominator approach. Rather than having the strongest sanctions regime, it means you will have the weakest sanctions regime." And that failure occurs even when the ambassadors don't hate each other. The results too often are watered-down, homogenized responses to world threats—responses that are as empty as the air they fill.

"It was hostile, but we are great at leaving the hostilities in the room and trying to forge a relationship on other issues, because we are working on other issues at the same time," explains Woodward, referring to some of the Oil for Food debates that would go on in the 661 Committee responsible for the program. "Sometimes we would leave 661 after a knock-down–drag-out on a Tuesday, but by Thursday we'd be together working on a different issue in a different context. That would help smooth things over. And then we wouldn't have a sanctions meeting for another ten days, and then again at the next one we would get right back into it and it would be the same thing all over again."

"Almost everyone among the ambassadors has good personal relations," says A. Peter Burleigh, the "chargé d'affaires" and deputy permanent representative of the U.N. mission who served as acting U.S. ambassador in 1998 and 1999. "Seldom do the policy disagreements ultimately get reflected in personal hostility or problems."

Ambassador Daniel Gillerman of Israel agrees. "One of the

frustrating aspects of being Israel's ambassador to the U.N. is the incredible discrepancy between the very warm and good and even intimate relations you forge with your colleagues, including some who have no diplomatic relations with Israel and some countries that are hostile to Israel, and the way those countries behave at the U.N. This is an analogy of what happens with the U.S."

But these personal relationships cannot be said to promote collective interest policies as orders come via e-mail from afar. "At the U.N.," another American diplomat says, "you engage in diplomatic combat for the maximum possible deal for your country."

"Your sole mission there," said a foreign diplomat, "is to go with a knife between your teeth and get anything and everything that you can get your hands on. That's how they send them. With a knife between their teeth. Go and get everything!" he said, laughing at the image. "Rape, pillage, and plunder. I'm still disappointed."

But out of this competition of self-interest, if a new U.N. purpose can be said to have emerged in recent times, it is one forged by nations that, acting in concert, seek to check the power of the United States. The goal, says Ambassador Burleigh from his experience, was "to reduce American clout." With the fall of the Soviet Union and the end of the cold war, the dynamics of the world stage shifted as the United States emerged as the sole superpower, and the only place our policies could be challenged was in the Security Council. No matter how often France, Russia, and to some extent China are referred to as "our allies" in order to keep up appearances, the truth is that they are rivals and competitors, if not exactly enemies.

The U.N., says Ambassador Burleigh, "is the one place, certainly among the veto-wielding countries, where they can actually take steps to rein us in and balance American power. They have aspirations for playing a more prominent role than they actually play, and the Security Council and the U.N. is one place where, because of the veto, they actually have clout that is in dramatic excess to their actual importance and the role they would otherwise play in the world. They have a guaranteed power position. If only by threatening to veto something, they then have to be taken into consideration and dealt with by us."

Yet French President Jacques Chirac dismissed this reality. In a CBS interview, he asked, "Why would France want to restrain American power? And even if she wanted to, how could she?" Actually, very easily. French behavior belied Mr. Chirac's contention that "it's an absurd, totally unrealistic argument" that France seeks to undermine the superpower.

"The French have a . . . clear-headed view that this type of U.S. power is, in effect, a menace," says Burleigh bluntly, and "it wasn't just the French." He says most of the nations at the U.N. "were uncomfortable about the dominant role of the United States." This uneasiness was quite apparent during the Clinton administration, in which Burleigh served, indicating that antagonism toward America is not unique to the Bush administration, though some of the aggressive post-9/11 policies and the Iraq war certainly exacerbated that perception. Even back in the Clinton nineties, says Burleigh, "the discomfort was not necessarily anti-Americanism, at least among the most sophisticated people, many of whom are our closest allies. They felt the U.S. was so powerful it didn't need to take in the viewpoint of others. I met very few people whom I would consider to be fundamentally anti-American. What they were and I think still are is uneasy with our degree of power. . . . Virtually all the other countries don't like that."

Another American ambassador admits that the "United States is less powerful [in the United Nations] than it is in the real world." He says the aim of the other U.N. members is to try and constrain "the eight-hundred–pound gorilla. They don't want to weaken it, because most of those countries need the strength of the gorilla to project military might to protect their own interests. But they all have the concern that this powerful primate [will act] in a way which they strongly disagree with. If they can find a way to circumscribe the gorilla, it's in their interests."

In U.N. World, we start five furlongs behind, which is a predicament most U.N. supporters would not have you believe. Charles Duelfer, the CIA Iraq Survey Group chairman, told a congressional hearing that the Security Council is "one of their last claims to fame these days" for France, Russia, and China, and he also lumps in the British. "They need the Security Council to remain an important and effective body in the world," he says. "From their perspective, they need a way of containing the United States, and the Security Council's a tool for that. It's a vital tool for them, where their veto position is important."

One notable example of the strategy to frustrate American aims occurred during the debate over Iraq in the Security Council, when the former Mexican foreign minister likened his and the other governments to the Lilliputians tying down the giant. "I like very much the metaphor of Gulliver, of ensnarling the giant," Jorge Castaneda was quoted as describing the strategy of U.S. opponents such as his nation. He advocated "tying it up with nails, with thread, with twenty thousand nets that bog it down; these nets being norms, principles, resolutions, agreements, and bilateral, regional, and international covenants."

Another Mexican diplomat, U.N. Ambassador Adolfo Aguilar Zinser, was recalled by his government for his outspokenness regarding the United States during the Iraqi war debate. He held that position during the fractured discussions in the Security Council when Mexico was one of the ten temporary members. After the war he denounced the United States, saying it wanted "a relationship of convenience and subordination" with Mexico and treated its south-of-the-border neighbor as a backyard. After Zinser was killed in a car accident near Mexico City in June 2005, Kofi Annan recalled that he had "served his country with dedication, wit, and independence of spirit at a crucial time for the multilateral system." The attempts to trip up America may also have deeper motivations. One American diplomat believes many smaller nations justifiably covet their U.N. status because "that meant they were a real country. If they could speak out against the big boys," they had arrived.

U.N. World's disposition toward America can best be summed up by a conversation Ambassador Burleigh says he had with the Palestinian observer to the U.N., Yassar Arafat's nephew, Dr. Nasser Al-Kidwa. "I remember him half jokingly but also half seriously saying, 'Peter, your country may control the world, but we control this territory,'" meaning the eighteen-acre U.N. headquarters and the decisions within.

Former U.N. Ambassador Jeane Kirkpatrick blames the U.N. for allowing America's ideological opponents to reach the highest levels of influence within the world body. She has suggested creating "a community of democracies which will be at least as strong as the community of dictatorships, which so effectively dominate so many U.N. activities." As of 2005, the group Freedom House counted eighty-nine democracies as U.N. members, leaving 101 tyrannies, dictatorships, and oligarchies to run the place.

While it would be bad enough if member nations of the U.N. opposed America out of misguided principles grounded in mistaken views of the United States and its role in the world, the situation is much worse. Anti-Americanism is often adopted merely for the benefits it will yield to those individuals who engage in it.

"It's not so much us against everybody else," says Woodward. "It's America versus 190 countries that each take their turn to be against us." He says there is an active Stop America movement within the U.N. system "no matter what it may be, just because we have one nation leading, and there are 190 countries left to follow." The media attention of a sympathetic world press corps doesn't help. Woodward says the prospect of publicly nitpicking the Americans can transform a sophisticated and worldly diplomat into just another city councilman at a zoning hearing who salivates at seeing his name above the fold in the morning paper.

"If you say something that tries to stop an American idea, if you say 'no,' you are propped up and you get kudos from your home country and from everybody else at the U.N., and it somehow pushes you and you say, 'Oh, I like that media attention. I'm going to do that again!' "

Dominique de Villepin, the dashing, gray-haired then-foreign minister of France, was the poster boy for that syndrome. He became a rock star in the words of one delegation member for his eloquent and impassioned opposition to giving full Security Council backing to military action against Saddam. Yet only four months before he served as Chirac's tackle, he sounded just like George Bush. In a commentary in *Le Monde* on October 1, 2002—the month before resolution 1441 was passed, unanimously warning Saddam of "serious consequences" if he did not fully cooperate—he wrote, "Yes, Iraq has defied the international community by concealing programs concerning these weapons: if she does not yet have nuclear capabilities, all the indications make us think that she has reconstituted biological and chemical capabilities." How do you say *amnesia* in French?

Less than six months later, after the war commenced despite the French objections, de Villepin was confronted by reporters in London and asked, "Who do you want to win the war?" According to the (London) *Telegraph,* the flamboyant Frenchman shot back, "I'm not going to answer. You have not been listening carefully to what I said before. You already have the answer." Did that mean America? Yet he called accusations that he was anti-American, "Laughable. I don't think it's even worth replying. I grew up, to a large extent, in the United States," he told the television channel France 3 on September 10, 2004. "I was educated partly in the United States. I have spent many years of my life there. It's a country I respect, I admire." He praised American "optimism. The Americans have a tremendous capacity to take up challenges." De Villepin was widely hailed across the globe for what was viewed as offering a principled counterargument against those belligerent

Americans and their narrow-minded leader who sought to challenge Saddam. Yet four months into the war, after his boss lost the ability to derail the long overdue consequences for Saddam, de Villepin claimed, "We were happy to see Saddam Hussein's regime fall."

Who's he kidding? "The French position," one foreign Security Council ambassador told me, "was not so much as being anti-American in the true sense of the word, as it was philosophically opposed to U.S. foreign policy on this one issue and at times on others also. Not agreeing with American foreign policy does not mean we are anti-American, but I do ask and expect Washington to listen to and consider our concerns. And at times that consideration is lacking."

"Americans too often do not have an appreciation that we respond to our own domestic concerns," explains another foreign nation's Security Council ambassador. "We have our own pressures. I've got the opposition party criticizing my government and my president, and we have to factor that domestic reality into our positions. Look at what happened after 1441 when the U.S. offered one more resolution to endorse an invasion. We [the Security Council] had the votes for it, we had the votes! The majority of the temporary members were going to support it, even the African countries. Then the French changed the rules with Chirac's veto threat and everybody said, 'Why should I stick my [neck] out on this if our French friends will kill it anyway?'"

Still others say opposition to American proposals is motivated by much simpler feelings—many just hate the pressure of having to achieve something. "What people at the U.N. want, in a very large part, is not to have to do anything," says Charles Hill, the former special assistant to Secretary-General Boutros Boutros-Ghali. "The U.S., because of who we are, can't sit back on every case, and the officials and ambassadors at the U.N. then get very annoyed when someone is trying to get them to do something. And whenever that is happening, it is almost certain that they are being called, or

badgered, or cornered in the delegate's lounge by the American ambassador, and they grow to resent it."

Is the annoyance of interrupted quiet time with *Le Figaro* what
drives anti-American sentiment?

Professor Hill says the prospect of delving into the world's most
intractable problems without any sureness of success carries with it
uncertainty and a result that could prove hazardous to the organization's reputation and, perhaps more importantly, one's own. After
all, many U.N. ambassadors are actually politicians in the governments of their home countries, so they're sensitive to what their
reputation and legacy will be long after they have departed the
shores of the East River to return to another (higher, they hope)
government post in their homeland.

The U.N., Hill says, "is a very supine organization that enjoys its
privileges, enjoys Manhattan, enjoys a veneer of high moral purpose that everyone there feels has descended upon them when they
are there. Having to do something is always troublesome, because it
means you're going to have to take sides, it means that somebody in
one way or another is going to get hurt politically."

The challenge for America, in the face of nations and individuals set against our initiatives, or action of any kind, is to find a way to
effectively realize our interests. Should we continue to operate in an
arena that can be hostile from the outset, or should the nation strive
to set the U.N. back on the course its founders intended it to follow?

The forum where the U.N.'s anti-Americanism and perception of it
has reverberated the loudest is in the U.S. Congress. Long after the
iconoclastic U.N. critic Jesse Helms had left the Senate, his succes-
sors in both houses took up the cause for which Helms had been re-
garded by many as something of a crackpot. For many years he was
viewed as being so far out on the extreme right that U.N. supporters could easily dismiss his complaints and criticism of their beloved
institution as those of some xenophobic Southern wack-job. He had
long lambasted U.N. officials as dysfunctional, called them cry babies,

and made it plain that Americans felt a lack of gratitude from the conclave for which they footed the majority of the bills. But with hindsight it has become clear that Helms had been on the money all along.

"The United Nations does not deserve continued support," he wrote in the esteemed journal *Foreign Affairs*, published by the elite Council on Foreign Relations in the fall of 1996. Helms wrote that the U.N.'s transformation from an "institution of sovereign nations into a quasi-sovereign entity . . . represents an obvious threat to U.S. national interests," that the organization cried out to be "radically overhauled. . . . Either the United Nations reforms, quickly and dramatically, or the United States will end its participation. . . . I am convinced without the threat of American withdrawal, nothing will change."

Within four years, as the chairman of the Senate Foreign Relations Committee, he delivered his message in person. "If the United Nations is to be effective it must be an institution that is needed by the great democratic powers of the world," Helms told the United Nations Security Council face-to-face in 2000, the first time a United States senator had been invited to address the Council.

"I am not a diplomat," he told them, admitting, "I am not fully conversant with the elegant and rarified language of the diplomatic trade . . . so I trust you will forgive me if I come across as a bit more blunt than those you are accustomed to hearing in this chamber."

Helms then read them the riot act. He told the Security Council that most Americans see "the majority of the U.N. members routinely voting against America in the General Assembly," that "Americans reject the idea of a sovereign United Nations that presumes to be the source of legitimacy for the United States Government's polices," and that a "United Nations that seeks to impose its presumed authority on the American people without their consent begs for confrontation, and, I want to be candid, eventual U.S. withdrawal."

He chastised the very diplomats who sat before him, saying, "The Security Council has utterly failed to stop Saddam Hussein's drive to build instruments of mass murder," reminding them that the "American people will never accept the claims of the United Nations 'to be the sole source of legitimacy on the issue of force' in the world." Perhaps Kofi Annan could have been reminded of this view when three years later he called the U.S.-led invasion of Iraq illegal, because it was not countenanced by the majority of the Security Council.

Perhaps Mr. Annan could have reviewed the lessons of history, as explained in the slow, southern drawl of the North Carolinian who told that same body, "International law did not defeat Hitler, nor did it win the Cold War. What stopped the Nazi march across Europe, and the Communist march across the world, was the principled projection of power by the world's great democracies. And the principled projection of force is the only thing that will ensure the peace and security of the world in the future. . . . More often than not," observed Helms, " 'international law' has been used as a make-believe justification for hindering the march of freedom."

Yet at the time, "Nearly every member of the Security Council challenged Mr. Helms's bleak portrayal of the United Nations and criticized the United States for letting it down," reported *The New York Times*. By today, the pool of U.N. critics and of those who pushed for reform has finally swelled to include politicians from both sides of the aisle as well as millions of Americans for whom the U.N. scandals only confirm that their long-held negative opinions have always been correct. The call for U.N. reform has become Kofi Annan's leading priority as a way to try and refurbish the U.N.'s sagging credibility while also addressing his baying detractors in Washington.

Richard Holbrooke (the former U.N. ambassador under President Clinton), who counseled Annan throughout the crisis of confidence in his stewardship, attacked the critics by claiming U.S. perception of the U.N. was "misinformed, misunderstood, and misrepresented." He released a letter the retired Helms wrote on February 17, 2005, to former Colorado Senator Tim Wirth, president of the U.N. Foundation. Helms, the longstanding U.N. boogeyman, wrote, "I know you would agree that if the U.N. did not exist, some-thing much like it would have to be created, because the nations of the world would have to have a place to talk through their differ-ences, and support each others' noble causes. For that very reason, I believe that we cannot give up on the U.N., but we must do the hard work of making the U.N. live up to its original promise."

Holbrooke led the chorus of U.N. supporters, sounding like the U.N. critics so championed by Helms for many years. But now it was Holbrooke who echoed Helms's demands that Congress strengthen a reformed U.N. Holbrooke said precisely because of "the lack of American engagement and leadership, the institution was hijacked by states whose practices are anathema to all that the U.N. stands for," claiming, "If we continue to under-fund, under-support and undermine the United Nations system, it will become progressively weaker and at the same time it will increasingly be-come a center of hostility toward the U.S."

But many others saw it as that already. "Most American taxpay-ers believe their hands are being bitten by the very people that our hands feed," countered Michigan Republican Congressman Thad-deus McCotter. "To hear talk about strengthening this particular or-ganization strikes me as odd . . . because I don't know who tries to get more power to a broken lamp. . . . I am very afraid to hear peo-ple saying we should strengthen a dysfunctional organization. As a parent, my view is when you reward bad behavior you get more bad behavior, and if you reward corruption by strengthening it, you get more corruption. We should not even talk of strengthening an orga-nization that appears not to be able to control itself, or manage it-self, let alone police itself."

That somber view led to congressional legislation called the U.N. Oil for Food Accountability Act, which would cut America's share of the U.N. budget unless the organization released all of the program's documents and removed diplomatic immunity of U.N. officials so they could face criminal charges in federal court. "The United States pays so much of the budget," said Nevada Republican

Senator John Ensign, who introduced the bill. "But every time we turn around, the United Nations is doing something that harms the United States. The United Nations seems to be working against . . . our policies. I don't expect them to be out there as our advocate in the world, but I certainly don't expect them to be our opponent in the world, and that is what they've become. No matter what the policy is, it's almost across the board; they try and form coalitions to lead the world against the United States!"

Ensign sponsored the legislation because he thinks U.N. reform can only be achieved with the threat of being cut off from Daddy. "The only way to make the United Nations accountable is by withholding funding," he says. "There is no other way. If you just give them the money and don't ask questions, they are not going to become accountable." That view, previously espoused by Senator Helms, resulted in a partial U.N.-reform program that did not go far enough.

Remember, in U.N. World, nothing is as it seems. If the reforms pressed for by Congress are not enacted, what can we do? Can we simply ignore the U.N.? Can we accomplish anything that way? Yes. It has been done before, successfully.

While many endeavor to improve the institution by engaging it, sidestepping the Security Council has, when appropriate, proven to be the best and only way to get something done. The love/hate relationship with the United States has proven that some bold or unpopular measures would never pass muster with other Security Council nations. After all, remove the label "Security Council" from the assemblage and one is left with the United States, France, Russia, China, and Great Britain deciding what course to take in world affairs for themselves.

In March 1999, the American government led a coalition against the Serbian slaughter in Kosovo that resulted in seventy-eight straight days of bombing under the auspices of NATO. President Bill Clinton ordered the air assault. He did not ask permission of the United Nations Security Council to launch the five-hundred-pound bombs from the F-14s. He did not seek a resolution granting him permission to launch anything. In fact, President Clinton completely bypassed the U.N. out of the realistic concern that the French, Russians, and Chinese would hog-tie the United States and NATO. Yet the president who waged war without the Security Council's blessing for dropping bombs has been hailed as the savior of multilateral diplomacy and revered as the symbol of respect for the international community. President George W. Bush, who went to the Security Council before taking military action, has been vilified. Go figure. But then again, in U.N. World, anything is possible.

In April 2005 Mr. Clinton was appointed as Annan's United Nations special envoy for tsunami recovery. He received his own U.N. office across the street from the headquarters building. His U.N. staff included his former White House chief of staff Erskine Bowles, who also settled into U.N. World. "President Clinton is so obviously the right person for this job," trumpeted Annan when he announced his new prize on April 13, 2005. "From now on, he will devote himself fully to leading the United Nations effort. . . . I know he and Mr. Bowles are also enjoying the United Nations colleagues who are on the team."

The team didn't last too long. By September, five months later, Mr. Bowles was no longer occupying his U.N. office, having returned south as president of the University of North Carolina. President Clinton was holding his own "Clinton Global Initiative" conference—seemingly in competition to the U.N.'s gathering during its world summit that fall—though he continued to serve the U.N. as special adviser and returned to the tsunami region.

But such trivialities were nowhere to be seen that promising April day as Clinton and Annan stood together in the service of humanity. In his autobiography, *My Life*, the former president describes Mr. Annan as someone "who had given most of his professional life in service to the United Nations, but he was not blind to its shortcomings, nor wedded to its bad habits." For his part, the Secretary-General introduced his new partner by saying, "From very early on, I looked for a really high-profile figure, with exceptional talent and qualities." Just leave it to Kofi to honor the commander in chief who dismissed both him and his organization six years earlier.

Back then, on the first night of the Clinton-led Kosovo attack that did thankfully halt the atrocities and ethnic cleansing, Annan declared, "It is indeed tragic that diplomacy has failed, but there are times when the use of force may be legitimate in the pursuit of peace." Notice the word *may*, not *is*. Annan went on to remind the world that "the Security Council has primary responsibility for maintaining international peace and security," leaving it unsaid that in his view the burden did not belong to Bill Clinton and his coalition of the willing.

As the bombing continued, Annan repeated his warnings. "Unless the Security Council is restored to its preeminent position as the sole source of legitimacy on the use of force, we are on a dangerous path to anarchy," he declared on May 19, 1999, in The Hague—familiar sentiments he would echo about Iraq four years later. He also warned, "Unless the Security Council can unite around the aim of confronting massive human rights violations and crimes against humanity on the scale of Kosovo, then we will betray the ideals that inspired the founding of the United Nations."

He also singled out "the emergence of a single superpower," and criticized "the preference for the so-called coalitions of the willing," to carry out joint military actions absent the Security Council's blessing. Perhaps such efforts would not have been necessary in both Kosovo and Iraq had the Security Council not repeatedly been the coalition of the unwilling.

Secretary of State Madeleine Albright told the Security Council where it could go. Asked by Jim Lehrer on PBS if an emergency session of the Security Council could stop the NATO bombing, she replied, "No." She hailed the nineteen-nation coalition (eleven fewer than President Bush assembled for Iraq): "The U.N. has spoken on it, and the reality here is if you hear what the Russians are saying and they're at the U.N., they would probably object to an operation like this. And the killing would go on. So I think that we are doing the right thing."

But when the fractured U.N. spoke out against the Iraq invasion in 2003, forcing President Bush to take it upon himself to carry out the council's neglected mandates, Albright, her boss, and their cohorts conveniently decided America was doing the wrong thing by taking action without the Security Council's blessing. "The perception here has been upside down," observes Professor Hill, Boutros-Ghali's U.N. special adviser. "Clinton did a lot of damage to the U.N. and didn't get any kind of heat for it, and Bush, in fact, tried to do a lot to bring the U.N. back to a responsible role and got pummeled for it." He says throughout the nineties, after the debacle of Black Hawk Down in Somalia in 1993, the Clinton administration "was openly and overtly scorning" the U.N. by, for example, excluding it from involvement in the Dayton Accords, the agreement hammered out in 1995 ending hostilities in the former Yugoslavia. The effort by the Republican-led Congress to withhold $1.5 billion in back U.N. dues unless the organization initiated reforms certainly did not help U.S. standing, leading to accusations that we were a deadbeat nation. Eventually Congress appropriated the money. Mr. Clinton took the credit, even though the management and financial reforms that were instigated were too few and did not nearly go far enough, as subsequent scandals have proven.

"There was a perception that Clinton was pro-U.N.," says Hill. "In fact he was doing considerable damage to it. I think the low point came in the Kosovo bombing." Yet President Clinton turns out to not be the only Iraq war critic who found it convenient to ignore the Security Council.

Jacques Chirac—who single-handedly destroyed Security Council backing for the Iraq war, who was the great critic of "unipolar" versus his beloved "multipolar" diplomacy, and who preached about the need for council approval for military forays—gave his fellow internationalists the cold shoulder when it suited his goals.

France never sought Security Council approval to send four thousand troops to the Ivory Coast or to then launch air strikes. "Nobody yelps about it," observes Ambassador Burleigh, because it's not the Americans disrespecting the U.N. "The important standard for the rest of them is that the U.S. has to meet the standards, and there can be exceptions made for the others," he says.

In November 2004, the military-ruled Ivorian government conducted bombing raids that accidentally killed nine French peacekeepers. Chirac approved retaliatory attacks that took out the tiny Ivorian air force. The Security Council acted *after* France's military action, imposing sanctions against the Ivory Coast military regime, including a travel ban on Ivorian officials, ironically the same punishment France refused to endorse when the United States sought one against Saddam's regime. Perhaps, if only the Ivory Coast's leaders had cut France in on more coca contracts, they would still be able to scarf down crêpes on the Champs Elysées.

The Security Council granted France another break it certainly would never have extended to the United States. It turned the French forces into U.N. peacekeepers but allowed them to act without consulting or obeying the United Nations' peacekeeping chain of command. In November 2004, they opened fire on protesters, killing seven and wounding two hundred, prompting demonstrators to attack a U.N. vehicle.

"Where are the BBC interviews with Secretary-General Kofi Annan declaring the French adventure 'illegal,' as he did . . . concerning Iraq?" asked Canadian columnist Lorne Gunter in Ontario's *National Post*. "The French have done it all without any deference to the multilateral consensus-building they so smugly demanded of the Americans and the British [regarding Iraq]. . . . Doubly galling is the silence—even complicity—of the U.N. and the international community . . . which so sanctimoniously and vocally obstructed the invasion of Iraq," wrote Gunter.

The hypocrisy within U.N. World is undeniable. Americans are at a distinct disadvantage. While paying more than any other nation for the privilege of membership, they are held to a higher standard, an unfair standard that seeks to compromise our national interests. And when we do break from the U.N., there are clearly political considerations behind whatever censure we receive. Presidents Bush and Clinton both did so, but only one was dragged through the mud by the world body. Ironically for the U.N., the one they've derided has been the one trying to return legitimacy to the laws and practices it attempts to enact. Unfortunately, during the Bush administration the U.N. has indeed chomped down hard on the hand that's been trying to nurture it back to life.

"The bottom line is that the United States has more enemies than friends" at the U.N., wrote Fred Gedrich, a senior policy analyst at the Freedom Alliance, a lobbying group founded by Oliver North. "The level of anti-American voting in the world body is longstanding and unsurprising. The U.N. has become a morally bankrupt and corrupt institution because it serves as a safe haven and mouthpiece for some of the world's most sinister forces."

The redundant proposals number in the hundreds, so many that the United States is continually in the minority voting against them. We are faithfully joined by our ally Israel in taking the principled stands, along with a powerhouse coalition usually consisting of Grenada, the Marshall Islands, the Federated States of Micronesia, and Palau.

When former Missouri Senator John Danforth showed up for his new but brief job as U.S. ambassador in 2004, he asked for a map to find out the location of all our tiny allies. It didn't take him very long to question the reasons for the General Assembly's existence. When it rejected U.S. and European resolutions condemning human rights violations, the exasperated and disgusted American representative reacted. "One wonders about the utility of the General Assembly. . . . One wonders if there can't be a clear and direct statement on matters of basic principle," he declared. "Why have this building? What are we all about? This to me is a very bad situation.

The message from the General Assembly is very simple and it is, 'You may be suffering, but we can't be bothered.'" Ambassador Danforth then, in a stroke of Midwestern common sense, quit after six months, returning to St. Louis to retire with his ailing wife.

Over the years, there has been some softening in the historic anti-Western stance of the General Assembly. It took sixteen years for the notorious Zionism-equals-racism resolution to be repealed as President George H. W. Bush and his administration applied massive pressure in 1991 to achieve that sign of progress. The point man on that victory was John Bolton, now U.N. ambassador. And in 2005, the General Assembly finally recognized and honored the Holocaust by holding a special remembrance for the six million victims. Incredibly, Israeli Ambassador Daniel Gillerman was elected as one of the General Assembly's twenty-one vice presidents, a largely ceremonial post but significant because of Israel's inclusion.

Yet as Kofi Annan has proposed an ambitious agenda aimed at reforming the troubled organization, no management fiat can change the ingrained anti-American attitudes that are as much a part of the building as the model of Sputnik suspended from the ceiling in the visitor's entrance, or the little airline-sized bottles of red wine that had been available from the vending machine just steps from the Security Council chamber.

Annan, however, insists that the U.N. is not anti-American.

He sat down with me for a half-hour Fox News interview in December 2003, thinking the storm of criticism over the war had passed—yet he was unknowingly on the verge of an even greater crisis that would soon engulf his domain, his family, and himself. He entered the wood-paneled Secretary-General's conference room on the thirty-eighth floor, just down the hall from his windowed office. A man of quiet dignity and elegance, he was very proper and answered my pointed questions with grace.

"The U.N. is not anti-American at all," he insisted. "When you go back to the creation of this organization, American leaders and American politicians played a very important role, and the U.S. and the U.N. for many years and on many occasions have worked extremely well together."

"But it did not happen now," I countered, referring to the failure of the Security Council to fully endorse the war.

"It did not happen now," he acknowledged. "The world is not made up of one event. I think one has to look at the record and the history, and I think we also have to be careful not to judge the U.N. by one event. We do a lot that impacts on every individual every day, but they don't see that. I don't think it is fair to generalize from the particular case of Iraq and dismiss the U.N. as ineffectual."

I reminded him that some consider him anti-American. He answered, "I think it is unfortunate that they get that impression. They have to understand that I have work to do, and I am the Secretary-General of the United Nations. I do not represent the United States in this building."

He conceded, "There will be times when I will take a position, which is at variance with the U.S. administration; it doesn't make me anti-American. It indicates I'm doing the work I'm here to do."

He then took a swipe at the critical news media coverage of the U.N. "There are many occasions where we see eye to eye but that doesn't make news. It's when you disagree that it gets exciting." Annan didn't think that was right. "I don't think it's fair, but I can't do much about it; it comes with the territory; it's part of the turf I cover at the moment. But I don't lose any sleep over it."

Perhaps as the Oil for Food revelations eventually tumbled out and stained his son, the criticism did cause some sleepless nights. But in the arena of international affairs, he insisted that he did "work well together" with the Bush administration. He also said they speak frankly, which is diplomatic lingo for disagreeing. "Where I have differences, I speak out just as they speak out." He also implied that the responsibility for the allowing of Saddam's abuses was not his but that of the diplomats. I reminded him that, "Saddam Hussein, for all those years, twelve to thirteen years, ignored the Security Council," that over the span of "seventeen resolutions, he did not completely provide" for what he was legally required to produce and to explain under the Security Council mandates.

"What does it mean when a tin-horn dictator, an evil man like Saddam Hussein, ignores the United Nations?" I asked Annan. For a moment he struggled with his thoughts, but put the blame squarely on the Security Council.

"I think the U.N. is as strong as the member states. We should not forget that when you look at the division of this current Iraq war, that it was the same United Nations that passed a resolution authorizing the first Gulf War, the same United Nations working with former President Bush and Secretary of State James Baker that created an atmosphere and basis of pulling together a coalition that went and removed Iraq from Kuwait. There are times when the governments come together and they work together. Iraq was one of those issues where there were genuine divisions among the membership, and that carried on through the war. We are trying to mend fences and heal the wounds as we speak."

The fact remains, however, that many in the United States have lost faith in the U.N. In many ways this Secretary-General and the next may be defined by their ability to reestablish the trust of the American people. I have asked him what he planned to do:

> **Me:** What would you say specifically . . . to the American people to try and convince them, who have been so disappointed the past couple of years with what they have seen here, to restore the goodwill of this organization?

> **Annan:** I think that the argument that comes through . . . is very clear: that we live in an interconnected world, in a world where we face many challengers, many threats—threats that no one country, however powerful, can face alone—and that we need to work together to contain these threats, whether it is terrorism, nonproliferation, or environmental degradation

and poverty that leads to failed states. And we also know that ignoring failed states creates problems that sometimes come back to bite us. So I think the collective effort of all of us working together is in the national interest of individual member states. I think that an effective and functioning United Nations is in the interests of the United States and its people, as it is in the interest of other nations and their peoples.

The words *collective* and *working together* rang in my ears. Judging by the accounts of insiders, in recent years the U.N. has been bogged down by dissention and disagreements while being buffeted by scandals that betray its purpose. We have watched the institution nearly implode and stall in paralysis. We have rediscovered the need for the United States and other nations to take action, to reform the stricken organization before similar crises further jeopardize its principles and American interests. There is much to learn from the past few years in U.N. World. From the leadership to the member nations, the administrators to the corporate partners, all the way down to the auditors keeping the books—global welfare and security have been compromised time and time again. The past few years in U.N. World say a lot about the organization . . . and, at the same time, very little.

– 5 –

HELPING THE ENEMY

If international law is to have any weight in the twenty-first century, the U.N. must realize its goal of producing binding agreements and policies that actually achieve some measure of consequence. If the United States is ever to put its faith in the world body, the U.N. will have to prove that it can maintain global security by restraining the reach and influence of those nations and entities that pose the gravest threats to that equilibrium. America can only hope that for some time there will not be a clearer case of the U.N.'s dereliction of duty than its handling of Saddam Hussein and his Iraq.

Ultimately, all of the resolutions, programs, sanctions, agreements, proclamations, propositions, and warnings in the world couldn't restrain the most infamous tyrant of the latter half of the twentieth century. Worse, a stunning testament to U.N. World is the fact that many of its actions served to support and enrich Hussein and to facilitate his ends.

The U.N. became a tool at the disposal of Saddam Hussein. He made a mockery of the humanitarian values the organization holds sacred while threatening the interests of the United States.

He had been hiding in his hole because the United Nations could not keep him out of it. When the hand of an American soldier, Fourth Infantry Division Task Force 121, firmly pulled Saddam Hussein out of his dirt-and-leaf-covered sanctuary, many celebrated the capture of an evil and murderous tyrant. But the United States's victory was the U.N.'s failure.

Saddam Hussein personally devised a strategy that created an impasse at the U.N. and paralyzed the Security Council. His country was on the edge of economic collapse because of the U.N. sanctions imposed on him after the first Gulf War as punishment for defying the council's resolutions. To maintain economic viability and domestic stability, Hussein retaliated by successfully seducing three Security Council members: France, Russia, and China. To seduce them, he had to achieve diplomatic dominance over the United States inside the U.N., despite his record of horrendous abuses. He could not have achieved all this without the oil revenue he took in under U.N. auspices. The Oil for Food program—the U.N.'s humanitarian gem—was his vehicle.

A staggering, nearly endless flow of riches poured Saddam's way thanks to the U.N.—riches vastly beyond anything he could have ever imagined. The tyrant's take from the program and from oil smuggling that the Security Council countenanced has been estimated at $10.2 to $22 billion, and the United States could only go along.

The Wall Street Journal estimates the U.N. actually let him control a far larger amount: "The total value of contracts under Oil for Food was more than $100 billion—or $64.2 billion in oil sales and $38.7 billion in humanitarian purchases . . . $100 billion worth of business that Saddam was able to steer wherever he wanted." The Volcker Committee concurred.

One hundred billion dollars!

More than the gross national product of 171 countries.

This while the average Iraqi's yearly income was roughly $600 and falling.

The idea was born of the best intentions at the U.N. The concept seemed so noble, simple, and achievable: sell oil, buy food. The U.N. says the program helped keep twenty-seven million Iraqis alive while reducing disease and malnutrition. But as we shall see, one must be deeply suspicious of the figures. Hussein exploited the program, manipulating the United Nations' goodwill and taking advantage of its naivety, stunning incompetence, and perhaps criminal complicity. Instead of just "sell oil, buy food," he sold oil and bought bullets, missiles, Mercedes, and Security Council votes.

In the hallways of the United Nations, I'd ask the diplomats about Iraq's spending from the U.N. program, and they would shrug their shoulders and reply, "It's the Iraqis' money. They can do what they want with it."

But, they would insist, thanks to the Security Council, Hussein was boxed in, incapable of again embarking on a global weapons shopping spree that would pose a threat.

Or so they thought.

Didn't anyone at the U.N. care enough to question a megalomaniac's expenditures? He certainly did not hide it. The world body's willful ignorance was absurd.

By 2003, seven years into the Security Council's sanctions, Saddam had managed to construct at least seventy-eight separate presidential palace compounds, built and paid for thanks to the Security Council's fecklessness. The display on such an obscenely self-indulgent scale seemed to be taken for granted by the world body. The over-the-top opulence has now been well documented. A Department of State report in 1999 estimated that Saddam Hussein had spent more than $2 billion on the palace projects alone. We have now seen the gold-leafed faucets, floors of fine marble, glittering crystal chandeliers, and oversized rooms that made the chambers of Versailles

seem quaint by comparison. Many were landscaped with lush manicured gardens, large man-made lakes and pools, and waterfalls. One
presidential palace spanned an area larger than Manhattan's Central
Park, with dozens of buildings. The Saddamiat al Tharthar, a massive
residential complex eighty-five miles west of Baghdad, was opened in
1999. The Department of State report called it "a sprawling lakeside
vacation resort [that] contains stadiums, an amusement park, hospitals, parks, and 625 homes to be used by government officials. . . .
There is no clearer example of the government's lack of concern for
the needs of its people." No wonder General Tommy Franks dubbed
the U.N. effort the Oil for Palaces program.

Hussein was also in the process of constructing the largest
mosque in the world, the Saddam Grand Mosque, which could hold
thirty thousand worshipers, complete with a lake in the shape of the
Arab world. Another mosque, the Mother of All Battles, contains a
monument of Saddam's thumbprint, with his initials monogrammed
in gold.

One hundred billion dollars!

Enough not only to build narcissistic monuments but, far more
serious and troubling, enough to buy nations and completely compromise the ethical mandate of the United Nations and the Security
Council. It is still not known exactly how much was earned through
bribes, payoffs, kickbacks, secretly controlled front companies, and
oil smuggling. But it was enough to keep Hussein in power.

"The dream of the United Nations has turned into a nightmare
of corruption and incompetence, and it's time for U.N. officials to
wake up," charged Congressman Dana Rohrabacher, Republican of
California, during House International Relations Committee hearings into the Oil for Food program. "What we had was blatant corruption, blatant and visible corruption that was ignored by U.N.
officials on the scene, and even worse, corruption covered up by
U.N. officials at U.N. headquarters."

"The U.N. cannot be governed by unaccountable international bureaucrats operating with little public oversight," added the

committee chairman, Congressman Henry Hyde, Republican of Illinois, or "abuses will continue to occur protected by neglect borne of indifference."

Democrats were more temperate in their criticism, but California Congressman Tom Lantos, a Hungarian Holocaust survivor, acknowledged his disillusionment, "The U.N. still looks very much like an organization created for a different time." He believes that "we need the United Nations more than ever," but concedes its repeated failures "harm our own interests."

We now know from secret Iraqi government documents that a laundry list of public officials, government agencies, prominent politicians, influential financiers and businessmen, selected private citizens, and journalists were all beneficiaries of Hussein's beneficence, many allegedly on the take, enriching themselves and the regime in a U.N.-run program that only emboldened and strengthened the failing dictator. Far from the confident denials of the deluded diplomats, Saddam Hussein was indeed exploiting the U.N.'s mandates by rearming his military.

The report by the head of the Central Intelligence Agency's Iraq Survey Group, Charles Duelfer, has exposed the U.N.'s hypocrisy and failure to contain Saddam.

Says Duelfer, "Saddam created a network of Iraqi front companies, some with close relationships to high-ranking foreign government officials. These foreign government officials, in turn, worked through their respective ministries, state-run companies, and ministry-sponsored front companies to procure illicit goods, services, and technologies for Iraq's WMD-related, conventional arms, and/or dual-use goods programs."

Here's a partial list of what Saddam purchased with U.N.-"supervised" dollars, and where he purchased the items:

Belarus: missile technology, satellite systems, radar and air defense technology, tank equipment, laser technology, rocket-propelled grenades, antitank ammunition, tank and Mig-29 spare parts.

Bulgaria: Kornet missiles, thermal imagers, combat vehicle launch units, spare tank parts, and shoulder-fired missiles.

China: missile gyros, inertial guidance systems, automatic weapons.

France: spare parts for Mirage fighter aircraft, Roland air-to-ground missile parts, electronic warfare technology.

India: missile program technology for solid propellant fuel.

Jordan: missile parts, global positioning systems, video gun sights, electronic countermeasures equipment, armored vehicles, thirty-mm cannon technology.

North Korea: infrared missile-jamming systems, missile gyros and navigation technology, ballistic missile technology, thermal-imaging equipment, ammunition, rocket systems.

Poland: missile system engines.

Russia: shoulder-fired missiles, advanced missiles, tanks, night-vision equipment, global-positioning-system jammers, missile-guidance systems and engines, Kornet antitank missiles.

South Korea: military computer systems, sophisticated communications and radar systems.

Syria: missiles, rocket-propelled grenades, machine guns, ammunition.

Ukraine: antiaircraft radar systems.

Yugoslavia: Mig-21 jet engines.

Not much on this list is edible, is it?

All while the U.N. was supposed to be monitoring and controlling Hussein's revenue to prevent him from rearming. All the while America hoped the U.N. would keep him in check.

"Saddam perverted the whole thing, corrupted it in effect," noted Vice President Dick Cheney, who said the Iraqi dictator "generated billions of dollars which he used partly to get around the sanctions by buying weapons of various kinds, conventional weapons in this case."

Others also blame America for letting Saddam get away with it. Democratic Senator Carl Levin of Michigan, the ranking minority member of the Senate committee investigating the Oil for Food scandal, cited "$10 billion in illicit income" that the United States and others allowed Saddam to rake in through permitted oil smuggling to Turkey, Jordan, and Syria. To Levin, this rip-off went down "in broad daylight," because the Clinton and Bush administrations endorsed oil trading "outside" of the program.

Levin branded those sales "blatant violations of the U.N. sanctions" that occurred as "the United States and other U.N. countries looked the other way." The end run wasn't secret—the State Department had officially notified Congress of the decision. The smuggling to Jordon and Turkey was permitted, one diplomat told me, "because Saddam's cheap oil ensured those nations' economies wouldn't implode." The result, of course, was another Security Council protected pipeline of funding that strengthened Saddam.

Volcker estimated that oil smuggling netted Saddam as much as $11 billion (that on top of $64.2 billion worth of oil sales from Oil for Food and $1.8 billion in kickbacks and payoffs sponged off the program). Volcker pinned the blame for smuggling squarely on the world body, saying it flourished "without any kind of inspection or oversight by the United Nations," and that the diplomats "turned a blind eye" to the violations "with no genuine effort by the Security Council to monitor" what was going on. The result, concluded Volcker, was that Saddam was yet again "emboldened by Security Council inaction." Even when the United States and Great Britain did try to limit the smuggling Volcker points out, "this effort failed in the face of opposition from China, France and Russia."

It wasn't supposed to turn out that way.

Saddam was supposed to have fallen; the Iraqi people were supposed to have been saved. Instead, the U.N. provided the money and the means for the dictator not only to exploit it but also to evade the reach of his greatest enemy, the United States of America.

Despite that perverse achievement, Secretary-General Kofi Annan continued to tout the program's success in feeding millions of Iraqis.

"I continue to believe that the Oil for Food program largely succeeded in achieving the goals set for it by the Security Council," Mr. Annan explained for this book. He admitted it "clearly needed oversight," but made it clear that "I also expect our critics to acknowledge the things that we do well, since that work is essential to the well-being, and even survival, of millions of people around the world." He acknowledged that there was a "justifiable need to get to the bottom of the . . . program's problems," and vowed he would "do all I can to make sure that the United Nations upholds the highest standards of conduct." But he lamented that the scandal was "overshadowing everything else that the United Nations does."

"For me," he explained, "the most difficult aspect of the criticism of the United Nations has been the way that it unfairly smears the valuable work that so many people do at the United Nations."

But it was also the United Nations' work—the work of some members of the Security Council in particular—that created the opportunity for the Iraqi dictator to dictate his terms to the powers that were charged with controlling him.

Saddam Hussein achieved implausible job security by recognizing that the real Gulf War was fought not in the Iraqi desert, but in conference room 7—a windowless, hushed, carpeted meeting room deep within the bowels of the United Nations Secretariat building in New York. Conference room 7 was the battlefield where he repeatedly fought the American forces arrayed against him, in the form of a succession of U.S. ambassadors: Madeleine Albright, Bill Richardson, Richard Holbrooke, and John Negroponte. The conference room 7 war ran for seven years, from 1996 to 2003, the lifespan of the Oil for Food program, and its lasting casualty has been the U.N.'s credibility and the lives of countless Iraqis.

The room is a nondescript, businesslike setting, a venue that certainly does not betray the remarkable string of strategic victories won within its walls by Hussein. It was in this unremarkable room that the 661 Committee, so named after the first resolution that established sanctions against Saddam on August 6, 1990, would gather once a month. This was the official U.N. group of Security Council representatives who would review, approve, or reject all of Iraq's thirty-eight thousand oil contracts. Their staffs had previously hashed out specifics at the nearby consulate of whatever country happened to hold the title of the Security Council presidency for that month. The diplomats would arrive, descending to the first basement level, walking down the lime-green-walled hallway, their wingtips clicking against the shiny tan linoleum, and then bear left under the metal letters announcing CONFERENCE ROOM 7/SALLE DE CONFERENCE.

Opening the heavy wooden door with the PULL/TIREZ handle, the officials would enter the worn brown-carpeted and tan-walled chamber, a sixty-by-forty-foot room, where they would proudly take their seats behind the Formica nameplates of their respective nations. At the horseshoe-shaped, pale, wooden center table, thin black microphones, notepads, pencils, and plastic translator earpieces awaited them at their chairs. Each ambassador from a Security Council country had the power to pass judgment. They included the five permanent members—the United States, Great Britain, France, Russia, and China—as well as the revolving roster of ten temporary nations that served Security Council terms of two years each. Of the forty-four nations that served as temporary members during the years the program existed (Chile served twice: in 1996–97 and again in 2003–04), Hussein did Oil for Food business with twenty-eight of them. It seems that even before the discussions began, the odds were in his favor.

Saddam triumphed for as long as he did by realizing that, while he could not be victorious on the military battlefield, he could be in conference room 7. He came to rely on another group of frontline troops who were dispatched in suits across the globe to subdued government offices, elegant company conference rooms, and busy bank branches. They were the ranks of Iraqi diplomats who concentrated their efforts on the "friendly" nations (most notably France, Russia, and China, three of the permanent members of the Security Council), who were seduced and co-opted at the expense primarily of America, Great Britain, and ultimately the starving people of Iraq.

Leave it to Saddam Hussein to pull off the largest heist in human history, right in midtown Manhattan, with the acquiescence of the "global community." By co-opting the Security Council, he had actually managed to use the U.N. for his own private version of the casino skim. Control the room, control the chips, control the customers, and take your cut off the top in the counting room.

The United Nations had made a major strategic blunder when establishing the procedures for the Oil for Food program. The world body gave Hussein the power to pick those from whom he bought and to whom he sold. The funds may have been deposited in a United Nations escrow account in the allegedly Saddam-picked French bank, BNP Bank Parabis, but by giving him the control over the suppliers, the Security Council abdicated its moral and fiduciary responsibility. That lack of oversight permitted Saddam, in reality, to run the program.

During congressional hearings in 2004, U.S. Ambassador Patrick Kennedy, our soft-spoken and exceedingly polite representative for United Nations management and reform, testified on Capitol Hill, starkly stating that our side had been overruled on that issue.

"At the insistence of many other Security Council members," he said, "the program permitted the government of Iraq to control the sale of oil and the selection and negotiation of contracts with suppliers of humanitarian items."

Those "other Security Council members" were France, Russia, and China.

"The Council members insisted that Iraq's national sovereignty and territorial integrity, and thus the right to execute contracts, be enshrined in the language of resolution 986. The 661 Committee reviewed the contracts that had been concluded between the Iraqi government and contractors to ensure that no items could be used for military purposes."

In other words, thanks to "those many other members," the Security Council gave Saddam the license to steal. They allowed that possibility—no, probability—in paragraph 18, the last one of the council resolution: "Nothing in this resolution should be construed as infringing the sovereignty or territorial integrity of Iraq." The U.N. let the prisoner serve as the warden.

That declaration was written below this empty promise: "[A]ll States shall take any steps that may be necessary under their respective domestic legal systems . . . to ensure that the proceeds of the sale are not diverted from the purposes laid down in this resolution." The diffusion of responsibility and negligence of U.N. authority left a void Hussein was all too willing to fill himself.

Explained Charles Duelfer in his CIA report, "The U.N. Oil for Food program saved the Iraqi regime from financial collapse and humanitarian disaster. When Iraq began exporting oil under U.N. Oil for Food in December 1996, the regime averted economic conditions that threatened its survival. The program also provided Iraq with unprecedented opportunities to earn significant amounts of hard currency outside the control of the U.N."

"Unprecedented opportunities . . . outside the control of the U.N." Saddam unknowingly echoed the legacy of the legendary George Washington Plunkitt of New York's corrupt political machine known as Tammany Hall. The old-line pol was immortalized in a book about his political philosophy and guiding principles that made him a millionaire through what he proudly called "honest graft." George Washington Plunkitt put it bluntly: "I seen my opportunities and I took 'em." Saddam saw his and did the same.

Only he did it better. Tammany had swindled the taxpayers of

New York City out of roughly $200 million by 1872, or almost $3 billion in today's dollars. Saddam grabbed at least seven times as much while his U.N. supporters looked the other way.

The United Nations enabled the continued reign of Saddam Hussein through a repeated lack of resolve coupled with naïve planning from the top down. The lesson of appeasement and lenience granted Saddam serves as a stark example of what America must avoid in future dealings with the U.N. As a result of the U.N.'s debacle, we are, to this day, picking up pieces of an Iraq shattered long before the arrival of U.S. forces. The U.N. imposed sanctions against Iraq four days after Saddam invaded Kuwait, on August 6, 1990. The Security Council decision, resolution 661, banned the sale of Iraqi oil and barred trade with Hussein's regime, save for food and medical supplies intended for the general population. Yet while the sanctions continued, Iraq repeatedly attempted to reject them and achieve a full removal of what it saw as restrictive conditions that violated its sovereignty. Iraq claimed the sanctions were devastating the nation, and blamed the U.N. and the United States for killing scores of its citizens, starving babies, and crippling the country. The humanitarian crisis was very real, but the effects were brought on by Hussein's defiance of the international order and his manipulation of the U.N.'s good intentions. His efforts at the blame game ended up being quite successful, garnering widespread sympathy in Europe, in the Arab world, and among like-minded Americans, which only increased the pressure on the friendly Security Council countries after several years to find a way to ease the sanctions' effects.

UNICEF estimated that five hundred thousand children had died under sanctions. The protesters and pundits largely blamed the U.N. sanctions, but seldom did they hold the tyrant responsible. In 2001, the Department of State noted that Hussein's lack of cooperation made it difficult to assess if food was actually being distributed properly. Even as many as five years into the program, the

United States was rebutting claims that sanctions were strangling Iraq. "Baghdad has been caught exporting dates, corn, and grain outside of Iraq while claiming the Iraqi people are starving," said the Department of State. The CIA's Duelfer report pointed out that "the sanctions did indeed have an enormous impact on Iraq. Saddam utilized and amplified that impact." Saddam's PR campaign involved everyone from government officials, journalists, and humanitarian groups to officials of the world body itself.

The well-publicized river of "starving babies," Duelfer points out, were the same unfortunate babies who may have succumbed to illnesses having nothing to do with the crises Oil for Food was established to alleviate. Of course, some babies died from malnutrition. But not at the rates Saddam was claiming. His regime was so perverse that it actually stored the bodies of babies who had died, and then repeatedly trotted them out for display in front of the international television cameras.

The *London Observer* reported in 2002 that "small coffins, decorated with grisly photographs of dead babies and their ages—'three days,' 'four days,' written usefully for the English-speaking media— are paraded through the streets of Baghdad on the roofs of taxis, the procession led by a throng of professional mourners." The BBC observed that because there were not enough dead babies to fuel processions, the regime prevented grieving parents from burying their infants immediately, as is the Muslim tradition. Saddam's regime needed them for propaganda.

An Iraqi taxi driver interviewed said, "They would collect bodies of children who had died months before and been held for mass processions." A Western source visited an Iraqi hospital and, in the absence of his "minder," was shown "a number of dead babies, lying stacked in a mortuary, waiting for the next official procession."

Hussein was "banking that images of dying babies would eventually force the international community to lift the sanctions altogether," explained Michael Soussan, who was an Oil for Food program coordinator from 1997 to 2000. He says that was a pretense

Hussein continued to maintain in his drive to end sanctions, claiming that five thousand infants a month were still starving to death, an unchallenged canard that continued through the life of the program.

"The U.N. did not stand up to this propaganda. It cowered in the face of this notion that the sanctions were killing Iraqi babies," Soussan told reporters after testifying before the first congressional hearing, held by the House International Relations Committee in April 2004.

"We should never have let Saddam Hussein win this propaganda war," he lamented.

But the U.N. did.

British Foreign Secretary Jack Straw observed that "While Saddam's propaganda machine bombards the international media with stories of spiraling death rates and worsening drug shortages, the truth is that we are doing what we can to help the Iraqi people, with little cooperation from the Iraqi regime. Saddam has the means to make life better for the Iraqi people but refuses to do so. And he has consistently tried to deceive world opinion about who is to blame."

In November 2000, President Clinton was asked by Pacifica Radio about the U.N. figures regarding "the five thousand children dying each month."

"That's not true, that's not true," countered Mr. Clinton. "If any child is without food or medicine or a roof over his or her head in Iraq, it's because [Saddam] is claiming the sanctions are doing it and sticking it to his own children. We have worked like crazy to make sure that the embargo only applies to his ability to reconstitute his weapon system and his military. . . . He has more money today than he did before the embargo. So if any child is without food or medicine, it's because [Saddam] has made a deliberate decision to let them die, to try to build up pressure to lift the embargo so he can spend that money however he wants. . . . He spends the money on his own military, on his own crowd, and he avoids spending it on a lot of kids who need it so he can blame us."

The numbers of the exact toll on the nation were wildly varying and suspect. Before Oil for Food began, UNICEF estimated that roughly forty-five hundred children under the age of five were dying from hunger every month. Two years into the program, by which time the deliveries of food and medicine should have shown an effect, Dennis Halliday, the United Nations humanitarian coordinator, who has branded sanctions "a war crime," claimed even more children, up to seven thousand a month, were being killed by sanctions.

But this is contrary to what the United Nations now claims. It says the program vastly improved the lives of Iraqis, leading to halving the rate of child malnutrition, and more than doubling the caloric intake of most Iraqis. The U.N. credits it with providing better medical care and reducing diseases such as cholera, malaria, measles, mumps, meningitis, and tuberculosis. The U.N. now says school attendance increased, they distributed 1.2 million school desks so Iraqi students no longer sat on the floor, and they helped to construct health centers in 120 towns. The U.N. now says that roads were improved, that the electrical supply system was strengthened, and that the phone system was modernized.

"The humanitarian program has contributed not only to arresting the decline in, but also in some areas improving, the living conditions of the average Iraqi," Secretary-General Kofi Annan proudly noted on March 13, 2001, adding, "The achievements of the program should not lead us into a sense of complacency."

Complacency? How about outrage!

In the six-month period before Annan issued that praise, the U.N. conceded that Iraq had actually not submitted one application to improve the health, water, sanitation, education, or oil facilities into which it was supposed to be pouring billions.

What the Iraqis were receiving was often not enough. Despite the U.N.'s lauding of the program, in October 2000 Tun Myat, the U.N.'s own humanitarian aid coordinator for Iraq, told a news conference that "people have become so poor in some cases they cannot even afford to eat the food that they've been given for free." He pointed out that for many Iraqis, the monthly food basket of rations amounted to their only income, and they would often sell or swap the items for clothes or other food.

The U.N.'s declarations focusing primarily on its achievements were mixed with Saddam's deliberate distortions and were then spread by a gullible media that rarely put the blame where it really belonged.

Even U.S. Secretary of State Madeleine Albright admits she was taken in when questioned by the venerable CBS newsmagazine, *60 Minutes*. In her autobiography, *Madam Secretary*, Albright recounts the time in 1996 when, as the ambassador to the United Nations, she was interviewed by Lesley Stahl:

> *I regret to say that I aggravated our public relations problems. . . . The segment included a visual tour of Iraqi health care facilities, with pictures of starving children and denunciations of U.N. policy by Iraqi officials. Little effort was made to explain Saddam's culpability, his misuse of Iraqi resources, or the fact that we were not embargoing medicine or food. I was exasperated that our TV was showing what amounted to Iraqi propaganda. Near the program's end, Lesley Stahl asked me, "We have heard that half a million children have died (as a result of sanctions). I mean, that is more children than died in Hiroshima. And you know, is the price worth it?"*
>
> *I must have been crazy; I should have answered the question by reframing it and pointing out the inherent flaws in the premise behind it. Saddam Hussein could have prevented any child from suffering simply by meeting his obligations. Instead, I said the following: "I think that is a very hard choice, but the price, we think, the price is worth it." As soon as I had spoken, I wished for the power to freeze time and take back those words.*

She could have blamed Hussein and the U.N. in that interview, but then Albright was involved in the establishment of the Oil for Food program as the U.S. ambassador to the United Nations in 1996. When she and the Clinton administration tried to defend their Iraq policy, the effort sometimes backfired. In February 1998, when Hussein again refused to cooperate with the U.N. weapons inspectors, the administration was considering launching military strikes on Baghdad. In an effort to drum up public support, Albright attended a CNN-televised town meeting along with Secretary of Defense William Cohen and National Security Adviser Sandy Berger. In a shocking display of disrespect by the audience, the forum turned into a heated and confrontational shout fest in which the three officials were loudly and repeatedly denounced by opponents of bombing Baghdad who, as usual, blamed sanctions and not Hussein for Iraq's crisis. Albright tried her best to direct the wrath to the culprit. "I am willing to make a bet to anyone here that we care more about the Iraqi people than Saddam Hussein," she said. "He has starved his people. We have provided food."

During an appearance at Yale University, she was nearly shouted down and almost "driven from the stage by student protestors denouncing her as a 'baby killer,'" recalls Professor Charles Hill, who served as the special assistant to Secretary-General Boutros Boutros-Ghali from 1992 to 1996, during which time Oil for Food began. "Madeleine Albright said you could drive a truck through this deal. And she was wrong because you could drive a whole fleet of eighteen-wheelers through it, which is what happened." Hill says, "Sanctions are a gift to the dictator. They simply gave Saddam Hussein greater control to get hard currency and dole out favors, to bribe and subvert all kinds of people around the world."

Yet, as was the case so often with the sanctions, truth fell on deaf ears.

Saddam was fooling the world, hook, line, and sinker. The sanctions could have been removed at any time had he cooperated with the U.N. Instead, he chose a path that brought his nation to the breaking point. By 1995, his economy was in a shambles and he himself was in desperate straits. It was at this point that Saddam relied on a proven lifeline that would save him: manufactured global sympathy. Standing by for his rescue was the reliable Security Council trio of France, Russia, and China. They were putting pressure on the United Nations to soften or end sanctions completely. "Iraq was in trouble," explains Charles Duelfer in his CIA report on Iraq. "The economy was in tatters, the middle class was decimated by the collapse of the dinar and the impact of sanctions. . . . Saddam had long refused to accept the option of exporting oil with constraints on revenues. He was concerned that, once started, the pressure on the Security Council to lift sanctions—his real goal—would be lifted. It was clear he was using the pain endured by his people, and the concern by some members of the Security Council about sustaining civil destruction, as pressure to get the Security Council to remove the sanctions. However, by 1996, it became apparent that the United States had a lock in the Security Council."

That's when Saddam found the key, and it was his acceptance of Oil for Food.

On May 20, 1996, Iraq agreed to a program that would place the U.N. in control of monitoring all oil exports in exchange for the purchasing of food and medicine. At first, Iraq was allowed to sell up to $2 billion worth of oil every six months. After the first year, it more than doubled to over $5 billion. By the end of 1999, the Security Council decided Iraq could sell as much oil as it wanted. The removal of any limit was the result of international pressure, a decision the diplomats would tell you was based on purely humanitarian goals. In reality, Hussein had once again bamboozled the U.N. The decision to provide him with an unlimited money spout only served to explosively increase his ability to gobble up even more.

"We were completely ignorant and blind at the time," recalls Professor Hill, who was in the U.N. executive suite at the birth of Oil for Food, "as to why Saddam and his guys were making the negotiations so insufferably, impossibly difficult. They were just playing with it all the time. They would cancel meetings, go back on what they agreed to; it was just driving everybody crazy." In time, everyone would see the mechanism, the truth pouring out from the files of Saddam's government offices after the war. That's when it became clear that the program also turned out to be a point of immense and unprecedented funding—for the U.N. itself.

As part of the arrangement, the diplomats tacked on a 2.2 percent administration fee that netted the organization a total of $1.4 billion over the years, an unprecedented bonanza that rewarded the U.N. with larger chunks of cash the more oil they let Hussein sell. The U.N. had a piece of the pie. Some would say it was a conflict of interest for the overseers to have one hand in the till instead of funding the program through independent means not connected to the program's revenue. The U.N. refuses to call the cut a fee or a commission, so I shall call it a tax in keeping with the time-honored practice of the mafia attaching garnishments to financial transactions under its purview. Even the five major New York mafia families were restrained enough to require a 2 percent "mob tax" on concrete construction contracts, an amount still less, slightly less, than the diplomats grabbed from Saddam. Who says crime doesn't pay?

The United States and Great Britain went along with the arrangement so as not to shell out separate funds from their own national budgets. In 2001, the Oil for Food program's head, Benon Sevan, reassured the Security Council that the 2.2 percent fee was actually modest.

"We have spared no effort to reduce our expenditures to a minimum," he said of the program's costs, insisting that the torrent of funds flooding into the bulging Oil for Food bank account would not turn "us into irresponsible officials squandering Iraqi money." That would be very difficult to determine. The U.S. Government Accounting Office found Oil for Food needed 160 auditors to properly monitor the spending. At most, the U.N. assigned two. And despite the audits performed by the U.N.'s special oversight division, the handling by Sevan's office of $40 billion worth of contracts was not examined at all.

The 2.2 percent account was an inexcusable conflict of interest for the U.N., determined the official hired by the post-Saddam Iraqi Governing Council, Claude Hankes-Drielsma. He pointedly called it a "cancer that lies at the core of the problem. For as long as members of the Security Council are party to corrupting the system, the U.N. will remain but a convenient tool for those countries who wish to operate without responsibility and accountability."

U.N. defenders say the fee was necessary to run the program, pointing out that the self-generating income made it a stand-alone project so the Secretariat would not have to hit up member states to pay for it. The U.N. Foundation also points out that of the 2.2 percent proceeds, "A substantial amount of this money went to pay the thousands of Iraqi employees who helped implement the program on the ground." But those employees also served as Hussein's spies, charges Entifadh Qanbar, one of the leading anti-Saddam exiles who went on to become Iraq's Deputy Military Attaché in Washington in the new government. Three thousand Iraqis worked on the ground in Iraq for Oil for Food, and Qanbar says that in order to be hired they had to be approved by Iraqi intelligence or pass muster with Saddam's Baath party. The U.N. may have provided a jobs program for the unemployed, but it also seems to have proved a boon for Iraq's internal spy network.

"The Oil for Food employees were recruited as agents by the Iraqi Intelligence Service," says Qanbar. "If you went to work for a foreign agency in Iraq without the IIS permission, you would be killed. In order to work for the U.N. you needed the government's permission, and the Iraqi U.N. employees were required to give Saddam's intelligence weekly reports about what they did, who they saw, and what was happening. It is unimaginable that the U.N. would be so foolish and naïve not to think that their employees were compromised."

The U.N. agencies had been "penetrated by elements of the

Iraqi Mukhabarat," noted Nimrod Raphaeli, senior analyst with the Middle East Research Institute, referring to Hussein's intelligence service. He told one congressional hearing that Saddam's spies targeted all the U.N. operations in Iraq, and tried "to recruit most of their employees, particularly the non-Europeans. Iraqi nationals would have difficulty serving in any of these organizations had they not agreed to collaborate with the Mukhabarat." U.N. supporters, and the organization itself, were often afflicted with a moral blindness that continually compromised their goals. The rationale seemed to be that any U.N. program dictated from U.N. headquarters was acceptable no matter what the reality or cost on the ground. Even Hussein's apparent infiltration of the U.N. system would not deter the U.N. supporters.

The U.N. Iraqi jobs program provided Saddam's thugs with opportunities to not only monitor but threaten U.N. workers with impunity. The Volcker Committee said U.N. staff members were fired on, a U.N. agency vehicle was bombed, and "Iraqi employees, some from prominent families, would caution the international staff not to bother Iraqi officials or 'bad things could happen.'"

There were "a lot of well-connected Saddam loyalists on the staff," recounted Dr. Rehan Mullick, a Pakistani-American from Illinois who landed in Iraq in September 2000 with the U.N. job of monitoring humanitarian conditions and reporting on the impact of the Oil for Food program. The articulate and thoughtful forty-two-year-old sociologist holds a PhD from Iowa State University. He was shocked by what he discovered to be the extent of the manipulation.

Dr. Mullick and others say that the local staff was populated by the wives, sons, and daughters of high-ranking Baath party officials, that the regime even "married" compliant Iraqis into the U.N.'s staff, which was an intelligence tactic reminiscent of Soviet-style deceptions during the Cold War. What's worse, he says that the spies even controlled the information flow that the U.N. relied on to run the program in the first place. As a result, completely false or misleading statistics were massaged by the regime's machine and spewed out under the supposedly objective cover of respected United Nations reports. Dr. Mullick was horrified at the level of the exploitation, so he says he submitted a ten-page report to his superiors exposing what he had discovered. In it, he noted specifics, such as the patronage appointment of Iraq's deputy foreign minister's son-in-law to oversee the reports on Oil for Food, as well as the diversion of billions of dollars worth of humanitarian goods to Iraq's military, and the reselling of Oil for Food-provided items on the black market.

Mullick says he received no response to his exposé from his Iraqi U.N. superiors, so he returned to U.N. headquarters and handed in his compilation of serious charges in person. Again, he contends, his revelations were ignored. But U.N. officials did take another action: they demoted him. The contribution of an American with a doctorate was reduced "until my only job was to run the slide projector at staff meetings," he ruefully says. Then they fired him. But at the United Nations, there's a euphemism for getting the ax: not having your contract renewed. Dr. Mullick blames what he calls the U.N.'s "old style mafia management" for burying the truth. The U.N., however, claims it has no information on what he discovered or why his contract lapsed.

Hussein's takeover of the program, says Dr. Mullick, means "the statistics quoted in the U.N. reports were often extrapolated with impunity and were often scientifically misleading." This helps explain why the uncertainty of the true numbers of "starving" children and the correct impact on infant mortality seem particularly questionable. Paul Conlon, who served as the deputy secretary for the Security Council on the Iraq Sanctions Committee, the precursor of the Oil for Food 661 Committee, says the U.N. would print whatever data the Iraqis provided under the cover of official documents, U.N. seal and all.

"Iraq occasionally forced the Secretariat to publish its [slanted] versions of what went on at committee meetings as official Security Council documents," Conlon testified before a House subcommittee chaired by Connecticut Congressman Christopher Shays. The U.N. played right into the hands of America-haters and those always willing to give the U.N. a break.

"I remember, over and over and over, various interest groups in this country claiming that the United States was intentionally engaged in starving little children," recalled Congressman Rohrabacher at a congressional hearing in March 2005. This while "the United Nations was permitting $1 billion a year minimum to go right down the black hole and not being used to help those children. This is a travesty and the fact that U.N. officials . . . didn't look at it as such is even more of a condemnation of the United Nations. We remember the speeches at the United Nations of people claiming that the United States and the West were responsible for starving those children. U.N. officials weren't even able or willing to act to see that the money was going where it was intended to go to help those people." It's not like they didn't know the extent of the spying within and the manipulation of U.N. agencies.

Rolf Ekeus, the Swedish diplomat who served as the head of the first U.N. inspections effort, UNSCOM (the United Nations Special Commission), remembers Tariq Aziz telling him in 1992, "You see, we know every word which is spoken in the closed session of the Security Council."

Ekeus's successor, the genial chief weapons of mass destruction inspector Hans Blix, once told me it was common knowledge that Iraqi intelligence had bugged and wiretapped the hotel rooms and phones of his operation. He chuckled at the thought of my expressing indignation, but had long ago accepted infiltration as a fact of life for the U.N. agencies operating in Iraq. That's how the CIA admits the Iraqis were able to clean up and clear out suspected chemical, biological, or nuclear sites before Blix's inspectors would arrive unannounced as part of their "surprise" visits. The Duelfer report even says that once, as the U.N. inspectors showed up at the front door, Hussein had himself hustled out the back. The inspectors never knew it.

The Iraqis had clearly compromised U.N. headquarters in Manhattan, true to Aziz's boast.

Paul Conlon also observed during his time in the Security Council that Hussein had "fairly good" information on "what went on" behind closed doors during secret Iraq sanctions meetings, and he says the Iraqis had even penetrated the Secretariat (Secretary-General Kofi Annan's offices) to such an extent that it "astounded the staff to learn how much the Iraqis knew."

The U.N. was co-opted by Hussein, and nowhere was that clearer than in the operation of Oil for Food. Its creation "was a key turning point for the regime," says the CIA's Duelfer. "Oil for Food rescued Baghdad's economy from a terminal decline created by sanctions. The regime quickly came to see that Oil for Food could be corrupted to acquire foreign exchange both to further undermine sanctions and to provide the means to enhance dual-use infrastructure and potential weapons of mass destruction–related development."

In other words, Hussein realized he could make a bundle right under the U.N.'s nose, pursue his dedicated mission of ending sanctions, and rebuild his weapons programs to dominate the Middle East. Yet the U.N. proudly pointed to their successes. Officials noted that the program provided $46 billion for humanitarian contracts, $16 billion to the U.N. compensation fund to repay Kuwait for the 1990 Iraqi invasion, and $2.65 billion to support the Office of Iraq Program, consisting of UNMOVIC (U.N. Monitoring, Verification, and Inspection Commission, the first weapons inspection program) and its successor UNSCOM (U.N. Special Commission) headed by Dr. Blix.

But a dictator was enriched. His people were starved and brutalized. The world suffered. The U.N.'s treatment of Iraq reveals its most pressing shortcoming—it cannot regulate, control, or effectively monitor the peaceful programs it designs to maintain global security, even to such a degree that the programs can have the opposite effect of that which is intended. America attempted to enforce constraints on Hussein through the Security Council in proposition after proposition, but the U.N. itself did nothing less than provide aid and comfort to the enemy.

In seeking to resolve this Iraqi crisis and the perceived threat to security that it represented, the United States had no choice but to abandon the broken machinery of the U.N. and to act independently of the institution, dropping the pen for the sword because the pen had no ink. By taking action America found itself with few friends. With the exception of Great Britain, our big allies were all lies—and, thanks in no small part to the U.N., they found plenty of reasons to fight us every step of the way.

– 6 –

ALLIES OR ALL LIES?

In the past several years, perhaps no U.N. entity has weakened American security more than the exalted Security Council. Charged with providing constraints on the worst of the world, the Security Council has become a disjointed, dysfunctional association of nations that too often wastes time rehashing old disagreements while only rarely reaching lofty goals. And no nations have compromised the integrity of the Security Council and the larger U.N. more than three of its permanent members: France, Russia, and China.

These three nations not only endeavored to prop up the dictatorship of Saddam Hussein, but also profited from it to the tune of billions.

That marked them as enemy collaborators.

Period.

They churned out stamped vetoes in exchange for billions in oil contracts that bought security not for the world but for Saddam Hussein. The deaths of our soldiers and of countless innocent Iraqis are the tragic legacy of the financial infiltration and corruption of the world body.

"This is where we have to connect the dots," urged Congressman Tim Murphy of Pennsylvania, "to find out if those companies within those member nations of the U.N. have blood on their hands against our soldiers."

Just follow the money.

France, Russia, and China cleaned up on a tyrant's dime.

In Paris, Moscow, and Beijing, the phone lines must have been burning up to the U.N. consulates in New York, carrying messages like "Make nice to Iraq. We need the dough." As the U.N. progressed in granting Iraq oil contracts to supposedly feed and care for its starving people, the goals of diluting U.S. power and someday ending sanctions against—and opening lucrative trade with—Iraq propelled the trio's ultimate agenda. For them, there was a lot to lose if Hussein fell and much to gain if he stayed.

In 2000, the Iraqi Trade Minister, Mohammed Mehid Salah, claimed that the U.N. sanctions imposed by Oil for Food had cost France $35 billion, Russia $40 billion, and China $25 billion in denied revenue. Iraq was also in debt to those countries: France, $6 billion; Russia, $8 billion; and China at least $1.1 billion. The International Monetary Fund pegged Iraq's foreign debt at $125 billion total. The regime was in hock to the tune of $40 billion to the members of the Paris Club, a consortium of nineteen nations that lend to developing nations, and another $80 billion to neighboring Arab countries. There you have 125 billion reasons for some people to keep Saddam in business.

As of 2002, the last full year that the program was operating, France controlled an overwhelming 22.5 percent of Iraq's imports, according to the CIA, while Russia and China weighed in at nearly 6 percent each. Billions more were promised to each country once sanctions were lifted. In other words, the jackpot was waiting if France, Russia, and China could outmaneuver the United States and Great Britain on the Security Council.

The Volcker Committee put France's purchases of Iraqi oil at almost $4.5 billion, Russia's at nearly $20 billion, and China's at just over $2.6 billion. Lucrative deals were cut between Saddam and 3,500 companies around the globe, the majority from the three Security Council enablers who were branded "the coalition of the venal" by Connecticut Congressman Christopher Shays during one of his subcommittee hearings on Oil for Food. Congressman Murphy was even more pointed about the behavior and motivations of the trio that Secretary of State Colin Powell, during his U.N. visits, would charitably call "our French friends . . . our Russian friends . . . our Chinese friends."

"The spineless U.N. produced paper tigers in the form of resolutions that had no teeth," observed Murphy, a freshman from Pittsburgh who had been a child psychologist and author before his leap into elective office. His training enabled him to analyze and diagnose the dysfunctional diplomats perfectly. "Time and again, the U.N. told Saddam Hussein and terrorists that the U.N. was all talk and no follow-through," Murphy declared.

"France and Russia had two choices: help us militarily, or intervene directly with Saddam Hussein to cooperate with weapons inspectors and stop his murderous regime. They did neither. Why didn't these countries step forward? Perhaps it had something to do with . . . Hussein's voucher scheme . . . and French companies close to President Chirac. . . . They were up to their ears in corruption, and the financial benefit of keeping Saddam Hussein in power weighed more heavily than their friendship with the United States." Murphy rightfully said Americans should "ask who our allies are and whom the U.N. is supporting."

"President Clinton didn't have the support of our allies. . . . It was somewhat of a joke," observed Shays. "When President Bush took office, he finally said, 'We've got to make this program work, and we also have to look at regime change if he doesn't cooperate,' and we still don't have the assistance of our allies. . . . It says to me, well, what's new?"

Shays addressed U.S. Ambassador Patrick Kennedy, the second in command at the U.N. mission in New York, who had plainly admitted that the other members of the 661 Committee resisted and blocked American moves.

"Isn't it true that you said the allies did not cooperate?" asked Shays.

Ambassador Kennedy replied, "I totally agree, sir."

As the Duelfer Report stated,

> *Saddam's strategy of unhinging the U.N.'s sanctions against Iraq, centered on [his] efforts to influence certain U.N. Security Council members, such as Russia, France, and China. . . . At a minimum, Saddam wanted to divide the five permanent members and foment international support of Iraq at the U.N. and throughout the World. . . . Saddam gave preferential treatment to Russian and French companies hoping for Russian and French support on the U.N. Security Council. He gave prominent vocal Iraqi supporters and willing influential U.N. officials lucrative oil allocations. He gave individuals a moral rationalization for their support and friendship. . . . The Regime's strategy was successful to the point where sitting members of the Security Council were actively violating the resolutions passed by the Security Council.*

It was no secret.

"There's no question Saddam Hussein understood the advantage of strategic purchasing," one diplomat chuckled. Our ambassadors witnessed pork barrel politics—U.N. style. "It was about money," said one American diplomat who was there. "France was never, never straightforward about their interests and objectives. France pretends their motives are different than they are. . . . There's no question they were driven by commercial and political interests."

"The U.N. is the last great home of dirty tricks," says John Loftus, a former Department of Justice prosecutor who is now president of

TheIntelligenceSummit.org, a group of former intelligence officials and operatives who study global power plays. He says, "What the French, Russians, and Chinese have been doing is stealing the moral imprimatur of the U.N. and twisting it for their national strategic purposes. They see the U.N. only as a big chess board and all the players are aligned against us."

Every Security Council 661 Committee meeting was a game. Department of State classified documents refer to 661 Committee meeting proposals with the comments, "Russia, China, France opposed." One classified memo revealed how "the French delegation" complained about U.S. and British efforts to crack down on what Iraq was attempting to import and, when we fought back, "Russian and Chinese reps made the same points as the French." As the secret diplomatic notes revealed, those "delegations were quick to criticize" U.S.-led efforts. France, Russia, and China even resisted cleaning up the illegal bribes.

Besides the billions of dollars that flowed thanks to the U.N.'s handiwork, Saddam also doled out his secret slush fund. The "oil allocation list" contained the names of 270 individuals, organizations, government offices, and political parties in fifty countries who Iraqi officials admitted were paid off in millions of barrels of oil for their support. It became a holy grail of greed, a detailed and specific menu of corruption that an unnamed top regime member revealed to agents of the U.S. Treasury's Iraqi financial assets team. It was nicknamed "Saddam's Bribery System." The majority of the recipients named in the paperwork were from France, Russia, and China because those three nations largely supported Saddam in the Security Council.

The investigators from Senator Coleman's Senate Permanent Subcommittee on Investigations even journeyed to Baghdad to interview Saddam's top brass, and reported that "senior members of the Hussein regime confirmed that 'the Saddam Bribery System' used oil allocations in an effort to buy political influence around the world." Former Iraqi Vice President Taha Yassin Ramadan told committee investigators that "the allocations were indeed 'compensation for support,' [that] another senior Hussein official confirmed the allocation scheme was 'buying influence,' [and that it] favored those individuals and entities from countries on the United Nations Security Council . . . namely Russia, France, and China."

A now declassified March 2002 Department of State cable warned the 661 Committee about what it diplomatically called gift giving, and asked if there was any way the U.N. could stop payment. Congressional and other government investigators gathered a massive amount of corroborating evidence from oil ministry documents, memos, letters, and financial transactions that verified Hussein's targets. They also spent hours conducting interviews with high-ranking regime officials who ratted out the alleged recipients, which further confirmed the allegations' accuracy.

While there were several on the list from inside the U.N., speculation in the hallways centered on former U.N. Secretary-General Boutros Boutros-Ghali as a recipient, especially after federal prosecutors filed court papers indicating money was paid to someone described as U.N. Official Number 1, at the start of the program in 1996. Boutros-Ghali publicly criticized the investigation as a "political strategy and drive to destabilize the U.N. and tarnish its work" in a letter to *The Financial Times*. He has denied receiving any payments, and Volcker found no evidence of a bribe.

The other notable character listed among the oil allocation recipients was the pugnacious radical British politician George Galloway, the royal subject who most loudly defied his government's will, aligning himself with the Iraqi sympathizers more commonly found on the other side of the English Channel. A masterful debater and unrepentant ideologue, he proved himself an articulate but thundering bully when he took advantage of his appearance before Senator Coleman's committee in May 2005 to push his antiwar and anti-Bush administration agenda. He brazenly used that opportunity to deny he was bribed, to denounce President Bush, to condemn the war in Iraq, and to bitterly criticize the investigation itself.

Galloway, even as an elected member of Parliament, would later praise attacks on British troops by Iraqi insurgents, saying the terrorists "are defending all the people of the world against American hegemony." In July 2005 he told the television network Al-Jazeera that "the biggest terrorists are Bush and Blair."

Galloway had visited Hussein twice, and as the most prominent Iraq proponent in Great Britain, had long fought to end sanctions. He was kicked out of Tony Blair's Labour Party for his rabid antiwar views, was reelected to Parliament under his own banner, and became a hero of Bush-haters and antiwar zealots. He had won a $300,000 libel suit from the British newspaper (London) *Telegraph* that claimed Iraqi documents implicated him in receiving oil bribes. The court ruled that Galloway was denied a "fair or reasonable opportunity to make inquiries or meaningful comment upon them" before the story appeared in the newspaper.

An article published in *The Christian Science Monitor* relied on documents that Galloway claimed were forgeries, so when he arrived after intense anticipation at the Senate hearing room, he was loaded for bear, able to discredit all news accounts of his improprieties as falsehoods, citing the *Telegraph* libel case. He said he never received any money, which Coleman's investigators said was laundered through two corporations and a charity Galloway had established to help Iraqi children. Galloway dismissed as forgeries the documents listing his name alongside twenty million barrels of oil, and accused the Iraqi officials who implicated him of lying.

"I have never seen a barrel of oil, owned one, bought one, sold one, and neither has anyone on my behalf," he bellowed. "What counts is not the names on the paper, what counts is where's the money, Senator? Who paid me hundreds of thousands of dollars of money? The answer to that is nobody." He also quite impolitely said of Senator Coleman, "He's a crazed, pro-Israel, prowar neocon hawk, and a lickspittle of George W. Bush." *Lickspittle* is a British phrase for boot licker, posterior pucker, or whatever definition of lackey you deem suitable.

The showdown was given front-page play around the world. Al-Jazeera said of Galloway's bombastic appearance, "A breath of fresh air sweeps into Hell."

Five months after Galloway's bravura performance, the Coleman investigators came up with more. They presented what the senator called "the smoking gun," reams of financial statements and bank records that the investigators said proved the money trail, along with the admissions of Saddam's top brass. They concluded that Galloway had indeed solicited oil allocations and the Iraqis had obliged by allegedly funneling through a third party $446,000 to Galloway's charity, and another $150,000 to Galloway's wife. The Volcker investigators came up with a separate $120,000 that they said went to the missus. As was his custom, Galloway loudly denied all and dared prosecutors to file charges.

If the evidence laid out by the Senate committee and its conclusions are to be believed, it would seem the case against Galloway and so many others named on the oil allocation list would be enough to pronounce them, as the jury foreman in Mel Brooks's *High Anxiety* put it, "incredibly guilty" of taking money to support Saddam. Congressional investigators had the admissions of thirteen Iraqi officials who had been questioned to corroborate the purpose of the list. Saddam's vice president Taha Yassin Ramadan told Coleman's investigators who went to Baghdad to interview him that Galloway had been given the oil allocations "because of his opinions about Iraq" and because Galloway "want[ed] to lift the embargo against Iraq." Ramadan admitted the allocations were "compensation for support." The whole point, said another official, was to "buy influence." Galloway, however, claimed Saddam's top brass should not be believed because they are incarcenated, some facing the death penalty, and would say anything to please "American investigatiors."

Tariq Aziz, Saddam's cigar-smoking Christian deputy prime minister, was cited by Duelfer and the Coleman investigators as one of the many sources who shed light on Saddam's corruption scheme. The Duelfer report said, "Aziz personally awarded several individuals substantial oil allotments" with the understanding that they would work to lift the sanctions or oppose "American initiatives within the Security Council." Coleman noted Aziz was a member of the Command Council, which decided who would receive the bribes before passing the names on to Saddam for approval. His investigators say Aziz was a troubleshooter for those who encountered problems with their allocations, citing one 2002 "face-to-face meeting in Moscow" after which an allocation holder was assured that "discrepancies regarding the allocation will be solved very soon."

But a week after Galloway's flamboyant performance, Aziz's defense smuggled out notes from the incarcerated prisoner confirming he was questioned about the Oil for Food scandal yet denying he bribed several specific officials. Maybe the lawyers got to him. Aziz scribbled on note pads leaked to the British newspaper *Guardian* that "I have not done anything contrary to law and human behaviour." He revealed, "I was asked if I had recommended giving money or oil to President Chirac or Petros Gali [Boutros Boutros-Ghali], Ekius [U.N. weapons inspector Rolf Ekeus, who has once said he was offered a $2 million bribe but turned it down]. My answer is no. The same to President Megawati [of Indonesia]—NO." While Chirac and Boutros-Ghali were not specifically named on the oil list, "the daughter of President Sukarno" was down for one million barrels and another one million as "Megawatti." Yet if the numerous documents were false, and multiple Iraqi officials were not telling the truth as Galloway so strongly insisted, why did someone else plead guilty to the contents in the same type of documents and claims and the U.S. Department of Justice use similar allegations as a basis for bringing Oil for Food–related criminal prosecutions?

Samir Vincent, a sixty-four-year-old Iraqi-born Virginia businessman who copped a plea in federal court, became the first person to admit guilt in the scandal. He conceded, as the oil allocations under his name had indicated, that he had received $5 million worth of oil and cash from Saddam in exchange for taking up his cause at the U.N. and across America as an influential friend and associate of many of Washington's most powerful, among them Jack Kemp and former President Jimmy Carter. He even allegedly played tennis with Ford administration Secretary of Defense Frank Carlucci.

Vincent had organized charity missions that delivered medicine to Iraq and, in 1990, he ran an antisanction tour of Iraqi clerics that met with Carter, evangelist Reverend Billy Graham, and John Cardinal O'Connor, the leader of New York's archdiocese at the time. Vincent, as the most prominent Iraqi-American advocate for ending sanctions, was a philosophical twin of Galloway. They both spoke out. They both ran humanitarian missions to Baghdad. They both met with regime officials. Only Vincent admitted he was paid for that support. Galloway steadfastly denies it.

Vincent also admitted that he was on the inside when Oil for Food was created, serving as a conduit between diplomats and Hussein's regime. "I met on a number of occasions with Iraqi officials in Manhattan and Baghdad," he conceded. "We discussed what would be acceptable to Iraq . . . and they gave me proposals to pass onto officials at the United Nations. . . . During the course of these negotiations, the Iraqi government promised to pay millions of dollars to me and others if a satisfactory agreement was reached with the United Nations on the implementation of an oil for food program. . . . Several millions of dollars in cash was sent by the Iraqi government to Iraqi government officials in New York. . . . Several hundred thousand dollars of this money was given to me, in Manhattan, and the rest was given to others, one of whom I understood was a United Nations official."

Vincent pleaded guilty to being an unregistered foreign agent for Iraq and was compensated by nine million barrels of oil allocated to his company, Phoenix International of Fairfax, Virginia, through Hussein's secret list. Both he and his company were listed by name, just as George Galloway was. The entries that Galloway claimed were forgeries reflected exactly what Samir Vincent testified to under oath. Federal prosecutors in New York also started making cases against others on the oil list.

The Houston company Bay Oil, run by Texas oilman David Chalmers, appeared repeatedly on Saddam's allocation list, and the feds indicted Chalmers and his company along with three others in connection with their oil deals, among them the notorious Koreagate fugitive from the 1970s Washington influence-peddling scandal, Tongsun Park. Park was convicted of earning $2.5 million from Saddam's regime. Chalmers and his firm were charged with paying kickbacks to the regime for his share of oil allocations, allegations that again mirrored the very same ones that Galloway says were concocted. Texas billionaire Oscar Wyatt, Jr., was also charged.

David Kelley, the United States Attorney for the Southern District who had impaneled the federal grand jury investigation, called the indictments "two more pieces in the Oil for Food puzzle" and promised "to wring the towel dry." Kelley, a ramrod-straight New York Irishman, had reached the pinnacle of law enforcement. He started his career as a police officer in the tony Long Island resort town of East Hampton, ticketing double-parked Porsches and pulling over Mercedes-driving motorists pickled by too many gin and tonics. He cut his teeth in federal courtrooms, putting away mobsters as head of the Southern District's organized crime division. The former made him familiar with the entitled Wall Street and entertainment barons who moved at the highest levels of American society in their ostentatious, manicured seaside estates. The latter trained him to follow sophisticated money-laundering schemes involving suitcase loads of cash stashed in secret bank accounts overseas or invested in nightclubs, gambling, drugs, and escort services at the direction of overweight men puffing on di Noble cigars and shuffling cards in dimly lit mob social clubs. Both roles proved to be mere apprenticeships for what Kelley would encounter exploring the U.N.-enabled scam. Yet his legal jurisdiction extended only to crimes that violated U.S. law, not the laws of other nations on the oil allocation list. Still, Kelley found plenty to work with, and the towel started twisting. In U.N. World, it almost seemed as if a job perk was an offshore bank account in which to hide your bribes.

Alexander Yakovlev, a long-serving official of the procurement department, was the first U.N. bigwig to get nailed. He entered the second guilty plea related to U.N. corruption after Samir Vincent had come clean seven months earlier. Since 1985, Yakovlev had worked in the division that spends billions for the world body and, said the Volcker investigation, "had responsibility for numerous high value contracts," including oil inspection contracts for the Oil for Food program. In August 2005 he copped a plea to money laundering and conspiracy, admitting he solicited hundreds of thousands of dollars from companies doing business with the U.N. The Volcker investigators said he had stashed $1.3 million ($950,000 from the U.N.-connected companies) in an offshore Caribbean bank account.

As part of his agreement with federal prosecutors, he apparently started to squeal, and within a month the feds indicted another U.N. official, fellow Russian Vladimir Kuznetsov, for conspiring to commit money laundering. Kuzetsov was chairman of the committee that advised the General Assembly on budgetary and auditing matters. He also opened an offshore bank account to "hide the transfer of criminal proceeds" in apparent payoffs from companies doing business with the U.N., according to the indictment filed by the U.S. Attorney's office for the Southern District. He pleaded not guilty.

Who knows how many U.N. officials were on the take but never caught? The Volcker Committee said Yakovlev "engaged in a continuous course of conduct of accepting payments from United Nations contractors in other United Nations programs." It must have seemed so easy and so acceptable. An indication of how confident Yakovlev felt that his U.N. overseers would never catch on is the revelation from Volcker that Yakovlev even transferred money from the offshore account right into his United Nations Federal Credit

Union account at the New York headquarters. In U.N. World there's no need to sully yourself with cash-stuffed unmarked envelopes. Just fill out a deposit slip.

The bribes may have reached into the United States, but the majority flowed to the three usual suspects seemingly beyond the reach of American prosecutors. Millions allegedly poured directly into the pockets of Russian, French, and Chinese officials, companies, and organizations. They accounted for 55 percent of the total disbursements from Saddam's secret list—30 percent to the Russians, 15 percent to the French, and 10 percent to the Chinese—and there was little or nothing the U.S. Department of Justice could have done about it. The French foreign ministry branded as "inaccurate" the allegations that economic interests influenced its Iraq policy. "It is completely inaccurate to say that France had major commercial interests in Iraq before the war."

The Russian foreign ministry stated, "Russia is incriminated by the very fact of its participation" in Oil for Food, saying the investigations "are trying to discredit the United Nations as a whole." China has said it abided by U.N. regulations and hopes for a "just, independent, objective, and transparent investigation," according to the Xinhua News Agency. Predictably, when the Volcker investigators came knocking on doors in Moscow and Beijing for help in their inquiry, those two Security Council members clammed up.

"Russia and China, while receiving investigators in their capitals, have not granted requests for important information and have refused to arrange access to some state-owned companies," said the September 7, 2005, report. Contrast that to the "significant assistance from the United States" for the probe.

The truth is hidden in the thousands of pages of 661 Committee meeting minutes. They will reveal what the Security Council members so diplomatically deny, and what was for so long covered up by the United Nations and the Security Council members, including the United States. The summaries, minutes, audio recordings of

244 meetings from 1996 to the war's eve remain marked "confidential." The U.N. and our government have it all but the State Department has classified the material as part of "the national interest" even out of reach of the congressional investigators trying to get to the bottom of the scandal.

The final report from U.N. investigator Paul Volcker offers our only glimpse into how the 661 Committee utterly failed, how "decisions were delayed, bungled, or simply avoided," and how the diplomats "did not ever discuss the existence of humanitarian kickbacks or strategies to combat them." They had warnings of wrongdoing almost as soon as the Oil for Food program started, as early as 1997, says Volcker, but only the Americans and the British "publicly expressed concern." It would prove to be a familiar and sad pattern. When the United States and the U.K. moved to stop Saddam's abuses they did so "over the objection of Russia and China," or "France and China" resisted the efforts, or "Russia and China protested" them, or they simply did not seem to respond. The meetings often ended with diplomats mired in "inaction"—diplomats who "did nothing," or who "took no decision."

Even when the Americans tried to investigate kickbacks, they were stonewalled. At the April 11, 2001, meeting, one United States official warned that businessmen "were making under the table payments." But, according to that official, whenever the subject was broached at 661 Committee meetings, "Russia typically would dismiss the information and stymie further investigation." Even when U.N. officials warned of possible abuses in a batch of 70 humanitarian contracts, 62 of them sailed right on through, adding another $10.2 million to Saddam's illicit booty. France says it told companies that kickbacks were "unacceptable." Russia claimed it knew nothing. China says it provided "written notification" against illegal payments.

The denials became so common that they evolved into something of an art. At the June 26, 2002, 661 Committee meeting,

China resorted to U.N. policy by fortune cookie. The Chinese representative resisted a British proposal (aimed at putting an end to the skimming) by citing an old Chinese proverb: "Man who is too critical has not friends; If river is too clean there is no fish."

Our "allies" certainly took that ancient wisdom to heart.

– 7 –

THE FRENCH CONNECTION

"France has emerged from the depths of the past. She is a living entity. She responds to the call of the centuries. Yet she remains herself through time." So wrote the leader of the Fifth Republic, Charles de Gaulle, in the opening lines of *Memoir of Hope: Renewal and Endeavor*, published in 1970. Had he lived through the past couple of years, he surely would have added, "'Herself' is for sale, by the way." The French heatedly deny it all.

"Indeed, the French government has sort of played the pimp to Saddam's efforts to prostitute the U.N.," says John Loftus. He calls the French the weakest of the Security Council's permanent five. "They are the most desperate and have abused the U.N. the most," he states. "The French colonies have turned against them. French business essentially consists of any nation that the U.S. condemns for rogue acts of terrorism and forbids trade with. That's where the French move in immediately and pick at the carcasses of dictatorships."

The French knew they were going to lose Iraq and the riches flowing to them through the U.N. Jean-David Levitte, the distinguished, respected, and well-liked emissary of Jacques Chirac, represented his nation in Washington, D.C., after serving his Gallic masters at the U.N., where he was charged with the stewardship of French policy in the 661 Committee, apparently making sure that checks with a Baghdad address wouldn't bounce at the Quai d'Orsay. There is no indication that Levitte was compromised by Saddam in any manner. His name does not appear on the Iraqi oil allocation list, as did the name of one of his predecessors at the U.N., and there is no evidence that he was motivated by anything other than carrying out the foreign policy wishes of Paris as he pushed his nation's interests in the Security Council. In a speech on October 7, 2004, Levitte lambasted the suggestions that his nation was on the take. He had been "outraged to read or hear in some media that France had opposed the war in Iraq because our vote might have been bought by Saddam Hussein."

"Frankly, this is outrageous," Levitte stated. "France was against this war because this war was not necessary. We said it at the time. There were no stockpiles of weapons of mass destruction threatening the security of the United States or Europe; there were no links between Saddam Hussein and 9/11. This is now clearly established, and is why we were against this war."

Levitte also blasted accusations that France protected Hussein by assuring the Iraqis that the French would employ their veto in the Security Council to block an American attack, something President Chirac did eventually threaten during his March 10, 2003, television interview. This was the most incendiary and potentially damaging suggestion: that Chirac's representatives secretly went out of their way to reassure Saddam Hussein that he would be diplomatically protected from American intentions.

The French ambassador focused his indignation on a front-page *Washington Post* article that appeared on November 3, 2003, entitled "Hussein Was Sure of Own Survival." The article said the

Iraqis had indeed been given the heads up and assurance of French backing. It reported on the claims of former Iraqi Deputy Prime Minister Tariq Aziz, who was being questioned extensively while in custody.

"Aziz has told interrogators that French and Russian intermediaries repeatedly assured Hussein during late 2002 and early this year [2003] that they would block a U.S.-led war through delays and vetoes at the U.N. Security Council." The article claimed "private talks with French and Russian contacts" while noting "the public record of French and Russian back-channel contacts with Hussein on the war's eve is thin and ambiguous, [and] the extent and character of French contacts with Hussein before the war is even less clear."

It would take another year and a half for the details to emerge, yet seven days after the story broke, the French ambassador fired off a stinging rebuke. "I deny those allegations as they are absolutely without foundation," Levitte wrote. "No French envoy was ever mandated to go to Iraq to meet with Saddam Hussein or give him any assurances. In its message to the Iraqi authorities during the period discussed in the article, France called upon the Iraqis to cooperate fully and actively with the United Nations."

Wiggle Room lesson number 1: Note the phrases *mandated* and *during the period discussed in the article*. Translation: No one was officially ordered to pass on our promise during that period of time immediately leading up to the war.

Perhaps the series of secret Iraqi Intelligence Service memos found by coalition authorities in the files of Iraq's intel headquarters should be brought to Mr. Levitte's attention. They methodically reveal Iraqi intentions and French complicity in crippling the moral authority of the Security Council. The Oil for Food investigation by the House Energy and Commerce Committee expanded on what Duelfer had also discovered regarding the official attempts to buy France's support against a war and the consequent French consummation of that promise.

"The President-Leader Saddam Husayn (May God bless him

and protect him) ordered the improvement of dealing with France"
in January 2002, the memos state. A February 5, 2002, memo entitled "Iraqi–French Relations" lays out Iraq's strategy to put the
French in its pocket. It orders that oil and trade "privileges will be
given to French political and individuals close to the center of political decision making" and urged "the possibility to support one of
the candidates in the French presidential elections after it becomes
clear who is going to win the elections, through the offer of oil contracts on the condition that the winner of the right represents a
good position for Iraqi and Arab issues."

A March 11, 2002, memo targets "individuals and businessmen
through whom we [IIS] will be able to approach the French President Jacques Chirac [who at the time was running for reelection]
and the Russian President Vladimir Putin." But perhaps most disturbingly, a memo dated two months later, May 6, 2002, describes
the very type of meeting Ambassador Levitte so strongly denied.
Dated the day after Chirac won reelection by the highest margin in
the forty-four-year history of the Fifth Republic, garnering 82 percent of the vote, it purports to detail a rendezvous between an Iraqi
intelligence agent and Roselyn Bachelot, described as "a French
Parliamentarian and the official spokeswoman for Chirac's election
campaign." Ms. Bachelot was a highly placed member of Chirac's
government who served as environmental minister.

In 2004, after Defense Secretary Donald Rumsfeld coined the
derisive phrase *Old Europe* to describe those nations—particularly
France and Germany—opposed to military action in Iraq, Ms.
Bachelot responded in the Pakistan *Daily Times*, "If you knew what
I feel like telling Mr. Rumsfeld . . ." She then fell silent, saying the
word would be too offensive. It apparently wasn't too offensive for
the French official to stand with a mass murderer, if the Mukhabarat
files are to be believed.

A memo (found in the files of the Iraqi Intelligence Service and
released by the House Committee on Energy and Commerce)
states,

1. The French Ms. Bachelot pointed out the historic relationship between the two countries, and the subject of Iraq will be the first in priorities and concerns of French politics on the condition that Mr. Chirac wins.
2. She assured that the French position opposed any American attack on the nation [Iraq] and France will use the right of opposition [veto] within the Security Council against any American decision regarding the attack on Iraq.
3. France will work throughout the upcoming period to lift the sanctions.

There you have it. The alleged French promise to protect Iraq with its veto more than a year before that vow was indeed fulfilled.

The Wall Street Journal went further, noting on October 8, 2003, that "one Iraqi intelligence report uncovered by Mr. Duelfer says that a French politician assured Saddam in a letter that France would use its U.N. veto against any U.S. effort to attack Iraq—as indeed France later threatened to do."

France indignantly said that was not so. There was no promise. No warning. No assurance it would protect Hussein. Ms. Bachelot, according to the *London Telegraph*, branded allegations "deplorable insinuations" and denied ever meeting with Iraqi intelligence agents.

Congressman Joe Barton, the chairman of the committee that released some of the most incriminating evidence against the French, noted that "at this moment, America's warriors are risking and giving their lives to defend the fledgling democracy in Iraq. We must not forget that if the U.N. had its way, Saddam would still be dispensing bribes, building his army, threatening his people, and invading his neighbors . . . as the 661 Committee watched the scam unfold." And, he might have added, it would have participated in it with the help of the French ringers placed inside the Security Council.

The secret Iraqi intelligence files were but one piece of evidence of the French sellout in the Security Council. But curiously, France had begun the sanctions process in 1991, standing alongside the United States and Great Britain as one of the original three enforcers.

"They were kick-butt tough," said one congressional source who reviewed the 661 Committee minutes before Oil for Food began. "The French were knocking heads," is how he put it, saying, "They were really cracking down, questioning everything, not giving an inch to Saddam."

But then something changed.

"Around the midnineties you can see the difference in their approach," said the source. "It's like they threw up their hands and gave up. They no longer challenged anything and their tone shifted. They started giving Saddam every break in the book."

The inexplicable reverse in the French attitude was marked by the veteran diplomats who were accustomed to Paris playing on Washington and London's side. After all, French pilots had patrolled along with other coalition warplanes when the Iraqi no-fly zones were established after the first Gulf War. The aerial enforcement, known as Operation Provide Comfort, established a safe haven for the Kurds in the north while Operation Southern Watch, starting in August 1992, protected the south from Hussein's aggression. But in December 1996, France dropped out, objecting to the further expansion of the no-fly zones without continued humanitarian aid to the Kurds. After patrolling Iraqi skies for five years, the French did not want to participate in anything that smacked of a purely military operation. On January 1, 1997, Operation Northern Watch commenced, and for the first time American and British pilots climbed aboard their warplanes and took to the Iraqi skies without the French. The French abandonment signaled the end of Security Council cooperation when it came to Iraq.

Why?

Jacques Chirac had been elected president of France on May 7, 1995.

Though denied by Chirac, it has been well documented that his relationship with Saddam Hussein influenced French foreign policy.

There is no doubt that Hussein found an old friend and supporter in the Elysée Palace who would go on to protect him to the very end, despite French howls to the contrary. As France's prime minister in 1975, Chirac visited Baghdad at Saddam's invitation, an official visit that was reciprocated the next year when the Iraqi leader journeyed to France. It was the only trip Saddam Hussein ever made to a Western capital, and it has long been part of "Jacques Iraq's" lore: He called the madman his personal friend, invited him to his country house, and took him on a tour of a French nuclear facility before selling Iraq two nuclear reactors and building the Ozirak nuclear plant destroyed during the Israeli raid in 1981. Chirac was quoted in the Manchester *Guardian Weekly* saying he was "truly fascinated by Saddam." He had a picture of him in his presidential office and there have been claims, not yet substantiated, that his political party, the Rally for the Republic (RPR), may have received funding from Iraqi sources. Iraq became France's number-one customer for arms and number-one exporter for oil. Just one year before the first Gulf War, French Defense Minister (and founder of the Iraq–French Friendship Association, which appeared on the oil allotment list) Jean-Pierre Chevenement visited Baghdad and told Hussein that he planned to "raise our bilateral relations to a higher level."

Oil Minister Amir Rasheed was quoted in the *Jerusalem Post* admitting, "Friendly countries who have supported us, like France and Russia, will certainly be given priority" when the lucrative contracts were to be awarded for Iraq's reconstruction after the lifting of sanctions. But Chirac, who sought to return to the French illusion of superpower status, would claim neither his own long history of ties to Hussein nor France's connections to his regime played a role in the veto threat.

"That is a myth," he told CBS's *60 Minutes* on March 19, 2003, six days after he drove a stake into the heart of Security Council unity. "I did indeed meet President Saddam Hussein when he was vice president in the midseventies but never since. But in those days everybody had excellent relations with Saddam Hussein and his party. . . . It was seen as progressive. Everybody had contact with them . . . including some important figures of the current U.S. administration who had contacts with Saddam Hussein as late as 1983, but not me." That is a reference to Defense Secretary Donald Rumsfeld's December 1983 visit to Baghdad as part of a Middle East tour as President Reagan's special envoy. He shook hands with Saddam, met Tariq Aziz, and established what the Department of State called a direct contact between the two administrations. That meeting would, twenty years later, be used by antiwar critics as proof of what they viewed as American hypocrisy.

As for the charges that his scandal-plagued party and election campaigns had been partly funded by Hussein, Chirac laughed in his interviews and called such allegations "preposterous, really. . . . Anything can be said about anyone. As we say in French, 'The taller the tale, the more likely people will believe it.' "

But the switch in French policy toward Iraq once Chirac took power was unmistakable. David Hanney, the British ambassador to the United Nations at the time, noticed that what became known as the "first serious breakdown in solidarity" in the Security Council coincided with Chirac's election.

"It began to erode," he recalled in his Yale University oral interviews, "and it got worse after 1995." He noted that "The French and the Russians do have their own national agendas, which relate to the resumption of trade, which relate to the payments of debts, which relate to their perception of Iraq as a key player in the region, and that played a role."

"France is looking at the long-term economic gains," observed Rolf Ekeus. The head of the U.N. weapons inspection team through most of the nineties pinned the blame on the economic incentives while noting the French leader's ties to the tyrant. "President Chirac was close friends with Saddam," Ekeus said. "He visited Baghdad once. But I think he has been very fair." Ekeus recalled a conversation he had with Chirac in 1995 regarding sanctions and keeping Hussein in check. "He was very supportive. . . . He said, "I promise we back you with support,' and they did."

A congressional briefing memo prepared for Congressman Christopher Shays noted that the chairman of the 661 Committee in 1999, Dutch diplomat Peter Van Walsum, put the turning point of French cooperation at October 1997, two years into President Chirac's term. That was when France completely switched sides and aligned with Russia and China in abstaining on Security Council resolution 1134, which condemned Iraq for obstructing the work of U.N. weapons inspectors. The resolution found that Iraq's "refusals to cooperate constitute a flagrant violation of Security Council resolutions," and demanded that Iraq allow the inspectors "immediate, unconditional and unrestricted access to any and all areas, facilities, equipment, records and means of transportation which they wish to inspect." It also proposed a travel ban on officials of Saddam's regime and expressed the council's "full support" of the inspectors. Russia, China, and France abstained. They did not support a strong message, did not support the United Nations' own efforts, did not support the Security Council's own resolutions, and did not support their "allies," America and Great Britain.

"In the sanctions committee," wrote Van Walsum, "France would consistently outshine Russia and China in criticizing the way the United States applied the sanctions regime. It almost looked as though France was engaged in a competition with Russia to be recognized as Iraq's most devoted friend, with France simply having to work harder as a former member of the Gulf War coalition. . . . I could not help feeling that more profoundly political considerations involving self-image were at play."

Van Walsum's views were published in the International Peace Academy book *U.N. Security Council: From the Cold War to the 21st Century*. Iraq had become "so emboldened by the growing division in the Security Council—and especially among the permanent five— that it resorted to ever more active obstruction of U.N. weapons inspectors," he noted.

As the sanctions continued and it became clear that Iraq would not abide by U.N. resolutions, Chirac broke the promise he had given to Ekeus. The French stopped enforcing sanctions through their participation in the no-fly zones and instead turned on the United States for doing so. By 2000, even the Clinton administration had had enough. Jamie Rubin, the Department of State spokesman, said, "The French government . . . ought to direct these comments to Iraq to stop Iraq from threatening American and British forces that are doing their job to protect the people of Iraq. . . . The French government would be well advised to inform the Iraqi government, as they have on many subjects, and they have a dialogue with them, to stop threatening American pilots."

Of course, the French government never did, at least not publicly. The Chirac government branded the no-fly zone monitoring pointless. Yet that position totally ignored the Security Council resolutions France supposedly supported and approved in New York. Iraq was obliged under resolution 686 to "cease hostile or provocative actions by its forces against all Member States including missile attacks and flights of combat aircraft." That requirement was far from pointless. Each time the Iraqis lit up their radar to track a coalition aircraft, they were violating Security Council mandates.

But France was known to be two-faced when it came to such matters. Even when Chirac's diplomats would actually vote in unison with other Security Council members to hold Iraq accountable, the French were breaking their own promises and undermining the U.N. on the ground in Baghdad.

The CIA Duelfer report found that at the same time France claimed it "continually monitored compliance with the sanctions" as Ambassador Levitte boasted, his junior diplomatic colleagues were engaged in the opposite behavior in Iraq. Duelfer found "French CAs [commercial attachés] in Baghdad, working to promote the interests of French companies while assisting them in avoiding U.N. sanctions." The French diplomatic corps was hand-holding French

businessmen and giving free lessons on how to skirt the very sanction protocols Mr. Levitte and his successor had piously supported.

In 2000, Duelfer noted that France felt threatened by the U.N.
weapons inspectors because, along with Russia and China, they
were concerned that evidence of their illegal transactions could be
discovered. "There are a lot of things they didn't want to come out,"
he said.

When Duelfer issued his voluminous report five years later, he
noted finding "evidence that French companies, after 1998, sought
and formed procurement relationships with Saddam's regime" in total violation of the Security Council. "These procurement transactions included offers and contracts for conventional weapons
systems and negotiations for possible WMD-related" systems. The
French knew no shame. "By 1999, recovered documents show that
multiple French firms displayed a willingness to supply parts for
Iraqi conventional military items," which included "spare parts for
the French Mirage aircraft, Iraqi air defense capabilities . . . western
manufactured helicopters . . . military related microwave, direction
finding, and passive radar technology." Not to mention "replacement parts for the Roland II surface to air missile system" with
which Major Jim Ewald had become so unfortunately acquainted.

The French went up to bat again, denying all as usual.

"France had sold no military equipment to Iraq since the summer of 1990 and it was furthermore impossible for Roland IIs to
have been manufactured in 2002, given the fact that they were not
manufactured after 1993," the embassy claimed. There was no explanation about replacement parts. Yet numerous documents recovered from the Iraqi Intelligence Service show that throughout the
life of Oil for Food, French defense firms were lining up to supply
Iraq.

"Iraq had a large inventory of originally French supplied equipment," said Duelfer. "Including Mirages, Roland missiles, and their
air defense system that was called Qari, which is Iraq spelled backwards. French defense contractors were quite anxious to supply

spare parts to refurbish the equipment." The massive amount of business corralled by French firms provided Chirac with an overwhelming incentive not to alienate Iraq, which would thereby endanger the massive payday awaiting French economic interests should Oil for Food have ended and sanctions been lifted.

The Heritage Foundation compiled a superb memo on France's financial interests:

- By 2003, French–Iraqi trade had topped $3.1 billion through Oil for Food.
- In 2001, France became Iraq's largest European trading partner. Roughly sixty French companies did an estimated $1.5 billion in trade with Baghdad in 2001 under the Oil for Food program.
- France's largest oil company, Total Fina Elf, has negotiated extensive oil contracts to develop the Majnoon and Nahr Umar oil fields in southern Iraq. Both . . . are estimated to contain as much as 25 percent of the country's oil reserves. . . . The two fields have the potential to provide a gross return near $650 billion. [When oil hovered at $50 a barrel the French take would have earned twice that, or $1.3 billion.]
- France's Alcatel company, a major telecom firm, is negotiating a $76 million contract to rehabilitate Iraq's telephone system.
- In 2001 French carmaker Renault SA sold $75 million worth of farming equipment to Iraq.
- More objections have been lodged against French export contracts with Iraq than with any other exporting country under the Oil for Food program, according to a report published by the (London) *Times*. In addition, French companies have signed contracts with Iraq worth more than $150 million that are suspected of being linked to its military operations.
- From 1981 to 2001, according to the Stockholm International Peace Research Institute, France was responsible for over 13 percent of Iraq's arms imports.

Colombo could solve this one.

No wonder Thomas Schweich, chief of staff at the U.S. Mission to the United Nations, accused several key members of the Security Council of "advancing self-serving national economic objectives" regarding their behavior toward Iraq.

Yet the French continually dug in.

In 2001, the foreign ministry reacted when Saddam's regime announced that France would lose its trade priority status with the Iraqis if it supported British efforts to clamp down on the Oil for Food program. "Our position," said Chirac's spokesman, "has never been dictated by commercial considerations but by our desire to meet our responsibilities as a permanent member of the U.N. Security Council. That same concern guides us today and will continue to guide us. As for French companies, their action is always carried out in accordance with U.N. resolutions."

The French talking points continued to put them on the defensive.

In May 2003, Ambassador Levitte spoke at Rice University in Houston and launched a spirited explanation of French motives, again denying that economic factors played any role in determining policy. He said, "If you look at the figures . . . you will discover, maybe with surprise, that France was before the war the thirteenth economic partner of Iraq. And Iraq represented 0.2 percent of our trade, 0.2 percent! You may say, 'Yes, yes, but there is oil.' Okay, let's look at the figures on oil. Our imports of Iraqi oil represented only 8 percent of the Iraqi oil exports. The U.S. imported before the war 56 percent of the Iraqi oil exports. So by far the U.S. was the number one importer of Iraqi oil. . . . I think it is unfair to say that France was interested only in economic interests when it was a question of principle, of international law. It was a question of peace and war, and not a question of oil. . . so please don't say our position was because of oil."

Levitte didn't mention the one priceless commodity France could trade: its coveted veto. In an open letter Levitte wrote to Washington power brokers at the time, he complained of an "unacceptable . . . disinformation campaign aimed at sullying France's image and misleading the public."

He continued to defend France's honor a year later, in April 2004, when he derided the continued "unfounded accusations . . . being spread by a handful of influential conservative TV and newspaper journalists in the U.S." He said, "These allegations suggest that the government of France condoned kickbacks—bribes, in effect—from French companies to the Iraqi regime in return for further contracts. They say Paris turned a blind eye to these activities. Let me be absolutely clear. These aspersions are completely false and can only have been an effort to discredit France, a longtime friend and ally of the U.S."

On April 7, 2004, Ambassador Levitte wrote an op-ed in the *Los Angeles Times* in which he declared his ignorance of Saddam's perversion of Oil for Food. "Was there corruption and bribery inside the program?" he asked. "Frankly, I don't know," he claimed.

✿   ✿   ✿

The French didn't know? The American delegation repeatedly told them, along with their Security Council colleagues, about the illegalities. Yet in a stunning exhibition of stupidity bordering on criminal neglect, the French, with the Russians and Chinese, allowed the wrongdoing to flourish.

Levitte, a special foreign affairs adviser to President Chirac, was appointed as his nation's ambassador to the U.N. in March 2000. After two years, he then moved on to the embassy in Washington as ambassador to the United States in December 2002. The allegations of corruption and kickbacks were brought to the attention of the 661 Committee in 2000 as Mr. Levitte assumed his duties in the Security Council, which of course covered the 661 Committee. On March 24, 2000, U.S. Ambassador William Cunningham, effectively the number two below Richard Holbrooke in

"A man I can do business with." That's how U.N. Secretary-General Kofi Annan described Iraqi tyrant Saddam Hussein after a 1998 visit to Baghdad. During their talks, Saddam smoked cigars like "a peace pipe," said Annan. Saddam broke seventeen U.N. Security Council measures from 1991 until the United States took action against him in 2003. *Corbis*

hrough "business" with the U.N., Saddam acquired the very truck terrorists eventually sed to bomb U.N. headquarters in Baghdad in 2004. The attack claimed twenty-two ves, including the Secretary-General's much-beloved personal representative and dear iend, Sergio Vieira de Mello. A scathing report later concluded the attack was ιccessful because of the U.N.'s own "dysfunctional" security, the "failure of U.N. ιanagement and staff to comply with standard security regulations and directives," and he lack of a culture of accountability." *U.N./DPI Photo*

Kojo Annan, son of the U.N. Secretary-General, reportedly pocketed $750,000 from oil-trading firms being investigated as part of the Oil for Food scandal and improperly received a diplomatic discount on a Mercedes. Kojo Annan has denied any wrongdoing, but Kofi says his son caused him "disappointment."
Studio Curchod

George Galloway, one of the British Parliament's most outspoken critics of the Iraq war, supported Saddam's efforts to end U.N. sanctions in exchange for twenty million barrels of oil, according to documents obtained from Saddam's regime. Galloway appeared before Senate investigators in 2005 only to insult them and President George W. Bush and deny all charges. *Corbis*

"I will talk to the [investigative] panel, not to you," retorted U.N. Oil for Food chief Benon Sevan, whose name appeared on Saddam's oil allocation list and who claims to have received mysterious large sums of money from his pensioner aunt. Sevan is believed to have returned to his native Cyprus, a nation that does not have an extradition treaty with the United States for financial crimes. And in the end, he never did cooperate with the panel, according to the Volcker Committee. *Courtesy Fox News*

addam's man in the United States, Samir Vincent, appears surprised by news cameras utside his Annandale, Virginia, home. Vincent pleaded guilty to federal charges stemming om the U.N.'s Oil for Food scandal. He admitted taking up to $5 million through addam's oil allocation list to try to influence American public opinion on behalf of addam's regime. *Courtesy Fox News*

The most vocal critic of the United States: French Prime Minister Dominique de Villepin. France rewards outspoken critics of the United States—Villepin received two promotions after his stint as foreign minister, the U.N. platform from which he argued against U.S. intervention in Iraq and thus elicited a rare round of applause from the Security Council. He later claimed to be "happy to see Saddam Hussein's regime fall," even though his nation vastly benefited at Saddam's trough.
U.N./DPI Photo

As the French ambassador to the United States, David Levitte blamed accusations of French bribes, kickbacks, and corruption in the U.N. Oil for Food scandal on "a handful of influential, conservative . . . journalists." For two crucial years, Levitte led French President Jacques Chirac's offense against American efforts inside the Security Council. *The George Washington University*

"Show us the money!" That's how one ambassador described former Russian Ambassador Sergey Lavrov's approach to the Oil for Food program in U.N. meetings. (Russia made the most of any nation from Oil for Food.) The suave, popular, and perpetually suntanned debonair Russian diplomat was dubbed the "George Hamilton" of the diplomatic corps. Like his French counterpart, Lavrov was promoted for his efforts against the United States, rising to Russian foreign minister one year after the Iraq war began. *U.N./DPI Photo*

Chinese Ambassador Wang Guangya and his counterparts usually wait to see which way the wind is blowing before committing to an issue, U.N. observers say. Communist China has routinely opposed American efforts in the Security Council. But its representative enjoys the fruits of American capitalism: Ambassador Wang lives in a lavish apartment in one of Donald Trump's high-rise buildings. *U.N./DPI Photo*

German Ambassador Gunter Plueger presided over the closing of the infamous 661 Committee, the Security Council subset that oversaw the corruption-ridden Oil for Food program. He "diplomatically" expressed his "sincere gratitude" to Benon Sevan, among others, and admitted while the program was important "for the survival of the Iraqi people . . . a final assessment of the sanctions against the former Iraqi regime still needs to be written." *U.N./DPI Photo*

Guilty: U.N. official Alexander Yakovlev (*left*) talks with me six weeks before he pleaded guilty in federal court to wire fraud and money-laundering charges for taking bribes from companies doing business with the U.N. Investigators said he stashed $1.3 million in an offshore bank account in Antigua—at least $950,000 of it from U.N. contractors. *Courtesy Fox News*

Another model U.N. employee? U.N. official Vladimir Kuznetsov, chairman of the U.N. Advisory Committee on Administrative and Budgetary Questions, chats with Secretary-General Kofi Annan. The U.S. Attorney's office indicted him in 2005 on charges of conspiracy to commit money laundering from "foreign companies seeking to secure contracts to provide goods and services to the United Nations."
U.N./DPI Photo

A look inside the "Insecurity Council," which too often is unable to live up to its task. Even the U.N.'s top nuclear official, Mohamed ElBaradei, conceded that "too often the Security Council's engagement is inadequate, selective or after the fact." Iran's billions have bought protection from Russia and China just as they, along with France, were blatantly bribed by Suddam Hussein's regime to keep his Oil for Food money flowing. The only permanent member to support the United States in Iraq was Great Britain.
U.N./DPI Photo

Iran President Mahmoud Ahmadinejad has repeatedly defied the Security Council's efforts to halt his nation's nuclear development. Perhaps he took a cue from his neighbor Saddam Hussein, who never met a Security Council resolution he paid attention to, or from Afghanistan, which ignored the Security Council's demands to turn over Osama bin Laden two years before the September 11 attack.
U.N./DPI Photo

Former U.S. President Bill Clinton has become the toast of the U.N. in his capacity as a money raiser for tsunami victims. Though he's given credit for his internationalism, he ignored the Security Council when he bombed Kosovo in 1999. *U.N./DPI Photo*

Like an American president, the Secretary-General enjoys calling a free mansion on U.S. soil home. This is the Secretary-General's elegant residence on Sutton Place, which could fetch at least $48 million in New York's real estate market. Were it to be sold, that money could pay for the polio immunization of 48 million impoverished children around the world. And that's the U.N.'s own estimate. *Courtesy of the author*

the U.S. mission, made the allegations of kickbacks so specific that fellow diplomats sitting in the Security Council didn't even need to put on their little translating earphones to get the message loud and clear.

Cunningham told them, "Hundreds of millions of dollars' worth of gas and oil are being smuggled out of Iraq, with the proceeds going not for Oil for Food humanitarian imports but to the regime and its cronies." His British colleague, Sir Jeremy Greenstock, added that they had also "heard convincing evidence that smugglers are also exporting oil through neighboring states including Turkey. The potential revenue from all these operations must now exceed $1 billion per year. Instead of being used to rebuild a hospital in Baghdad or provide clear water for a village, the money is being spent by Saddam Hussein's regime for the sustenance and comfort of the Iraqi elite and military."

The French didn't know?

Perhaps Ambassador Levitte should review his own words, as reflected in previously classified Department of State cables. He was serving as president of the Security Council in September 2001 when the U.N. overseers reported that Iraq had been illegally demanding extra fees of from thirty to seventy cents per barrel and "The revenue was not going to the Oil for Food escrow account as originally intended for use in improving the humanitarian situation in Iraq."

U.S. Ambassador Cunningham, sitting near Levitte, said the profits were "being manipulated by Iraqi officials," and the money was "not going to Oil for Food" or "being used to support the humanitarian needs of the Iraqi people." The U.S. Department of State's secret cable said, "Ambassador Cunningham and most other council members voiced serious concern of the problem posed by illicit oil surcharges."

"Levitte," reported the cable, "said the French government opposed the imposition of illegal surcharges on Iraq oil exports, a practice which deprived the Oil for Food escrow account [program] needed revenue to deal with Iraq's numerous humanitarian concerns."

The French didn't know?

Their U.N. ambassador practically conceded the point.

Equally suspect for a nation so "disengaged" from the process was Levitte's proposed attempt to change the 661 voting procedure from unanimous consensus to a majority vote, a move that would effectively have ensured a loss for the United States and Great Britain on every vote. Thankfully, only Jamaica supported him.

In meeting after meeting, the Americans and British practically begged their fellow council members to crack down on the corruption and violations of their own resolutions, and in typical U.N. fashion nothing was done. In a March 17, 2000, meeting the Americans warned of illegal oil exports through the Persian Gulf, and as usual the French and the Russians sat on it. "No consensus emerged on how to deal with the issue," according to a council report.

The Americans and the British faced down their French counterparts for more than a year, but the time spent hammering away at the illegalities resulted in little more than a nod to common sense from the 661 Committee. "The committee decided to keep the issue of oil smuggling under review." In U.N. World, getting the basics can be a small, sad miracle.

Congressional testimony of October 5, 2004, reads,

> **Congressman Tim Murphy:** Was there any role or awareness, for example, of the French, the Russian, Chinese governments of these kickbacks going on?
>
> **Ambassador Patrick F. Kennedy:** We informed their members of the 661 Committee.
>
> **Murphy:** So they were informed. Back in what year? Mid-nineties?

Kennedy: In 2000, sir, when it came to our attention. It was first raised, I believe, in the July 13, 2000, meeting of the 661 Committee.

If France had indeed been the ally it claimed, the record would reflect something more than a continual undermining of American policy. Their protests are empty, which is why within the diplomatic community in New York, the French insistences of innocence have collapsed like a pierced soufflé.

In 1998, five years before Levitte was forced by the public Oil for Food revelations to become a one-man assembly line of denials, U.N. Weapons Inspector head Rolf Ekeus had made the French motivations crystal clear during his U.N. Yale oral history interview. "They would like to come in first," he said of the French. "They would like to have Total Fina Elf, the oil company, involved in exploration and the enormous profits that come from this. Of course they are anxious to be number one, and they also compete with the Russians." Ekeus's comments came barely two years into the program and five years before France double-crossed the United States.

"If you want to see who's interested in oil, look at French policy," Richard Perle, chairman of the Bush administration Defense Policy Board Advisory Committee, told *Fox News Sunday*. "It is entirely self-concerned, and it has to do with oil contracts and very little else."

Others have likewise said that France's foreign policy is in many areas motivated by money.

"If one looks at France's involvement in peacekeeping," observes one ambassador, "those missions it supports or strongly pushes are almost always linked to some French economic interest. They were willing to cut and run in East Timor. They have no interest in Sierra Leone. But when you talk about places like the Ivory Coast, where they have financial interests, they wrap themselves up in the U.N. charter with highfalutin rhetoric to dress up their financial goals." The ambassador spoke with disgust of the French opposing sanctions on Charles Taylor's Liberia in an effort, he said, to protect France's mahogany trade. "The French put lipstick on a pig and danced it out there," he said, to further French financial stakes in Africa.

Nowhere was this thinking more on display than in Iraq.

"Chirac personally saw Iraq as their foothold to be a player in the Middle East," noted one American ambassador. "There were commercial and political reasons to open up the floodgates to Saddam. I think it would be fair for a critic to say they were reckless in how they did this. Their judgment was seriously flawed, and that contributed to the phenomenon, especially by the late nineties, where they basically said, 'Come on, let's start doing business again. Let's open up the bazaar.'" He said French officials "felt if they got in there early, they could corner the market and squeeze out the United States." Yet by being obstinate at the U.N. while currying favor in Baghdad, France, he noted, "wound up on the wrong side of history."

❊   ❊   ❊

Ultimately, it took the freshman congressman and former child psychologist Tim Murphy to diagnose the dilemma America faces with France and its actions through the U.N. Murphy observed at a congressional hearing on the Oil for Food abuses,

> The United States gave millions of lives to France in World War I, World War II, and Vietnam. Yet they turned their backs on us when faced with Hussein's ever-increasing threat to the international community. . . . They have given us the cold shoulder. France has repeatedly turned to us for help. In response, they have turned their backs on us. The Oil for Food corruption scandal may be the answer why.

The betrayal in the Security Council at the hands of our nation's oldest ally may have been the most disturbing realization about the climate of corruption, but it was by no means the only one. While the United States and Russia have had a tenuous relationship since the days of the Soviet Union, it took the U.N. to facilitate our latest look at unbridled Russian ambition and greed. While America is looking to keep the world secure, Russia seems to be panhandling for a few bucks, plain and simple.

– 8 –

THE RUSSIANS ARE COMING

"The Russian vote was for sale."

With that assessment Ambassador Woodward sums up the horse trading that went on in the Security Council during the 661 Committee meetings. One might have mistaken the participants as Wall Street commodities traders or haggling merchants in an Arab bazaar. For the United States and Great Britain, the debate might have been about ethics, but for others it was largely about money. No one, multiple sources confide, made that clearer than our Russian friends. No one was a better example than the Russian ambassador, Sergey Lavrov, the dapper veteran first posted to the U.N. in 1994.

"Lavrov is a smart guy," observes another American diplomat. "And he never lost focus on what was important, which was the money."

The ambassador recalls a meeting in the Secretary General's office with Mr. Annan and other Security Council representatives where he says Lavrov "was brutally frank about his concern in Oil for Food—the financial arrangements." While the U.S. delegation viewed the Security Council as a way to enforce principle, the Russians used it as a cash register to squeeze as many rubles as possible from the Iraqi regime.

"That's the way their elite system is built," observes Woodward. "You pay to play."

"Any country or any person who was owed something would be a fool if he or she wouldn't like to get the money back," Lavrov admitted to the researchers at the Yale University U.N. Oral History Project. By the start of the war, Saddam had racked up roughly $8 billion in debts to his Russian patrons, and the Kremlin did not want to appear foolish.

"We have never been trying to get this money back through illegal means," claimed Lavrov. "We have been stressing that we want sanctions to be lifted through the Iraqis' implementation of Security Council resolutions."

And on the flip side, observed Charles Duelfer, "Saddam's regime needed both Moscow's political clout in the U.N. . . . and its economic expertise and resources to sustain his regime."

It was a rewarding relationship.

"Saddam granted one-third of the Oil for Food goods contracts . . . to Russian firms," noted California Congressman Tom Lantos of the financial pipeline that generated roughly $4 billion a year from the Oil for Food program alone. "It is truly infuriating to discover the depth of the contempt and greed displayed by . . . France and Russia," Lantos added, saying both "evidently jumped at the chance to participate in Saddam's crimes against the international community."

The CIA's *The World Factbook* nailed Russia's extensive incentives that Ambassador Lavrov perhaps kept in mind as he boxed with his American and British counterparts over ending the sanctions:

- Russia's Lukoil negotiated a $4 billion, twenty-three–year contract in 1997 to rehabilitate the fifteen-billion–barrel

West Qurna field in Southern Iraq. Work on the oil field was expected to commence upon cancellation of U.N. sanctions on Iraq.

- In October 2001, Salovneft, a Belarus company, negotiated a $52 million service contract to drill at the Tuba field in Southern Iraq.

- In April 2001, Russia's Zaruezhneft company received a service contract to drill in Saddam, Kirkuk, and Bai Hassan fields—a contract worth over $11 billion, according to the CIA.

- Russia's Gazprom company over the past few years has signed contracts worth $18 million to repair gas stations.

- From 1981 to 2001, Russia supplied Iraq with 50 percent of its arms.

The Duelfer report was unsparing: Hussein "sought a relationship with Russia to engage in extensive arms purchases and to gain support for lifting the sanctions." Billions were promised when sanctions were finally lifted by the Security Council, creating "a significant economic interest in pushing for the removal of sanctions."

The relationship would also offer the Iraqis perhaps their closest Security Council companion. "Tariq Aziz in particular had close contacts in Moscow," said Duelfer. There he would get insight on "what the prospects were for actions in the Security Council." As early as 1997, two years into Oil for Food, Hussein held out the lure of a $12 billion energy deal to Russia that, of course, could only begin when sanctions ended.

The double dealing continued even as the Bush administration was lining up diplomatic support to force Iraq to abide by U.N. resolutions. Merely seven months before the war, the Russians signed a $40 billion five-year economic agreement with Saddam's regime, in effect shoving it in Washington's face as it tried to corral support against Hussein on the Security Council.

The Washington Post reported on August 17, 2002, that the Iraqi ambassador, Abbas Khalaf, who had once been Hussein's personal translator, boasted that the deal was sealed to thank Putin's government for its "support." "Russia was, is and will be our main partner," he said. "What we need from Moscow is moral, political and diplomatic support."

Iraqi Foreign Minister Naji Sabri, who had been crisscrossing world capitals with a stop at the U.N. to try to forestall military action, hailed the Russian agreement. "We have given full priority to Russian companies in Iraqi oil trading," he said, citing "the traditional friendly nature of relations between the two countries."

The *Financial Times* noted that this development came as Russia also announced increased nuclear cooperation with Iran, and prepared for a state visit by North Korea's despotic leader Kim Jong-il, making Moscow practically "the axis of evil's" convention city.

The Iraqi embassy in Moscow was turned into an ATM machine. The Duelfer report says Russian firms that did business with Saddam dropped off at least $61 million in cash there, a practice of using diplomatically protected missions as bank branches. It was not at all unusual to see oil suppliers and traders bringing large suitcases full of hard currency to embassies and Iraqi military offices so that the payments would be untraceable. There was so much money being moved that the U.S. Department of the Treasury accused the Iraqi ambassador to Russia of stealing $4 million in cash, and has since taken action to recover the loot for the Iraqi people. One former Iraqi diplomat described to CIA investigators how embassy personnel routinely abused their U.N.-sanctioned diplomatic privileges by smuggling cash, radar jammers, global-positioning jammers, night-vision devices, and small missile components on weekly diplomatic flights to Baghdad from Moscow. The Russian plane would leave laden with illegal material on Monday and return to the motherland Wednesday. "The flight was not inspected by the U.N.," notes Duelfer, who also claimed one weapons delivery man was the Iraqi ambassador to Russia, who "personally delivered GPS jammers to the Iraqi embassy in Damascus during April 2003 . . . concealed as diplomatic mail," one month into the war.

Russian firms were also attempting to sell Saddam military hardware to fend off the Americans, according to Duelfer. This included forays similar to those the French allegedly used to supply Saddam's military with missile parts that would be used to shoot down American warplanes. The only difference was that the Russian supplies were intended to target U.S. tanks. Less than one month before the war started, the Russian government firm Rosoboronexport "offered to sell and deliver several weapons systems to Iraq . . . Igla-S shoulder-fired SAMs and Kornet antitank missiles available for immediate sale." Air defense systems and Russian tanks were also offered. Four contracts for the material were signed, according to investigators, and "Russian officials offered to send equipment and technical experts to Iraq under the cover of Oil for Food contracts."

The Duelfer report confirmed that some of the equipment was shipped to Iraq. Within two months of the last meeting that supposedly took place on February 21, 2003, a pair of American M1 Abrams tanks were reportedly destroyed by Kornets. While Central Command did not confirm it, many news reports and military analysts claimed the first Abrams destroyed in battle were hit "by a sophisticated Russian antitank missile called a Kornet." *The Baltimore Sun* cautioned, "Russian and Ukrainian officials have denied selling such a weapon to Iraq."

American investigators have chronicled a variety of schemes the Russians employed to underhandedly gut the very sanctions its diplomats were trying to weaken in New York. Duelfer's probe concludes that Oil for Food contracts were supposed to be the "cover" to slip in prohibited military items disguised as humanitarian "illumination devices, water pumps, and assorted agricultural equipment."

It was not as if the Russians always hid their goals. The Ministry of Foreign Affairs, on December 13, 2000, said, "Russia has consistently advocated and will continue to advocate a line for the suspension and subsequent lifting of sanctions in the context of compliance with the Security Council resolutions." One American diplomat says the Russians employed "diplomatic extortion" to get their dough. "They came to us bilaterally," recalls the diplomat, meaning the Russian delegation held a sit-down with only our folks, and "at very intense decibels argued that if we didn't look at their contracts that were pending and find a way to release a very significant number, they intended to make business impossible for us at the U.N.."

It wasn't quite the horse's head in a bed, but the Americans got the message. The next time the 661 Committee met, "There were a fair number of contracts that we let go on through, and not just for them but also for the French, because the French knew what the Russians were doing," explains the diplomat. The French hid behind the Russian threat to get their way too. "It's politics. It's not much different from members of Congress who are trying to get legislation through 'extorting' things out of other members if they want to get their votes."

Well . . . sort of, but worse. Another member of the American delegation, U.N. Mission Chief of Staff Thomas Schweich, says the Russians were particularly adept at making up tons of excuses to get their way and to keep the money flowing. "They had a variety of tactics that they used. The principal one was lack of proof of the surcharges. That was a common statement that the Russians made, that, 'Yeah, you've interviewed a few people, but how do we know anybody is really paying?'" The Russians refused to acknowledge the evidence the Americans presented to them. "There was substantial proof " of the surcharges and kickbacks, says Schweich.

The U.N. had even interviewed numerous oil suppliers who did not want to pay the illegal kickbacks, but Saddam's sycophants in the Security Council refused to acknowledge the truth. "There was very, very strong evidence and of course in retrospect we were correct about that," says Schweich.

While Russia was squeezing the Americans and millions were allegedly being funneled to the highest offices in the Kremlin, Russian Foreign Minister Igor Ivanov visited Baghdad, met with Hussein, and hailed their relationship: "Russia believes that the time has come to take practical steps to lift sanctions," he noted. "President Saddam Hussein commended Russia's efforts in this direction. . . . As you know, as a result of a decade of sanctions, Russia has also sustained considerable losses amounting to tens of billions of dollars. We have informed the U.N. Secretary-General of this." There's the kicker.

The Duelfer report was blunt: "Iraq promised to economically reward Russia's support by placing it at the head of the list for receiving U.N. contracts under the U.N. Oil for Food Program." In Beijing, *People's Daily* euphemistically noted that it was a "gesture of gratitude" for Russian opposition to the American-proposed "smart sanctions" in 2001, when Hussein "rewarded Russia with more than $10 billion" worth of humanitarian contracts within the Oil for Food deal. This was followed by a Russian–Iraqi trade agreement worth another $40 billion.

The Iraqi ambassador to the U.N., Feisal Amin Istrabadi, a U.S.-born Iraqi from a prominent political family who spent thirty-three years in exile while the Baathists held power, blames the economic carrot dangled by Saddam. "There were certainly commercial and political interests involved," he told *The Washington Post,* "and Russia behaved like any other state in looking after itself."

Hussein, it seemed, tried to bribe nearly everybody.

"Iraqi attempts to use oil gifts to influence Russian policy makers were on a lavish and almost indiscriminate scale. Oil voucher gifts were directed across the political spectrum," said Duelfer, pointing to one deal that returned a $10 million profit. The Duelfer report lists allocations in oil vouchers to prominent Russian politicians, government agencies, and political parties including the Communists, the Liberal Democratic Party, the National Democratic party, and even the Russian Orthodox Church and the Moscow Science Academy.

Two of the most startling names on the list were at the highest levels of Russian politics. One was Vladimir Zhirinovsky, the ultra-nationalist lawmaker described by Congressman Tom Lantos as "one of the most odious and fantastic personalities of our time." He was alleged to have received $8,679,000 worth of oil, enough to supply the entire United States for a period of four days.

Zhirinovsky "praised Adolf Hitler's ideology . . . advocates military aggression against Russia's southern neighbors as a way of achieving political stability in the region . . . [and] made headlines by threatening to take Alaska back from the United States, nuke Japan, and flood Germany with radioactive waste," says Lantos. Zhirinovsky has called America, NATO, China, and Turkey adversaries, and published a book entitled *Spitting on the West*. When in 1995, he traveled to Baghdad, he was greeted by Hussein. According to a study by Indiana University, he sent volunteers to help the Iraqis during Desert Storm.

The other newsworthy name was Alexander Voloshin, a former top adviser to both Boris Yeltsin and Vladimir Putin who served as Kremlin chief of staff from 1999 to 2003. He was allegedly paid $16 million worth of oil vouchers through the Russian presidential council. The Coleman investigators said the "oil allocations awarded him had been approved by Saddam," and "given to Voloshin." Like the lineup of other implicated politicians, Voloshin predictably denied the accusations. "I have never been to Iraq and never had any direct or indirect contacts with Iraqis. I was never engaged in Iraqi oil transactions," he was quoted by the Russian news agency RIA Novosti. The Volcker Committee did question the authenticity of Voloshin's signature on a letter relating to oil allocation.

Zhirinovksy parroted the "Who, me?"

"I did not sign a single contract, I did not receive a single cent from Iraq, not a kopeck," he told Ekho Moskvy radio, adding that he "never saw any Iraqi oil, not a drop." This despite the Senate Permanent Subcommittee on Investigations' claim to have found "six letters signed by Zhirinovsky himself that openly discuss the allocations and more than thirty documents of the Iraqi Ministry of Oil that expressly identify Zhirinovsky and his political party . . . in connection to the allocations."

Senator Coleman said the Russians were awarded the lion's share of the illegal oil allocations because of their support of Hussein, and that Vice President Ramadan confirmed, "Zhirinovsky did receive the oil allocations." Another Iraqi official told Coleman's investigators, "Of course Zhirinovsky would make a profit. That's the whole point." The committee said that in one case Zhirinovsky even paid the required kickbacks for his oil to Iraq "by transferring ownership of a building in Moscow to the Iraqi embassy." The list of other reputed Russian recipients reads like a Kremlin phone book: the speaker of the Supreme Soviet Parliament under Boris Yeltsin, the head of the Russian Communist Party, the chairman of the Russian Solidarity with Iraq lobbying committee, the chairman of the Federation of Trade Unions, and the former presidential deputy chief. There was even a listing for the "son of Russian ambassador in Baghdad."

Every Russian official who has been reached by reporters has denied allegations of illegality, but Iraqi officials have admitted their motives. Vice President Ramadan told the CIA investigators that favors were handed out because "he believed the Russian government was sympathetic to the plight of Iraq and strongly against the sanctions . . . and that most of the parties of the Russian Parliament [Duma] supported Iraq's position."

Perhaps the alleged payoffs were the reason Russia first tried to block the U.N.'s own investigation of the scandal, refusing to support Paul Volcker's Independent Investigation Committee. Kofi Annan had to personally intervene and persuade his old Security Council friend Sergey Lavrov, by then bumped up to Russia's foreign minister, to enlist the Kremlin's endorsement.

One member of the American delegation recalls a telling revelation during the intense and unsuccessful struggle to get Russia to join the United States and Great Britain in military action against Iraq. He had been invited to a cocktail party at the Upper East Side apartment of an American oil trader, a millionaire many times over, who was frank and to the point. "He did most of his oil trading in Russia," he recalled. "So he was certainly an expert on how Russia

deals with the oil business. This guy says to me, 'You State Department people are idiots. All you need to do is play the Russian game.
You need to guarantee that they get future oil. Sign a deal with
them! You need to pay them off. You need to cut a deal with their
largest oil company so that they're involved.' He said, 'It's easy doing
business in Russia. It's all about who you pay off.'"

Here stood the diplomat, white wine in hand, staring at the real
world.

"Future oil deals . . . the Russians were looking for that," he
admits.

Another American diplomat told me that what infuriated him
the most about the antiwar "no blood for oil" chant was just how easily that rationale can be proven wrong. "If the war was really about
oil," he reasoned, "we would have done what the French and the
Russians did—make deals and carve up the oil fields. We didn't
have to go to war for the oil, just end the sanctions and slice the pie!"

So while the French pretended to play high-minded politics as
they stuffed their pockets, and the Russians went straight for the
vault, what about China? In contrast to its friends, China managed
to leave a nearly paperless trail, but one blazed with equal self-
interest and even more deceptive cunning.

– 9 –

CHINESE TAKEOUT

"China is encouraging its companies to carry out cooperation with Iraq under the Oil-for-Food program. China is satisfied with its cooperation with Iraq and is grateful to the Iraqi government for its support given to the Chinese companies in the project. . . . China and Iraq . . . boast bright prospects for cooperation in oil, electricity, communications, and other industrial sectors."

That was Chinese Trade Minister Shi Guangshengas talking, reported by Beijing's *People's Daily* on July 11, 2001, before the Oil for Food scandal erupted. In return, the "Iraqi Oil Minister hoped for more progress" and "promised to continue to support Chinese companies to implement their contracts in Iraq." During the Iraq debates inside the 661 Committee and the Security Council, China routinely sided with France and Russia but was not as vocal as they were. Resolutions and proposals aimed at watering down or removing sanctions against Hussein included China as the third sponsor. And although the Chinese have largely escaped the scrutiny of their two Security Council partners, they were cleaning up. During a 2001 Security Council debate, Ambassador Wang Yingfan endorsed a Russian proposal aimed at helping Saddam; the intended result was, as the others hoped for their nations, an opening of Iraq's economy to Chinese firms.

"Iraq's normal interaction and normal trade relations with other countries should be allowed to resume. Foreign companies should be allowed to invest in Iraq and be allowed to sign service contracts with Iraq," he declared. Wang put his nation firmly in the anti-American camp by adding, "The no-fly zones must be abandoned as soon as possible," and air strikes aimed to force Saddam to finally cooperate with the U.N. "should stop."

"The Chinese are a very subtle enemy," observes John Loftus. "They don't believe as the Russians did in brandishing the big sword. There is an ancient Chinese proverb that states, 'It is a wise eagle who hides his own claws.' They have been very subtle. They believe in war by surrogate. They use other surrogate states [because] they are not bold enough to confront us directly." Loftus says that is why they do not appear as blatant about their Oil for Food abuses as France and Russia.

The majority of illicit trade with China involved communications equipment and missile systems. While Charles Duelfer pointed out, "There is no evidence to suggest the Chinese government complicit in supplying prohibited goods," his report made clear that many Chinese firms violated sanctions to build up Saddam's military by using front companies or simply being discreet. "Ultimately," concluded Duelfer, "it provided Iraq with prohibited items. . . . [T]his relationship allowed Iraq to improve its indigenous missile capabilities. . . . Chinese companies willingly supplied these types of items to the Iraqi regime." The systems enabled Hussein to upgrade his ability to shoot down coalition pilots patrolling the no-fly zones.

The most glaring example of this Chinese trade harmful to the United States was a huge fiber-optic telecommunications project designed to upgrade Baghdad's telephone and communications systems.

Because the fiber optics were laid underground, intelligence sources widely feared they could be used to evade and defeat interceptions by American and coalition forces during a war, as well as to direct radar and missile units.

As it did with France and Russia, Iraq dangled contracts with the Chinese that would go into effect only when the Security Council lifted sanctions. The Chinese foreign ministry claimed, "China has all along strictly adhered to the relevant United Nations Security Council resolutions on sanctions," on November 26, 2002. The Chinese had earlier dismissed any military application. How clever.

"Chinese enterprises and corporations have not assisted Iraq in building the project of fiber-optic cable for air defense," claimed Foreign Minister Tang Jiaxuan in 2001. "The Chinese government has always been very serious, very strict and always very responsible in implementing the relevant U.N. resolutions on Iraq. . . . We have a very good track record in the United Nations."

Like its brethren, France and Russia, China welcomed opportunities to sell to Iraq and also worked to remove the sanctions. A November 2000 visit to China by Iraq's Deputy Prime Minister Tariq Aziz further cemented those efforts, when Chinese Vice Premier Qian Qichen supported Saddam's push to have sanctions lifted. "China supports Iraq's efforts in removing sanctions," said the government. "China, as a permanent member of the Security Council and as a friend of Iraq, will continue to make unremitting efforts alongside Iraq" to lift the sanctions. Qian also "encouraged Chinese entrepreneurs to participate in the Oil for Food programme. . . . China stands ready to explore new ways for expanding trade cooperation with Iraq."

Follow the money.

Less than two years later, in January 2002, Qian met again with Tariq Aziz along with Chinese Premier Zhu Rongji. The Chinese told Aziz that while they supported the ending of sanctions, they also hoped that "Iraq would strengthen its cooperation with the U.N.," according to the CIA. At that meeting the Iraqis apparently raised the ante and "threatened to end trade relations with China if Beijing agreed" to the American- and British-led effort in the 661 Committee to enumerate specific items forbidden to Saddam's regime. China, as usual, decided not to support us.

The CIA's *The World Factbook* reported, "China National Oil Company, partnered with China North Industries, Corp., negotiated a 22-year long deal for future oil exploration in the Al Ahab field in southern Iraq. The Chinese Aero-Technology Import Export Company [CATIC] had been contracted to sell meteorological satellite and surface observation equipment to Iraq."

In addition, $23 million worth of telecommunications equipment was sold to the regime by China. Russia was the largest supplier of weapons to Iraq for twenty years; China was the second largest. The motivation of his Chinese colleagues was simple, says Woodward. While they are much harder to read, and at times as frustrating as the French, he thinks China was motivated "in making sure that the Americans didn't get their way. That's it, much more of an attitude to try and bring America down one notch." A variety of observers in the diplomatic community who confided in me explained that the Chinese government was not bought off—as France and Russia were—but cast their vote with the majority to counter the United States for geopolitical reasons.

Tang Jiaxuan attended the final Security Council meeting before the war but did not threaten, as Jacques Chirac had, to use China's veto against military action. He said his nation would "judge the matter on its own merits." Of course, China aligned itself very publicly against the United States with France, Russia, and Germany by endorsing their opposition to a war.

The Chinese have not received the attention of investigators at the level of their French and Russian friends. Perhaps this is due to the closed, impenetrable nature of the still-Communist country, but it is also probably due to the absence of the tantalizing evidence that implicates those in the highest echelons of French and Russian society. Unlike those two nations, there are no appearances on the oil allocation list of Chinese government officials, politicians, or po-litical parties. No recognizable names emerge that suggest a blatant compromising of the nation's foreign policy. The oil allocation list includes such obtuse entities as China National Oil, Sinochem, Unipec, and Hauken. There are repeated listings of only two indi-viduals, a "Mr. Joan" and Zhuhai Zhen Rong, both of uncertain and undetermined origin.

The Wall Street Journal reported that at least $5 million of Mr. Joan's estimated $12.5 million from the oil allotments allegedly went to a former executive of a large Chinese arms maker, Huang Ruzhen. According to the *Journal*, Mr. Huang confirmed that he negotiated for the oil with permission of the U.N. and the Chinese government, but claimed he did nothing in return to help Iraq.

I posed several questions to Secretary-General Annan for this book, only two of which he refused to answer.

> **Me:** Regarding Oil for Food, you have said that you do not believe Security Council votes "were bought" by Saddam's contracts. Do you believe the billions of dollars that his regime granted to France and Russia through the program or through the oil allocations influenced their policies and stance against the resulting war? Do you think economic in-terests influence policies of member states?
>
> **Annan:** No comment.
>
> **Me:** What do you think are the lessons of what went wrong in the Oil for Food program, in the sense that sanctions were busted and the Iraqi regime was able to manipulate the good-will and efforts of the international community for its own means?
>
> **Annan:** No comment.

– 10 –

U.N.-CIVIL SERVANT

Given the fact that nations aggressively pursue their own interests at the U.N., and that the United States has few friends who can truly be considered consistent allies, we can only hope that the U.N. civil servants who carry out the world body's decisions will act in a manner that reflects a concern for the greater good of the world. We can hope that above all the bickering of nations, the U.N. officials themselves serve as a check to guide the organization toward its goals of stabilizing and improving the condition of the world order.

But if experience shows us anything, it's that while the laws and proclamations of the U.N. can be drafted with infinite righteousness, they can also be undermined by the very U.N. administrators drafted to enforce them.

In the fall of 2003, I greeted Benon Sevan with relief.

The white-haired veteran U.N. diplomat projects a brittle,

no-nonsense air. U.N. officials would tell me he was "a good boss who worked incredibly hard." Sevan clearly relished having returned to U.N. headquarters in one piece as he warmly accepted my sympathy.

"I was in my office when it happened. It was terrible," he recalled of the U.N. Baghdad headquarters bombing a few weeks earlier that had taken the lives of so many of his colleagues and destroyed the U.N.'s aura of invulnerability. "I came this close to being killed," he emphasized, holding his thumb and forefinger barely apart. I told him how glad I was that he had survived and expressed my sincere gratitude both for his dedicated service to the Iraqis and for the willingness of diplomats like him to carry out their duties amid danger. It's how we'd like to think of all the U.N. officials around the world.

The next time we saw each other was May 10, 2004. He was hurriedly striding down a New York City sidewalk, as I peppered him with questions—microphone in hand with a television camera recording the confrontation—asking if he took bribes from Saddam Hussein.

Sevan, the sixty-six-year-old hot-tempered Oil for Food program director and four-decade U.N. veteran, came to represent the face of the scandal. He started the defense of his honor in the late fall of 2003, as questions started bubbling up in the media about some nebulous U.N. program called Oil for Food that many didn't know anything about. The extent of the scandal exploded in January 2004, when a newspaper in Baghdad, *Al-Mada,* took on the investigation of the mess with the fervor of Woodward and Bernstein's *Washington Post.*

The paper splashed on its front page the list of those who allegedly received oil allocations from the Hussein regime. For the diplomatic corps inside the U.N., the sudden revelation was a bombshell. Here for the first time were the details—names named, including the numbers of barrels of oil allegedly distributed as part of a massive influence peddling operation the U.N. didn't even know about. The appearance of a "Mr. Sivan—U.N." sent shock-waves through the Secretariat.

"Who's that? It can't be Sevan. It's not even spelled right!" they would tell me in protest. Deny and defend. Defend and deny.

It was Sevan, according to the flood of paperwork later dug up by investigators. Detailed transactions, meetings, memos, and phone calls seemed to show that Sevan had taken a bribe of oil allocations. Saddam had set up a system where he personally approved each name on the list. He even personally ordered the bribe of a U.N. oil inspector who allegedly was paid more than one hundred grand to look the other way when the oil tanker *Essex* was overfilled. Investigators say that sweet little deal earned Iraq an extra illegal $9 million. The inspector, forty-six-year-old Armando Carlos Olivieira of Portugal, worked for the Dutch contractor Saybolt. The investigation led by Minnesota Senator Norm Coleman released a memo from the Iraqi oil minister to the deputy prime minister, advising him that "in compliance with the order of the president leader, may God protect him"—Saddam—"we have approved . . . an agreement with the oil inspector to award him 2 percent of the total of additional quantity for his services. . . . The total of $105,819 was paid to the oil inspector [Mr. Armando Carlos]." The targeted inspector has denied that he was bribed.

It seems remarkable that the feared despot "the president leader, may God protect him" ruling over a nation of twenty-four million people would involve himself in the intricacies of administrating a payoff. A measure of Saddam's desperate greed and the importance of keeping the Oil for Food billions flowing can be found in his widespread attempts to reach whoever would help, from world capitals to individual U.N. employees.

Saddam would sit down with his advisers to hash out to whom he would sell oil. The meetings were known as the Command Council, and, according to Volcker's investigators, they included Iraqi Vice President Taha Yassin Ramadan, Deputy Prime Minister

Tariq Aziz, Finance Minister Hikmat Al-Azzawi, and the Minister of Oil Amer Muhammad Rashid. In keeping with Saddam's strategy to spread the money around to supporters of the regime's goals, "The Command Council gave priority to oil contractors from certain countries that were thought to be more favorably inclined toward lifting sanctions," states the first Volcker report. "The Command Council began to increase the number of special oil allocations for the benefit of particular individuals or entities that were perceived to support or be politically favorable to Iraq." Benon Sevan seemed to be a perfect target.

As the Oil for Food head, he held enormous sway over the spigot that supplied Saddam's lifeblood. This was reflected by the comments of former Oil Minister Rashid, who told U.N. investigators the Command Council allocated oil to Sevan because "he was a man of influence." It was hoped that he would go to bat for Iraq to try and prod the 661 Committee to release more spare parts needed to increase the output of Iraq's decrepit refinery facilities.

The Security Council did just that and approved an increase. Two days later, on June 21, 1998, Sevan went to Iraq for two weeks. The council had passed a resolution authorizing the spending of up to $300 million to import oil exploration and production equipment— good news for the demanding Iraqi officials. During Sevan's visit, he met with the oil minister twice, on June 22 and 30, and with the vice president once, on July 2. Both are members of the Command Council. The Volcker investigators say that at one of the meetings with the oil minister, Sevan "solicited an oil voucher."

Surely there was a good reason for Sevan's request. It was made, supposedly, "to help a friend," according to a letter dated September 26 from the director of Iraq's government division SOMO, the State Oil Marketing Organization, which processed Iraqi oil transactions. That "friend" was Fakhry Abdelnour, an Egyptian cousin of Secretary-General Kofi Annan's predecessor, Boutros Boutros-Ghali. Abdelnour ran an oil company called AMEP (African Middle East Petroleum Company), which had been having business problems, according to investigators. The firm was registered in Panama, but had "no offices, refineries, facilities or employees there." It was really based on the French Riviera, in Monaco, a bastion of wealth, gambling, and excess. Abdelnour lived in Geneva, Switzerland. Such was the international coterie also benefiting from Oil for Food.

Sevan denies that he recommended "his friend." He conceded to investigators, "I might have mentioned, I don't know." But, he added, "Even if I had mentioned it, it was never meant as a recommendation. Because I never made recommendations to anybody." At the same time Sevan was in Iraq talking up the oil minister in Baghdad, "his friend" Abdelnour sent his first letter to the Iraqis to try and get in on the U.N. program. This would eventually lead to an oil deal worth $144 million.

When Sevan returned from his June–July 1998 visit, he appeared before the Security Council and did exactly what the Iraqis had apparently hoped he would do. He told the Oil for Food overseers that Iraqi officials had urged him and the Secretary-General "to spare no effort in ensuring the approval of the contracts for essential spare parts concerning the oil industry as well for other sectors, which had been delayed far too long." There was no mention of "his friend." His plea was effective.

By that fall, the Oil for Food program boasted, "Record number of oil spare parts contracts approved by sanctions committee. Benon Sevan has emphasized to the Security Council and the 661 Committee the importance of expediting approvals in the oil sector and reviewing further contracts put on hold." Spare parts contracts weren't the only deals being approved. The Volcker investigation revealed that Sevan continued to press the Iraqis for more oil allocations for "his friend," and the oil continued to flow into Abdelnour's company with a second allocation in the spring of 1999. In fact, Abdelnour really didn't have to do much of anything, because he would turn around and sell the oil to the big petroleum companies for an instant profit.

Sevan persisted, say investigators, dogging Hussein's henchmen when he saw them. He must have become a pest because records show he personally buttonholed the oil minister in Vienna several times as well as in Iraq, and even hit up an Iraqi diplomat at the U.N. mission in New York. But the Iraqis apparently didn't think they had gotten their money's worth from him. When Abdelnour's company received the second oil allocation, it was for a smaller amount than the first, one million barrels instead of the expected 1.8 million.

Iraqi officials "did not believe that Mr. Sevan had been helpful," so Sevan "complained" about the cut. But it was to no avail. Three months after "his friend" signed the contracts for the lesser amount of oil, Sevan learned he perhaps really had reason to be angry about being exploited by the Iraqis. The $300 million figure for oil equipment earmarked for Iraq had actually been increased by another $85 million. Sevan rushed back to Baghdad, he told the Security Council, at the request of the oil minister to discuss increasing Iraq's oil production even more. He said he "was received very warmly by the vice president and all the ministers." The meeting now seems to have been very fruitful, because just six days after Sevan returned from that trip, yet another oil allocation popped up on the Iraqi list. This time it was under his name. The amount: two million barrels, double what the Iraqis had previously provided to "his friend." What did Sevan next do at the Security Council? He appeared before it just ten days after the Iraqi oil list included a "Mr. SIFAN—U.N." for the very first time and promptly doubled the estimate of what the Iraqis would need to rehabilitate their oil infrastructure from the $300 million figure to $600 million. The pattern seemed to have been set.

Sevan became perhaps the most forceful advocate for Iraq and the Oil for Food program inside the U.N. besides the Iraqi ambassador himself. Continually, throughout his stewardship, he forcefully pressed the Security Council and the 661 Committee to increase the amount of money Iraq could pump into its oil industry and lift the number of "holds," or blocks the United States and Great Britain put on Iraqi imports. The Americans tried to restrict material Hussein could use for military or other purposes, but Sevan fought for increasing the number of Iraq's imports, and for a while he often got his way. On March 31, 2000, the Security Council agreed to his request to increase the amount of oil production, spare parts, and equipment Iraq could buy to produce more oil. Just like the amount of the second oil allocation from the Iraqis, the allowance for Hussein was doubled by the Security Council.

Sevan continued to appear before the Security Council members, and his pleas for increasing Iraq's oil production were always couched on behalf of the Iraqi people. "I'm sure some of you will now tell me: 'Benon, come on, not again, you sound like a broken record!'" he told one Security Council meeting. "Every hold placed on an application for an essential supply affects the implementation of the program. Or to put it another way, it hurts the Iraqi people."

He begged for them to provide "the essential needs of the Iraqi people," to "spare no effort in meeting the dire humanitarian needs of the Iraqi people," and "not to lose sight of the human dimension and fully bear in mind the humanitarian needs of the Iraqi people at this very difficult period."

His demands were echoed by Secretary-General Kofi Annan, who also often spoke of the urgent need for the 661 Committee to approve as much as possible to "benefit the Iraqi people." If only it did benefit just the Iraqi people. While the U.N. claimed "the humanitarian situation in Iraq has improved considerably" thanks to Oil for Food, not much was said publicly about the suspected skimming, stealing, and smuggling that started to slowly emerge in the fall of 2000, four years into the program.

No doubt, to some degree, Annan's views stemmed from sincere and genuine fear of a humanitarian nightmare. But it didn't seem to register anywhere that the more money that cascaded into Iraq, the more money Hussein had at his disposal, the more money the U.N. received to bolster its well-being, and the more money schemers had access to through bribes and payoffs.

✵   ✵   ✵

The suspected Sevan oil allocations from Iraq flowed throughout the life of Oil for Food, right up to just four months before the program ended with the March 2003 coalition invasion. The Volcker investigation revealed that Sevan's name continued to appear on SOMO (State Oil Marketing Organization) documents allocating oil or in those of his "friend's" company, AMEP, until November 17, 2002. This was four days after Hussein accepted the tough new unanimous Security Council resolution 1441 that found him "in material breach" of his responsibilities to the U.N. and threatened "serious consequences" if he did not fully cooperate with the sixteen resolutions the Security Council had let slide since his defeat in 1990. The shadow of war was approaching, with President George W. Bush and Prime Minister Tony Blair making it clear that Saddam at last would be forced to live up to his empty promises.

The November 17 allocation reserved 5.5 million barrels of oil in Sevan's name, according to U.N. investigators. The list was compiled two days after Iraqi forces continued their repeated violations of U.N. sanctions by trying to kill American and British pilots patrolling the no-fly zone. The Iraqis had fired surface-to-air missiles and antiaircraft guns at the allied warplanes, a violation of resolution 1441, just days after it was enacted.

Sevan was apparently in line for more of Saddam's generosity just one day after "the president leader, may God protect him," issued an open letter to the rubber-stamp Iraqi parliament. Hussein declared that the U.N. order was an "alliance between Zionism and the American administration and their satanic lackeys." He told them, "Your enemy has returned, once again, to camouflaging its schemes under the cover of the Security Council which has . . . infringed upon all that may represent the conscience of international unanimity." U.N. investigators have found that in all, Saddam diverted 14,300,000 barrels of oil allocations in connection with Sevan, giving "his friend's company" a profit of $1,500,310. Sevan denies he asked for or received oil money or anything else from Saddam's regime.

✤ ✤ ✤

As the details saw the light of day in the aftermath of the American invasion of Iraq, Sevan found himself on the defensive.

"I will talk to the panel, not to you!"

That was Benon Sevan's curt response when I confronted him on camera for Fox News on the Manhattan sidewalk, and he wasn't entirely forthcoming.

He talked to them but didn't say much. The Volcker investigators note that Sevan first met them on May 18, 2004 (the week after he uttered his vow during our sidewalk encounter) but "was unwilling to discuss the allegations against him at that meeting." It wasn't until eight months later that he sat for a "formal questioning session" and the publicly released transcripts reveal his evasive and meaningless answers. "No," "I don't know," "I don't remember," and "I might have" predominate Sevan's explanations about his efforts on behalf of "his friend." The highest-ranking U.N. official responsible for the largest humanitarian program in the organization's history, who had been personally appointed to his sensitive post by Secretary-General Kofi Annan, was unable to even remember some of the basics when questioned by the U.N.'s own investigators. After promising cooperation in words seen on television from Utah to Uzbekistan, he did not cooperate.

One month later, in June of 2004, a leaked e-mail from Sevan was given to *The New York Times* by a U.N. official. Addressed, "My Dear Friend," Sevan's letter constituted his defense to his colleagues. He claimed he was the victim an "intense smear campaign," saying "there was no alternative to the program," and blamed the program's problems on others. "It could have been better administered had we been allowed by the member states to do so," he wrote. He vowed, "to fight it out and clear my name as well as the name of the organization."

I read another e-mail he sent to a friend, in which he branded the allegations "defamation" and lamented how shabbily he felt the organization had treated him, especially since he was nearly "blown up" that day in August in Baghdad, when the terrorists claimed they had succeeded in killing him, and especially after all the faithful service he had given to the U.N. over nearly a lifetime.

Yet Sevan had a curious way of fighting it out. The Volcker investigators say he "met with the Committee" eleven more times through 2004, and only consented to a "formal" interview in early 2005, just before Volcker released his first report. Sevan's lawyer, Eric Lewis, points out that it was his client who requested the first meeting, and he brands Volcker's account of others as "misleading at best." Lewis says those "meetings' consisted of Volcker's staff picking up "boxes of documents, records and personal papers" that they retained into early 2006, and he cites the U.N.'s flip flop on covering Sevan's lawyer's fees and its refusal to give Sevan complete access to his own records after they were provided to the committee as the reasons for the delay in Sevan's meeting with Volcker's team. Lewis also says that Sevan offered to respond to written questions from Volcker at any time, but none were ever sent. In the end, Lewis suggests that the only real meeting with Volcker's team was at the end of the process, in January 2005.

That may be, but the findings of Volcker's Committee are what they are. And Lewis is left to blast them as "politically charged," branding it an "incompetent investigation" that issued "insupportable and biased findings" against his client in order to provide "cartoon villains, not the truth." He accused the committee of sacrificing his client "in a misguided attempt to deflect attention and placate U.N.-Bashers," and he hailed what he called Sevan's "openness and cooperation" with Volcker's investigators.

His statements couldn't lead directly to any criminal prosecution by Volcker because the esteemed panel lacked subpoena power and was not a law enforcement entity. No matter what Sevan spilled, the former United States attorneys who made up the muscle of Volcker's investigatory staff had no ability to accomplish anything that would directly put someone in jail. They couldn't file charges. They couldn't go after bank records in Panama to see if Sevan's "friend" funneled Oil for Food proceeds to him. They had no prosecutorial ability to lodge any charge against him (as they had the mafia bosses and white-collar criminals they had pursued in the service of the Department of Justice before signing on with Volcker). While the evidence that they did uncover was turned over to prosecutors, the Volcker staff could only issue a report, and in the end Sevan and his lawyer would answer the findings by sending a letter to Volcker that wasn't even made public. "Mr. Sevan's response was provided on a confidential basis and is therefore not contained in this report; the Committee will publish the response on its Web site upon Mr. Sevan's written request."

The Volcker report concluded that Sevan indeed had "solicited and received" oil allocations worth approximately $1.5 million. They branded his behavior "a grave and continuing conflict of interest" that was "ethically improper" and said that he "was not forthcoming to the Committee." Since the U.N. and Volcker's Committee do not have the ability to issue subpoenas, determining whether Sevan was criminally on the take would only be up to a prosecutor's office such as the U.S. Attorney for the Southern District, which could have jurisdiction. Nevertheless, Senator Norm Coleman praised the Volcker Committee for exposing Sevan's actions. "He repeatedly lied to investigators," he said. Senator Coleman was convinced that there was "probable cause that Mr. Sevan's actions rose to the level of criminal liability." The senator again demanded that Annan strip Sevan of his diplomatic protection "so that a criminal prosecution can proceed."

The U.N. response was predictable. As always, the spokesman for the Secretary-General said the information was all part of the ongoing Volcker investigation and that everyone should let it run its course.

Annan had steadfastly promised to remove the protection of diplomatic immunity for any U.N. official if there was evidence of wrongdoing. He just never said what level that evidence had to reach before he would act. The U.N. insisted, though, that immunity would be removed so criminal charges could be filed if requested by a prosecutor. While Coleman was more than convinced that a criminal case could be brought immediately against Sevan in the fall of 2005, no law enforcement agency then acted.

Authorities were left with Sevan's explanations and Volcker's opinions. Because of the constraints on the Volcker Committee and its inability to subpoena financial records, the only clue investigators could rely on was a series of curious and tantalizing morsels Sevan had included on his United Nations financial disclosure forms.

So we are faced with what has become an all too familiar status quo in U.N. World: persuasive evidence of potential corruption and possibly crime, and absolutely nothing that can be done about it within the organization aside from censure and expressions of dismay. If you look at the trail of evidence Sevan left behind, ignoring it amounts to condoning it.

If Sevan hadn't listed the cash payments, no one would have raised the question. But for a period of four years, from 1999 to 2003, he claimed he received a total of $160,000 in cash from his elderly aunt, Berdjouchi Zeytountsian. She was a retired Cypriot government photographer who, the Volcker investigation noted, had lived for the past twenty years on a modest pension. "Nothing about Mr. Sevan's aunt's livelihood suggests that she possessed large amounts of disposable cash income," declared the investigators, saying she "had never shown signs of having access to large amounts of cash and would not have been expected to carry large amounts of cash outside the country. During her retirement, Ms. Zeytountsian lived in a small, plain two-bedroom apartment in Cyprus that had been purchased by Mr. Sevan." That suggests she didn't have enough money to buy her own place.

Her modest pension and government insurance netted her approximately $1,200 a month. Her "few withdrawals" from her bank account ranged from about $100 to $1,000. Her life savings amounted to one certificate of deposit worth roughly $85,000 in U.S. currency. Yet this was the elderly pensioner who Sevan maintained had given him $50,000 in cash in 1999, $45,000 in 2000,

$30,000 in 2001, and $35,000 in 2003. Sevan told the U.N. investigators she would bring the money into the United States "to help defray the expenses of her annual stay with [him] and his family in New York." Were they putting her up at the Waldorf?

The total over the four years amounted to $160,000.

The Volcker Committee was not impressed with Sevan's story. "Mr. Sevan's statements regarding the source of the additional cash income, which he disclosed on his United Nations Financial Disclosure Form for the years 1999 to 2003, are not adequately supported by the information reviewed by the Committee." Senator Coleman was not as circumspect. "Benon Sevan broke the law," he said. He later portrayed the allegations as part of a much wider culture at the "highest levels of the U.N. Greed and power, rather than compassion and comfort, guided their actions."

Sevan's attorney responded to Volcker's findings by launching a scathing attack on the investigation. "Mr. Sevan never took a penny," declared Eric Lewis, a Washington, D.C., lawyer retained by Sevan to react to the committee's findings by accusing the Volcker Committee of having "succumbed to massive political pressure." He called his client a "scapegoat."

Lewis is a veteran of high-profile international financial rip-offs. He represented the liquidators in the notorious Bank of Credit and Commerce International case in the early 1990s. BCCI (Bank of Credit and Commerce International), an Abu Dhabi bank with heavy Middle Eastern investments, became the largest bank collapse in history, an estimated $17 billion global scandal. Authorities found BCCI stole billions, bribed government officials across the globe, financed terrorism and arms smuggling, and even "managed" prostitution.

Now Lewis had a client at the center of another massive international scandal. He attacked the Volcker Committee for its questioning the veracity of the elderly aunt story. Mr. Sevan had been "entirely forthcoming with respect to the timing and manner of income received from his late aunt." Lewis noted investigators had relied on "a conversation with someone in Cyprus who purports to be familiar with the finances" of Mr. Sevan's aunt for their suggestion that Sevan was hiding the truth.

The biography of Mr. Lewis provided by his law firm (Baach, Robinson & Lewis) notes that he is "an expert in asset tracing in international fraud cases." Perhaps he can trace the $160,000 in cash payments back to Sevan's elderly aunt and provide the documentation and hard evidence that support his client's claims to a suspicious senator, doubting investigators, and skeptical public.

The Volcker investigators uncovered "additional evidence [that] reveals more reasons to doubt Mr. Sevan's claim" that the dough came from his aunt. The dates of her visits to New York "bear little correlation to the dates of the Sevans' cash deposits," with only one-fourth—$33,400—being made when the aunt was even in the United States. The paper trail also revealed about half of Sevan's bounty came during one fifteen-month period when his aunt hadn't even come to visit him.

The investigators also presented a compelling case for why he needed extra money. They say, "The Sevans' finances were frequently stretched thin from the monthly burden of funding two residences, debt obligations, credit card charges and related living expenses." At times, "The monthly balances in their checking accounts hovered at or near zero." His bank account, notes Volcker's team, "went into overdraft status forty-five times and Mrs. Sevan's Chase checking account was overdrawn 153 times" prior to his allegedly asking the Iraqis for an oil allocation. The investigators say Sevan then "used the cash deposits to pay off all debts but his mortgage," including "several thousand dollars on his Optima credit card."

It is unfortunate that Ms. Zeytountsian was unable to corroborate her devoted nephew's contentions. The month after Mr. Volcker was appointed to head the panel to investigate the program run by her beloved relative, with a mandate to start digging into whether Sevan was corrupt, she fell down an elevator shaft and died. Investigators were never able to talk to her. At the time, the U.N. told us that Sevan suddenly had to return to Cyprus to attend his aunt's funeral. Were it not for the hand of fate, perhaps an eighty-four-year-old spinster could have come to the rescue of the accused and explained how she managed to scrape up an amount equal to 133 times her monthly pension, to carry the bundle with her through customs to New York every year, and to hand it over to her loyal and trusted relative as a thank-you gift.

The Volcker revelations hit the U.N. as a body blow to Kofi Annan's inner circle. Sevan had not merely been his handpicked head of Oil for Food but also carried the title of Undersecretary-General. Volcker had struck close.

"I am reluctant to conclude that the U.N. is damaged beyond repair," said the venerable Illinois Congressman Henry Hyde, "but these revelations certainly point in this direction."

Annan reacted by suspending Sevan along with another U.N. executive, Joseph Stephanides, his fellow Cypriot, who served as head of the U.N.'s liaison with the Security Council. Volcker determined that Stephanides had violated U.N. rules by helping a British company improperly land an Oil for Food contract, and he was fired. But Stephanides fought back, believing that as a midlevel official he was being sacrificed as the scapegoat to protect the U.N.'s higher-ups. He heatedly denied the allegations, saying he was completely following the directions of his bosses and the Security Council Iraq Steering Committee, which weighed in on the contracts.

Stephanides produced several memos that seemed to support his contention and conflict with the U.N.'s conclusions that had cost him his job. The memos clearly showed he informed and received approval for his actions from his superiors, but after twenty-five years he was out, just months shy of his retirement at age sixty. But even when Annan did do something about the scandal, it seemed he still couldn't get it right. A U.N. panel later ruled that the SG had made a mistake in canning Stephanides, and Annan refused its recommendation that he provide the unfairly fired official with a public apology. But Annan did agree to rescind his decision, and he issued a letter of censure to Stephanides.

Along with Stephanides, Sevan was barred from returning to U.N. headquarters unless the visit was related to his defense. He was allowed to retain his protective diplomatic immunity, a status bestowed on him by Annan as part of his continuing service at an honorary salary of $1 a year. Sevan lay low, living with his wife on his forty-year U.N. pension (having retired on a previous salary of $125,000). He apparently spent his time shuttling between his apartment on Manhattan's swanky Sutton Place and his beach house in the Hamptons. In the end, the Volcker Committee was able to trace a total of $147,184 in confirmed cash deposits in the Sevans' bank accounts. He resigned from the U.N. in August 2005 and apparently skipped the country, forfeiting his $1 a year and presumably the diplomatic immunity intended to keep him in the United States and to ensure his cooperation with Volcker—which the lanky former Fed chairman said Sevan failed to fulfill. Just days before Volcker released the allegations in August 2005, Sevan was apparently ensconced back in his native Cyprus, enjoying the protection of his country, which does not have an extradition treaty with the United States for financial crimes.

He had become persona non grata in the organization he had served "proudly" for four decades. "The Secretary-General is shocked by what the report has to say about Mr. Sevan," said Annan's new British chief of staff, debonair former political reporter, media consultant, and World Bank official Mark Malloch Brown. Formerly head of the billion-dollar United Nations Development Program, he had been brought in as Annan's new number two after Annan's previous right-hand man, the long-serving "Chef de Cabinet," seventy-year-old Iqbal Riza, "retired" amid the continuing scandal.

Later it would be revealed that for eight months Riza had been shredding Annan's files—mere duplicates, according to the U.N. Yet because he had already left the U.N.'s service by the time the Volcker Committee made the document destruction public, no action was taken against him.

At one hearing on the scandal held by the House International

Relations Committee in May 2005, Congressman Dan Burton of Indiana stared at the witness, Malloch Brown, and incredulously asked him point blank, "Do you really think the world is going to believe that?" His voice rising in anger, Burton continued, "After all the scandals we have seen in Washington where they were destroying documents in the past? That was very slick, very smooth that they were duplicates. I don't think anybody buys that." Burton stared directly at Malloch Brown and pronounced, "You're good, you're very good."

All Malloch Brown could do was try to reassure the skeptical congressmen that Riza's shredding was not untoward and that the U.N. was intent on fixing the mess. In his eloquent British voice, Malloch Brown was contrite and courteous as he explained there is "a sanction for lying and for criminality as there is in any organization," even though no one in the scandal had as of that time been subject to it. Malloch Brown told the panel, "I am as appalled by Oil for Food as you are." He said, "We want to make sure that never again do we appear before a committee such as yours having to explain away an Oil for Food program, because it's not a happy situation to be in when you are entrusted with public money and the program went wrong."

He blamed the scandal on "management lapses" and "political deals and decisions that were largely outside the Secretary-General's control. . . . I don't think our lapses were as bad or certainly as criminal in character as some suggest. But any lapse in an organization like the United Nations is a fall from grace. We do have to be better than the best, and we clearly aren't."

Malloch Brown's influence was felt from the first day he was appointed. At his introductory news conference, he immediately started spinning the scandal away from his boss, saying, "This is a very big story of which the U.N. is one small, sad part." He seemed to be implying that little wrong had happened in the building. He also moved swiftly to replace the old guard. The top echelon of besieged U.N. officials started to retire as Malloch Brown moved to clean house. Annan resisted all calls for his own scalp, saying he intended to fill out the remaining nearly two years of his term, which expired on December 31, 2006.

The bunker mentality left it to Sevan's lawyer to be the lone voice that would willingly speak out in his defense, and for that service he was to be well paid . . . by the U.N. It seems incredible that a U.N. official accused of personal criminal actions would be protected by the very institution he allegedly betrayed, but Sevan was supposed to have enjoyed that benefit. The reported $300,000 in legal bills were going to be covered by the Oil for Food piggybank provided by the U.N.'s 2.2 percent administration fee—which means not only would Sevan profit from the very oil revenues he was accused of abusing, but he would also use the Iraqis' money to defend himself from allegations that he had ripped off the Iraqis. Iraq's U.N. ambassador Samir Sumaidaie was "shocked and dismayed" at the decision and demanded the Security Council "stop this blatant misuse of funds" that was "adding insult to injury."

It is curious that the decision to reimburse Sevan was apparently the only one like it. U.N. spokesman Fred Eckhard termed it "exceptional," as reporters noted that no other accused U.N. official was afforded the same financial courtesy. The decision was made by Secretary-General Kofi Annan. The U.N. at first claimed Annan granted the windfall to ensure that Sevan would stay in New York, rather than return to his native Cyprus, so that he could cooperate with Volcker's investigators.

They had to back off from that excuse after Volcker took the unusual step of publicly disputing that logic, and the embarrassed Malloch Brown admitted, "We bobbed." The offer was then rescinded, to Sevan's displeasure.

Investigators weren't buying Annan's reasoning, even though it was based on the opinion of the U.N.'s office of legal affairs. It seemed clear that Annan's long relationship with Sevan had protected his position throughout his stewardship.

"It was the Secretary-General who picked Mr. Sevan to run the program," noted Ambassador Richard Williamson, one of the former U.S. diplomats at the United Nations. "It was Mr. Sevan who was one of the closest associates of the Secretary-General who established the bureaucracy that allowed what appears to be a pattern of sweetheart deals and kickbacks and other things that eroded the program."

A quite different view came from Sevan's paid-for mouthpiece. Lawyer Lewis credited his client with running a program that "literally saved tens of thousands of innocent people from death by disease and starvation." He said Sevan only had one aim in his constant nagging of the Security Council and the 661 Committee: to increase the amount of spare parts Iraq could use for its beleaguered oil facilities. "Mr. Sevan's goal throughout the life of the program was to expedite the pumping of oil in order to pay for urgently needed humanitarian supplies in full compliance with the mandate established by the Security Council."

The Security Council should be ashamed of itself.

In a payoff, it's a simple matter of following the money. And while, after the fact, journalists and investigators have been able to do just that, the public is left with the conclusion that the U.N. has not bothered to follow the money itself. And so a nagging question arises. What other monies has the U.N. lost along the way? And to what ends of the Earth have they wandered?

– 11 –

$400,000 IN A DESK DRAWER

Given the U.N.'s difficulties in keeping its house, its nations, and its people in order, one is almost afraid to ask about its finances. Yet we're compelled to do so—not only because of how much the United States shells out every year to keep the organization humming along, but also because of the need to see if it hums a functional tune. The money the U.N. spends is in large part the money of the U.S. taxpayer. And the money the U.N. spends has a direct effect on American security. The important question is not only whether or not the U.N. is accounting properly, but also whether Americans are buying a product that undercuts their interests. Unfortunately, on both counts, the American citizen can end up getting a raw deal.

"There's no flaming red flags in this stuff . . . no smoking gun," declared Paul Volcker in February 2005, as he released audits the world body never intended anyone outside the Secretariat to see.

But as I flipped through the thousands of detailed pages, my fingers were getting powder burns. Wasted millions, cash carried around in paper bags, an untold amount of U.N. property "unaccounted for," under-the-table sweetheart deals, no-show workers. The findings exposed a consistent failure of proper management and oversight on a shocking scale with nary a public peep.

A hidden glimpse of the real story of Oil for Food was squirreled away in a heavy batch of fifty-eight audits only released because of public pressure. Had the U.N. had its way as usual, no one outside of the Secretariat, the U.N. bureaucracy headed by the Secretary-General, would have ever known about what was so politely described as the "lack of approved work plan, organizational structure, and key performance indicators, inadequate communication," and all the methodically detailed management failures and mistakes.

"Our preliminary review of these audits only underscores my long held concern about fraud, mismanagement, and lack of adequate oversight," said Republican Minnesota Senator Norm Coleman, chairman of the Senate Permanent Subcommittee on Investigations. Coleman, a Brooklyn-born conservative Democrat turned Republican and former mayor of St. Paul, served as the state's chief prosecutor for seventeen years. He can smell a crime when he sees one. That experience led him to become one of the U.N.'s sharpest critics on Capitol Hill. Relying on his Midwestern common sense and New York moxie, he bore into the U.N., becoming in December 2004 the first congressional voice to call for Kofi Annan's resignation.

Annan, meanwhile, hailed Volcker's release of the previously secret audits. He claimed they showed "the program was being audited, and that attempts were made to get a manager to try to correct whatever weakness there is in the system," adding, "I'm happy that we have now been able to release these documents." Happy? Then why hadn't the U.N. ever released them before, even blocking their distribution to the Security Council? Under U.N. rules, the audits would only go to the in-house head of the department that was being audited and circulate within a very small upper-management circle of the Secretary-General. It was the perfect setup. Don't tell the Security Council, the General Assembly, the governments, the media, the U.S. Congress. Certainly don't tell the American people, for heaven's sake, who pay nearly $1.8 billion a year of the U.N.'s whole budget. Keep it all quiet, hidden, and under the rug. We'll deal with it ourselves.

The U.N.'s annual report to the member states would include a largely sanitized version—but not the full audits. The program, said Fred Eckhard, Annan's spokesman, "has been audited to death." But it turned out that of the audits that were conducted on Oil for Food, only one examined the office at U.N. headquarters. None examined the thousands of contracts with the oil companies and Iraq or the thousands more providing humanitarian goods. None investigated *anything* Saddam Hussein did. In other words, the U.N. audits completely *avoided* auditing the guts of the program. Perhaps here's why. What follows is what your money went for:

- The U.N. overpaid the Gulf War reparations to Kuwait by $2 billion and will never get it back.
- Building inspectors in Iraq were paid $500,000 to inspect buildings that did not exist.
- The three major consulting companies hired to monitor Oil for Food transactions overcharged the U.N. by nearly $2 million, and the auditors found countless other violations that went unreported.
- "Mismanagement" and "neglect" caused the U.N. to lose at least several million dollars "and could result in additional financial losses in excess of $10 million."
- Hazard pay would be shelled out even if U.N. employees were sitting at home watching TV.
- Some $400,000 was stashed in a U.N. office in Ebril, Iraq, which had "unrestricted access" so anybody could walk in. U.N. staff would delve into funds for cash "loans," and there

was no indication that the U.N. ever asked for its money back.

- Another U.N. agency office handled $119,950 in cash with no burglar alarm or safe.
- In America, an armored Brink's truck would transport cash between offices. In Iraq, if you worked for the U.N., hundreds and hundreds of thousands of dollars in cash was normally driven by U.N. staffers in their cars. Sometimes the cash was even carried "in a paper bag." The auditors determined the practice "poses a serious security problem" because "international U.N. staff members do not take security issues seriously."
- U.N. staffers would go to liquor stores and cigarette shops to exchange cash. During one audited period, the amounts exchanged ranged from $150 to $4,000 each time.
- The U.N. paid an unnecessary $1.2 million, an amount that "appeared excessive," to buy equipment that was already provided by a U.N. contract.
- A sum of $625,000 was shelled out to pay "local personnel" even though they were not employed by the U.N. to do anything.
- One hundred assistant site engineers were hired who should not have been, costing "an unjustified expenditure of approximately $470,000."
- The United Nations office of the Humanitarian Coordinator for Iraq was "overwhelmed" by its financial duties. The audit found there was only one official who could approve expenditures, and he was saddled with sifting through upwards of $40 million a day of bills while he also covered another U.N. agency. Then the guy left.
- The chief finance officer of one U.N. agency was sent back to his home country with full pay for five months, at which point he attained the mandatory age of retirement and did just that. The reason? Other U.N. officials explained he "did not properly conduct his work responsibilities and had poor relations

with both the administration and the mission's personnel." It seems that at the U.N. you don't really get fired, you get retired and then rehired. The day after that official's ignominious departure, he was given a new job as chief financial officer of yet another U.N. operation.

- The U.N. was billed $123,844.50 by a Baghdad restaurant to feed Iraqi government guards for 2003, despite the fact that there was a war and U.N. operations had been scaled back. Why was the U.N. footing the bill for Iraqi government employees anyway? In the end, the U.N. could not even confirm how much food was actually delivered or to whom.

- After the deadly bombing of the U.N. Baghdad headquarters that destroyed most of the building, the U.N. continued to "incur monthly expenses at the full rate for cleaning services."

- The U.N. couldn't even get its own gym built. It hired a firm to add one to the Baghdad headquarters, to be completed by December 2002. By the time the building was blown up eight months later, the gym had yet to be constructed and the contractor owed the U.N. an unpaid penalty of $135,000.

- One U.N. agency spent $1,381,000 to buy seventy-six cars and trucks and not only didn't use them all, but didn't even know how many it actually needed.

- The U.N. paid what appeared to be "an exorbitant" price of $42,518 for office furniture in Amman, Jordan. It turned out the seller was actually a former U.N. employee who the auditors said simply swiped the name of a legitimate furniture dealer. No official action was taken.

- Twenty-nine vehicles worth $601,210 were improperly junked.

- The U.N. overpaid by $622,893 for voice, fax, and communication services.

- In only one agency, $430,000 worth of assets "could not be located." In another, $100,994 worth of U.N. property "could not be properly accounted for." In other words, more than half a million dollars worth of stuff was plain missing.

- The United Nations Development program bought diesel generators as a backup system in northern Iraq and then realized it would cost $10 million to bring in the fuel.
- The U.N. habitat office bought but never used fifty-one other generators, wasting $670,821.
- Two U.N. agencies blew $299,117 on one hundred computers they didn't need and never used.
- The U.N. could not keep track of private phone calls placed on U.N. satellite phones.

All this, and more, from a small and very limited examination of how the U.N. spent its money in Iraq.

Another audit found massive overpricing on Oil for Food contracts. The Defense Contract Audit Agency reviewed just 10 percent of all the contracts and found 48 percent, or nearly half, were inflated, some by as much as 35 percent. The potential amount bilked out of the program was more than half a billion dollars, and that loss represents an examination of just a slice of Oil for Food's total business. Who was minding the store?

"What's missing from these audit reports speaks volumes about United Nations oversight," explained Connecticut Congressman Christopher Shays, chairman of the Subcommittee on National Security, Emerging Threats, and International Relations. "Key elements of the Oil for Food Program, like U.N. headquarters management and humanitarian contract terms, were never examined."

The American auditors especially questioned how suffering Iraqis were aided by their government using $16 million of Oil for Food money to buy three hundred "high-end Mercedes Benz touring sedans . . . items of questionable utility for use by the Iraqi people." This program was the U.N. gem that was portrayed by its controversial director, Benon Sevan, as having been properly audited hundreds of times. Sevan constantly reassured reporters that

Oil for Food was run according to the "strictest administrative standards."

Then again, the U.N. kept the truth hidden. We would never have known the real story had the Third Mechanized Division not rolled into Baghdad.

How can the United States invest any faith or money in an organization that has shown so little respect for the public trust? Without a sound and transparent system of self-regulation, the U.N. cannot guarantee anything. There is a troubling paradox to the modern U.N.: it touts the virtues and necessity of the rule of law for the international community, yet fails to govern itself by this most cherished of principles—even at the basic level of accounting.

The pervasive culture of unaccountability at the U.N. has led to potentially criminal financial negligence. Wracked by fraud and a dangerous disinterest, the organization has lost track not only of the money it is charged with spending in a responsible manner but also of the ends that money is meant to serve. The U.N. has allowed its funding to be directed to some of the most nefarious agents and intentions of our time.

– 12 –

HOW THE U.N. FUNDS TERRORISM

Terrorism is the most critical issue facing the American public today. As we currently fight terrorism abroad and defend against it at home, the nation is unified at least on the principle that it is a grave threat to our way of life. How outrageous it is, then, that we *fund* it by failing to hold the U.N. accountable for what it does with our money. Some have asserted that there is a pressing need to withhold U.S. funding to the world body until we are certain that we are no longer using our money to gamble with our security. We must come to realize that, in the current state of affairs, gambling is precisely what we are doing. Whether it is the Security Council's inability to constrain Iran and North Korea and effectively confront terrorist organizations, or allowing U.N. funds to be used in support of causes in direct opposition to American and democratic interests, we are financing the sources of our worst fears.

❖ ❖ ❖

It was a cool December evening. The Sabbath had ended, and the sons and daughters of Jerusalem bade good-bye to their parents and flooded outside to have fun with their friends on a Saturday night. Many gravitated to one of the most popular hangouts, the Ben Yehuda mall, a cobblestone street lined with shops and cafés where hundreds of teens liked to congregate for carefree nights of joy and laughter. In the crowd was Assaf Avitan, a fifteen-year-old tenth grader who had just been accepted into a special program for gifted children. He studied advanced physics and computer science in high school and planned to pursue a career in science.

"He was brilliant beyond his years," says Assaf's mother, Miri. "He could have a conversation with people much older than he was about pretty much any subject, and they would be shocked with his span of knowledge."

Assaf joined his friends that night to celebrate the sixteenth birthday of twins from his Jerusalem neighborhood. He was accompanied by his buddy, fifteen-year-old Golan Turgeman, and they had arrived after bowling nearby, deciding to drop by the birthday party before heading home. "Assaf had gone there so many times before, I didn't think this time would be any different," laments his mother.

It was 11:30 P.M. and Assaf and his pal had been standing on the sidewalk for about fifteen minutes chatting with their friends when two dark-haired young men—who surely in another age and at another place would have engaged Assaf and Golan in a game of soccer or the sharing of sodas while talking about sports and girls—blended into the crowd of teens and blew themselves up.

Assaf and Golan, so full of promise, were killed that night, and their deaths are due in part to the negligence of the United Nations.

The pair who approached them were two Palestinian suicide bombers. The explosion sent searing metal fragments and ball bearings shooting into the flesh of the giddy kids, killing eleven of them and wounding—astonishingly—180 others. A car bomb exploded twenty minutes later, intended to kill and maim the police and paramedics who responded to the carnage.

The U.N. Security Council paid for the bombings. It contributed to the murders of Assaf and Golan and the other nine victims that night, the youngest fourteen, the oldest only twenty-one. The Security Council also provided the ability to massacre hundreds more who have fallen victims to Palestinian terrorism. The dignified diplomats in New York didn't intentionally provide the funding, or knowingly offer the impetus for those terrorists and the many others who engaged in mass murder, nor would they understand or agree that the United Nations should be held responsible for such terrorist attacks. But the buck stopped there, and the Security Council let millions more flow into the hands of terrorist organizations and their supporters.

First, with respect to the recent actions of the Security Council, it is no stretch to realize how the negligence of Russia and France facilitated kickbacks from Iraqi oil contracts that were used as illicit funds to pay for terrorists and to reward their families for the human consequences. Numerous government investigations have shown that Iraq relied on the corruption of the Security Council to promote and fund terrorism.

It is a matter of record that the American diplomats warned France and Russia, along with the other members of the Security Council 661 Committee, that Saddam Hussein was soaking up kickbacks, only to have the warnings dismissed. It is not inconceivable that, if the Security Council had done its duty and turned off the Iraqi spigot, some portion of the financial aid to Palestinian terrorists could have dried up. But instead, eighteen months after the council members were alerted by the United States about the illegal diversion of U.N. dollars, the families of Assaf and Golan's two killers were rewarded with Iraqi oil money for their carnage.

While Security Council diplomats denounced terrorism in the august chamber, two floors below, inside the 661 Committee's conference room 7, they might as well have been approving direct deposit to Hamas, Hezbollah, Islamic Jihad, the Popular Front for the Liberation of Palestine, and the Arab Liberation Front.

"The United Nations is partly responsible for the death of my son," wails Miri, fighting back tears. "Money that was meant for the Iraqis got to Saddam and he wrote a check to reward the murderers of my kid."

The House International Relations Committee revealed that the Hussein regime laundered the proceeds of Oil for Food contract kickbacks to pay rewards to the Palestinian families of suicide bombers. Starting with the beginning of the Intifada in 2000, Iraqi officials, say the congressional investigators, diverted funds from the 10 percent kickbacks and deposited the illegal revenue in an account in the Rafidain bank in Amman, Jordan. The account also held revenue from other program payments. The money was then transferred to another account controlled by the Iraqi ambassador to Jordan, Sabah Yaseen. Investigators say he and other Iraqi officials would then cut checks to the Palestinian families to honor and encourage the murder of innocent Israelis. Over a two-and-a-half-year period, from September 2000 to just before the war began in March 2003, Iraq shelled out $35 million for the families of Palestinians killed or wounded, providing bounties ranging from $15,000 to $25,000, along with a certificate with Saddam's smiling mug and that of Yasser Arafat. Roughly a hundred terrorist attacks claimed nearly five hundred Israeli lives through the four-year intifada, and Hussein distributed a bonanza to the families of terrorists and of those Palestinians who died or were wounded during Israeli military actions.

"It helped enforce the culture of terrorism," says Assaf's mother. She largely blames "the Palestinian Authority under Yasser Arafat for allowing and enabling Hamas to commit terrorism. But Hussein's checks were a part of all that," she says. "And now I am told he got the money from the U.N. Oil for Food? It makes me furious." The families of Assaf and Golan's two killers, say authorities, received $15,000 for their sons' handiwork only one month after the attack, on January 22, 2002. The public ceremony to honor the young murderers was held in Ramallah and sponsored by the Baath party office, known as the Arab Liberation Front, the vehicle that bestowed money diverted from the U.N.'s program. The official martyrdom certificates known as the President Saddam Hussein's Grant were embossed with Saddam's signature and solemnly distributed along with the checks, words of thanks, kisses, hugs, and handshakes for a job well done.

The Israeli family of another young victim of the Ben Yehuda attack also blames the financial incentives provided by Iraq that came from the private terrorist piggy bank funded partly by the U.N. Shoshi Cohen, whose seventeen-year-old-son, Ido, was killed, says the $15,000 thank-you check spurred the terrorism that claimed the life of her son and so many others.

"Nothing is going to bring Ido back now," she says. "But funding terrorism needs to be stopped. I think both sides, Israelis and Palestinians, are suffering, but that's not an excuse for this. The funding from Saddam helped kill Ido."

Ido had been sitting on an a bench with his older brother, David, who got up and walked over to buy a slice of pizza for Ido. The bombers struck. David and Ido's mother was at home when the telephone rang, the chilling call every Israeli family dreads in the immediate hours after the attacks. She rushed to the hospital, but because Ido had been separated from David and did not carry any ID, there was no information on where he was. The medics had found him with metal shrapnel lodged in his back and a massive, bleeding head wound. As is the custom of Israeli authorities, photographs are taken of the unidentified victims and passed to the families of those not located. Shoshi sifted through the gruesome images but did not recognize her son. There was, however, one victim in the intensive care unit who matched Ido's description. She rushed over and saw a young body connected to life-support machines and asked a nurse to show her the patient's back, for Ido had a unique birthmark there. The nurse refused, explaining that such a move could kill the boy. Ido's mother identified him by his shoe size. Ido Cohen lingered on life support for one week before he died.

"It was the most devastating thing imaginable," says his mother.

"To have your child stolen from you so quickly. An innocent kid. It wasn't worth it for me to continue living, but I still had other children and they needed me. . . . Somehow I made it until now, but it still pains me every single day." Ido Cohen and his mother's grief remain a testament to one of the modern "successes" of the United Nations.

Saddam Hussein was a savvy tyrant happy to find as many "enemies of his enemies" as he could. He not only rewarded millions in the name of slaughtering Israelis and Americans, but directly tried to cut terrorist groups in on the action pouring from the 661 Committee's negligence inside U.N. headquarters. The U.N. amounted to something of a silent partner. The Department of State estimates that since 1970, about seven hundred Americans have been killed and sixteen hundred wounded in terrorist attacks, excluding 9/11. The bombing on Ben Yehuda street that killed Assaf, Golan, and Ido also injured five Americans: seventeen-year-old Ziv Brill of Long Island, New York; nineteen-year-old Temima Spetner of St. Louis, Missouri; Jason Kireshenbaum of New Rochelle, New York; and eighteen-year-old Israel Hirschfield; and twenty-nine-year-old Joseph Leifer of Brooklyn. A bombing on the street in 1997 killed fourteen-year-old Yael Botwin of Los Angeles and injured ten other Americans, while killing four Israelis, among them two fourteen-year-old schoolgirls.

The list of entities assigned special oil allocations, the ones that we are told Hussein personally approved, include some of the world's most notorious terrorist organizations and supporters. The argument that Iraq had no terrorist connection is bunk. The list of oil allocations approved included the PFLP (the Popular Front for the Liberation of Palestine), a terrorist organization responsible for the murders of countless innocent Israelis as well as Americans. The PFLP was founded in 1967 and carried out some of the most infamous terrorist operations in the Middle East, from the infamous airline hijackings of the 1970s to numerous deadly suicide and car bombings, shootings, stabbings, and even a strangling. PFLP terrorists took credit for the assassination of Israel's tourism minister as he left his wife having breakfast in October 2001, and a plot to destroy a Tel Aviv office building in April 2002.

The PLO itself and its political bureau were allocated their own oil, which provided them with funding to support and encourage their terrorist activities at the height of the wave of terror. But perhaps the most curious and offensive listing belongs to that of Palestinian Liberation Front leader Abu Abbas. He was the notorious mastermind of the *Achille Lauro* cruise ship hijacking in 1985 in which wheelchair-bound New York retiree Leon Klinghoffer was shot and rolled overboard in front of the horrified eyes of his wife. Abbas had taken part in the operation himself and had been captured by U.S. forces along with his terrorist colleagues when President Reagan ordered the interception of their flight by the U.S. Air Force as they flew to Algeria. Abbas was released, however, because the Italian government confirmed he had an Iraqi diplomatic passport. He was later sentenced in absentia in Italy to five life terms but found sanctuary in Baghdad.

"Abbas was a vicious terrorist who was responsible for countless deaths of innocent people—men, women, and children—throughout the Middle East," said Klinghoffer's daughters Ilsa and Lisa after Abbas died in U.S. custody, apparently of a heart attack, in March 2004. He had been captured just outside Baghdad almost one year before. A trial, said the Klinghoffer sisters, "would have sent a clear message to terrorists everywhere that, if they kill an American citizen, they can run but they can't hide." Abbas and the PLF "settled in Iraq and became an instrument of terrorism in the hands of the Saddam Hussein regime," declared the Israeli foreign ministry. The Israeli Defense Force released an extensive documented review of the relationship between Abbas and Saddam, and found that there was extensive support and training for terrorists by the regime beyond what had previously been known.

The rewards to terrorist families paid out of U.N.-facilitated kickbacks were merely the public displays of support. The IDF found that Hussein's regime "recruited and trained Abbas activists in camps in Iraq, equipped them with arms and sent them to carry out terrorist attacks . . . including in the Republican Guard base in Tikrit." Arrested PLF terrorists admitted to Israeli authorities that they had received such training in Iraq and, with "the direct support of Iraq," were directed to attack both military and civilian targets. They "wore uniforms, used code names, and masked their faces," and were taught how to detonate bombs, assemble exploding cell phones, install remote-controlled car bombs, make Molotov cocktails, use an exploding suitcase, fire rocket-propelled grenades, and handle machine guns. One suspect said he was trained in Iraq to "attack a kindergarten or school and to kill the children without mercy."

The Israelis fingered Iraqi Vice President Taha Ramadan, the point man for Iraqi oil who chaired the Command Council that distributed the oil allocations, as the head of terrorist financing. That is not a coincidence. Oil provided the terrorist money. Ramadan had his hand on the flow of oil millions and could direct the U.N. runoff to the terrorists. According to captured documents, Ramadan headed the Palestine office that distributed the checks. "He is in charge of implementing the policy of rewards and prioritization in the framework of the Oil for Food arrangement," said the IDF, making "Saddam personally involved" through Ramadan. "The money coming from the outside . . . is the oil fueling the terror industry," concluded the IDF report. The Israelis raided the offices in 2002 and started to put the pieces together, tracing the results of numerous terrorist attacks back through the killers' families, through the financial network that rewarded them, and finally to the bank accounts of the Hussein government.

As President Bush applied pressure on Iraq both publicly and through the United Nations in 2002, Hussein started to feel the heat. He reacted by more than doubling the terrorist rewards, clearly hoping to incite more violence in Israel that would distract the Bush administration from focusing on him. On March 11, 2002, two days after thirteen people were killed in a suicide bombing in an Israeli restaurant, Iraqi Deputy Prime Minister Tariq Aziz was quoted by Reuters as announcing, "President Saddam Hussein has recently told the head of the Palestinian political office, Faroq al-Kaddoumi, his decision to raise the sum granted to each family of the martyrs of the Palestinian Uprising to $25,000 instead of $10,000." The next day a twenty-one-year-old Israeli soldier on his way home for a holiday was shot dead by a Palestinian terrorist, and the day after that six more were killed when Palestinian gunmen opened fire on cars near the border with Lebanon.

Aziz proudly defended the rewards. "The Iraqi leadership believes that the Palestinians . . . are not terrorists," he told the Middle Eastern MBC network six months later. "It is a legitimate activity which we support explicitly and not in secret." Among those whose families were rewarded with Iraqi financial aid, according to the captured documents, were the suicide bomber who killed fifteen people and wounded thirty-three at the Matza restaurant in Haifa (among the dead, fifteen-, sixteen-, seventeen-, and eighteen-year-old high school students, a sixty-seven-year-old prominent architect who had arranged meetings between Palestinian and Israeli leaders, a fifty-two-year-old television producer, and a thirty-two-year-old waiter whose wife was expecting their second child); the suicide bus bomber who killed eight passengers and wounded fifteen (among the dead an eighteen-year-old girl who had just graduated from high school, a twenty-six-year-old Yeshiva student, and a twenty-seven-year-old who planed to announce his engagement); a suicide bomber who detonated his explosive belt on a bus killing seven and wounding thirty (among the dead a twenty-eight-year-old photographer "who loved to surf," a seventy-five–year-old grandfather of thirteen, and a nineteen-year-old who had a two-year-old brother); the suicide bomber who walked into the crowded Moment Café across the street from the prime minister's home on a crowded Saturday night, killing eleven and wounding fifty-four (among the dead a twenty-eight-year-old who planned to marry her boyfriend the next month, a twenty-five-year-old who also planned to marry his girlfriend the next month, a twenty-eight-year-old named for his grandfather who died at the hands of the Nazis, and a nine-month-old baby girl sleeping in her baby carriage). This is but a small sample of what investigators say U.N. program proceeds helped accomplish.

"The monetary awards provided by the Hussein regime were a means of encouraging Palestinian terrorist organizations across the spectrum," noted Yudit Barsky, director of the Division on Middle East and International Terrorism at the American Jewish Committee. "It had the effect of placing a bounty on the heads of potential Israeli victims. The message was: If you kill an Israeli, you will receive a reward." Besides the public ceremonies broadcast on Palestinian television showing the distribution of the checks and praise for Hussein, the Iraqis also provided scholarships for the suicide bombers' sons and brothers to study in Iraq. They funded anti-American propaganda that was distributed throughout the Palestinian territories, including a tape titled *USA: The Enemy of Humanity*, and posters warning "the Bush Administration, the British Government and Zionist entity . . . not to continue the attack and pain they cause to our fighting and suffering Iraqi people."

Another infamous international terrorist, Abu Nidal, was also harbored by Iraq. His organization, known by his name or Black September, was responsible for attacks in London, Rome, Vienna, and Pakistan dating back to the seventies. He died under mysterious circumstances in Baghdad in August 2002. The Iraqis claimed he committed suicide while being treated for cancer, but then came reports from the (London) *Telegraph* that he actually "was murdered" on regime orders after refusing to train Al-Qaeda fighters to attack American targets. There is no evidence that he earned the right to receive benefits from the oil allocation list or kickbacks from Oil for Food, while so many others apparently did.

"It's too sickening" for Dani Turgeman to realize that the bounties investigators say were the fruits of a U.N. program were in fact funneled to support so many terrorist attacks. "It is very difficult to find out that it wasn't just the Palestinians, but Saddam also paid the family of the terrorist who injured me," he says. The thirty-year-old electrician went to the trendy Moment Café with six friends on that fateful night. The place was packed, so they were waiting outside, debating what to do, when the bomber struck. He and his friends flew in different directions.

"I was conscious," Dani remembers. "I saw my hand was bleeding and had shrapnel in one of my eyes. I was lying on the street in total shock. I don't think I realized I was badly injured." He tried to walk to an ambulance but collapsed. He was rushed to surgery and lived, but his condition worsened. Within three days, his entire body became paralyzed. He remained in the hospital for six months, and slowly regained some movement, but his left hand was amputated and he lives in constant pain.

"It's hard for me to think about who did this to me and who paid for it," he admits. While he has resumed working in his craft by using just one hand, "It's a huge struggle. . . . I'm in such pain and try to focus on just getting through each day. It gets me too upset when I start to think about the evil that did this, and I lost good friends in the attack. I am so angry at everyone who supported terrorism against us," he says.

On June 23, 2000, the family of Hamas terrorist Ismail Ahmade Al-Hurani received their $25,000 thank-you as part of "the President Saddam Hussein Grant."

It had been nearly two years since the American diplomats had sat in the Security Council and 661 Committee meetings and raised their concerns about Saddam's Oil for Food kickbacks. Apparently, it was deemed not worthy enough to investigate.

Alleged kickbacks from oil allocations were not limited to Middle Eastern terrorist causes. Other favorites were radical Marxist and leftist political organizations around the globe. Among those named on Iraq's Santa Claus list were the Communist parties in Ukraine, Bulgaria, and Belarus; the Socialist parties in Serbia, Bulgaria, and

Yugoslavia; the radical parties in Serbia and Yugoslavia; and Brazil's October Eight Movement—communist-related revolutionaries who kidnapped the American ambassador to Brazil in September 1969 and traded his freedom for fifteen rebel prisoners held by the Brazilians. More recently, at the International Communist Seminar in Brussels in 1999, the October Eight Movement signed a declaration promoting "socialist revolution" and condemning "U.S. imperialism" that included "the aggression against Iraq."

As disturbing as the U.N. connection to terrorism is, it gets only worse the deeper one digs. Terrorism threatens our interests both directly and indirectly. And as terrorists have more boldly targeted the United States, Americans have awakened from their slumber to address the threat posed. But as we struggle to do so, and as we now engage terror on its front lines, most Americans do not realize that the U.N. has us swimming in quicksand, at times neglecting its duty to aid us in our quest, and at times serving as a complicit aid to those who wish to do us harm.

"It's all about money."

Charlie Viccia knows money, especially sophisticated, international money-laundering schemes. He is a senior special agent for the ICE, the Immigration, Customs and Enforcement division of the U.S. Department of Homeland Security, and he blew the whistle on one of the most egregious abuses of the U.N. that ever reached into the United States—the buying of a $174 million Russian-made anti-aircraft missile system intended to shoot down and kill American pilots patrolling the Iraqi no-fly zone. The Iraqi paperwork said it was a boiler system.

"That's what they were showing everybody, that they were going to buy this elaborate boiler system. They even had the specs on the boilers."

Charlie is furious at the U.N. He is a fifty-two-year-old, nearly three-decade veteran of federal law enforcement, a Bronx-born and -raised pro with a master's degree in law enforcement. Having dedicated his life to hunting down the bad guys, he now traces the intertwined financial dealings of drug dealers, white-collar criminals, and terrorists out of the Customs and Border Protection office in Tampa, Florida. They had received a tip from an informant, but instead of the expected million-dollar cocaine shipment, the lead involved a deal to finance the missile system for Iraq from Oil for Food revenue. When it hit Charlie's desk, he pushed for the U.N. to do something about it, but typically, he says the diplomats sat on their thumbs.

"When I saw nothing was happening, and I knew $174 million was about to be flushed out of Iraq, I knew then that the Oil for Food program didn't stand for anything. They didn't even know about it. There was no watchdog as far as I was concerned."

Charlie was digging into a vast and covert international conspiracy that would lead from Washington, D.C., to U.N. headquarters in New York, to the United Arab Emirates, and eventually to the Hussein regime in Baghdad.

The missile system was the S-300PMU-1, a Soviet-era-designed defense shield that is the military rival to the American-made Patriot missile batteries. It is capable of taking out "low-altitude air-breathing targets, such as cruise missiles and aircraft," reports the Center for Nonproliferation Studies. First debuted publicly at the 1992 Moscow Air Show, one unit can "contain up to 48 missiles . . . on 12 self-propelled . . . transporter-erector-launcher vehicles . . . each carrying four missiles in sealed canisters." The system is so sophisticated that its radar can "guide up to twelve . . . surface-to-air missiles (SAMs) to simultaneously engage up to six different targets."

"It was massive," says Charlie. "To get it out you're talking box-cars." He says it was going to be transported by rail through Syria, with the U.N. paperwork claiming the freight was washing machines, refrigerators, and household appliances.

"Everybody's feelings at the time was that there was nothing the U.N. was going to do or enforce."

But no one counted on Charlie Viccia.

"The case was . . . stalled because we couldn't figure out which U.S. laws applied, so they assigned it to me, and I began researching what laws could apply to the case. I started following the money to see if the money went through U.S. banks."

Bingo. The funds had been wired through New York to an Abu Dhabi bank that has a branch in Washington, D.C. That gave Charlie, and the entire U.S. Department of Justice, the hook they needed to seize the money, stop the sale, and prevent Hussein from acquiring a weapons system that would have improved his ability to defend himself.

The money trail, says Charlie, led to a bank in Jordan, which transferred a $43.5 million deposit through New York to the Abu Dhabi National Bank, which in turn deposited the funds into an account for the Al Wasel and Babel General Trading Company.

Charlie pulled the corporate papers and discovered that two Iraqis owned 49 percent of Al Wasel and Babel. Strangely for minority shareholders, he says, they were the only ones who had power to write the checks.

"It was like a typical drug-money-laundering case," says Charlie. "They were misrepresenting who they were, because when we looked at who was the signatory for the banking, it was only the Iraqis. They were the only ones that could sign for the money coming in and out of Al Wasel and Babel, so any purchases of that magnitude had to be approved."

The investigation revealed that one of the Iraqis who was licensed for trading on behalf of the company, Hikmat Jarjes Bahnam, had a passport that identified him as a government official. One of the first deposits came in December 2000. It was for $7 million, and then, over the next year or so, more money started mysteriously flowing into the company's accounts until it totaled the $43.5 million.

A bank official admitted that the citizen of the UAE who was listed as the principal of the company "had no control over the monies deposited, and that the Iraqi government and its agents are the real owners" of the company.

Charlie figured the diplomats at the U.N. would know what was going on, so he started poking around. After all, any Iraqi trade outside U.N. auspices was illegal, especially when you're talking missiles disguised as boilers.

"I went to our representative at the U.N. and asked him, 'Were there any contracts on file for Al Wasel and Babel that would allow them to spend this money for Iraq to purchase a boiler system?' I gave them the contract numbers. The answer was no. So my question was, 'Isn't that a violation of the Oil for Food program?' At that time nobody was looking into it, so I asked, 'Why aren't we going after them for violating the Oil for Food program? Who handles it? Who brings it forward?' I had never dealt with anything like that before. Who goes after people violating the Oil for Food program? They had transferred the money without the U.N.'s permission . . . multimillions of dollars as a down payment for the contract, and I was trying to freeze the money." Charlie got the runaround. He says he was told, "It would have to go before the U.N. . . . and nothing would probably be done."

Charlie Viccia was pounding the pavement, asking the questions. He should have applied for a search warrant and called the Seventeenth Precinct to get an ESU (emergency services unit) truck over to First Avenue. The boys could have used a battering ram on conference room 7's closed doors, arrested everybody for a RICO (Racketeering, Influenced and Corrupt Organizations Act) violation, and marched them down to central booking for fingerprints and mug shots. They could have held the American and British ambassadors as material witnesses. But then, the U.N. has diplomatic immunity, and Charlie had no legal jurisdiction. Even the fire department has to be invited onto U.N. property.

Undeterred, Charlie says he went to federal prosecutors, who had not yet woken up to the fact that the biggest heist in human history was going down every time the 661 Committee met about two miles north of the New York Southern District courthouse.

"I brought it to the assistant U.S. attorney and his [reaction] was, 'Well, with seventeen resolutions already on them, where we gonna go with it?' " It took four years and a war for the Feds to be able to go someplace.

"We are unmasking the financial façade of the former Iraqi regime," declared Juan Zarate, the Department of the Treasury assistant secretary for terrorist financing and financial crimes, in 2004. Zarate, a thirty-four-year-old California-bred, Harvard-educated former federal prosecutor, knew his stuff. His success at unpeeling the intricacies of Iraq's money machine led him to lead the new Office of Terrorism and Financial Intelligence. Then, in June 2005, he was tapped as a special assistant to President Bush for counterterrorism.

"Saddam and his cronies used a global network of agents and businesses to pilfer from the Iraqi people and to underwrite their tyranny," said Zarate.

At Treasury, one of Zarate's jobs was to find Hussein's stolen money and give it back to the Iraqi people. By 2004, Treasury investigators determined that the real owner of Al Wasel and Babel was Saddam's regime itself. Calling it a "commercial front for the Iraqi Intelligence Service," they identified Iraq's Deputy Prime Minister and Finance Minister Hikmat Mizban Ibrahim al-Azzawi as the primary official who "controlled" the company and the man investigators believe had directed that first $7 million deposit into the Al Wasel and Babel bank account.

Besides trying to buy the missile system, investigators say al-Azzawi also used Al Wasel and Babel as one of many similar companies to collect 10 percent kickbacks for the regime. He was eventually captured on April 18, 2003, and had earned the designation the Eight of Diamonds, number twenty-eight on the Deck of Cards of the most wanted Iraqis. Yet time after time, the company had done business with the Security Council 661 Committee without apparently raising any suspicions.

The diplomats and the U.N. Secretariat repeatedly let Al Wasel and Babel contracts sail right on through. Claudia Rosett, the journalist in residence at the Defense of Democracies, who zeroed in on

Oil for Food early, estimated Al Wasel and Babel conducted at least $145 million in Oil for Food business altogether. Much of that could have been pure profit the U.N. let flow into Saddam's hands. No one knows the exact amount, and Al Wasel and Babel has not responded to my numerous attempts for information. It turns out the firm was but one of dozens of front companies the feds say were employed by the Iraqi regime to acquire illicit material, with another two hundred Iraqi-controlled firms that they believe did illegal business with Oil for Food.

Congressional investigators from Henry Hyde's International Relations Committee uncovered what they said were an additional two thousand shell bank accounts in Jordan, each one used only once to shift money from kickbacks to Hussein. Another Iraqi front company allegedly bilked Iranian pilgrims traveling to Mecca out of $500 million each year, while other firms doing business were actually run by the Iraqi Intelligence Service. But nothing compared to the $174 million missile system.

Charlie credits the PATRIOT Act for helping him break the case.

"I was able to go to the UAE bank that had a branch here in Washington, D.C., and say, 'You need to give me the paperwork you have on this because we are conducting an investigation and the PATRIOT Act mandates that you have to provide the information.'" The bank's lawyers agreed. "We couldn't have traced this all back to Iraq without the PATRIOT Act. I wanted to go and grab the money then, and we could have. We had the ability to freeze the money, under the PATRIOT Act."

But Charlie says the Department of State stood in his way. He blames the public criticism of the PATRIOT Act, which he says raised sensitivities in Washington and stymied its full use. By early 2003, the war had started and Charlie says his pleas went unheeded. He says he was told by Foggy Bottom bureaucrats, "Why are you so worried about seizing this money now? We're already in Iraq. What's the difference?" "It was frustrating. I was banging my head against the wall," he says. "That money's there, it's sitting in the account of Al Wasel and Babel. That money will go to Iraq, and it could end up funding the rebels who could be fighting us forever afterwards. That's why we need to seize that money now."

It wasn't until April 15, 2004, four years after Charlie had begun digging, that the United Nations finally took action against Al Wasel and Babel, but by then Hussein had been deposed, and the missile deal had long been abandoned. After the United States officially designated the firm as "an Iraqi front company," the U.N., under Security Council resolution 1483, directed the United Arab Emirates' authorities to freeze the company's assets. But, as Charlie feared, it was too late. The $45 million deposit for the missile system was long gone. Charlie suspects the money was transferred back to Iraq and is likely funding the killing of American troops and innocent Iraqis.

The big shots agree.

"As for the billions soaked from Oil for Food," Juan Zarate, the Department of the Treasury's assistant secretary for terrorist financing, told Congress, "it is likely that some of these funds ended up in the coffers that are now available to fuel the Iraqi insurgency and terrorism inside and outside of Iraq."

The Department of the Treasury awarded Charlie with a well-deserved letter of commendation. I'd bet he'd trade it in for a letter having authorized the snatching of that $43.5 million any day.

The vagaries and complexities of the international system may demand the debate, the politicking, and the diplomacy that we have all come to recognize in the application of international agreements and policy. However, when it comes to matters of terrorism, terrorists, and the states that harbor the practice and its practitioners, there cannot be a gray area. There is too little margin for error. For Americans reminded by the hole in the New York City skyline, for Londoners recounting that awful summer day in 2005, for Spaniards haunted by the train bombings, or for Jordanians who sifted through the rubble of hotels, it is evident that terror has become enemy number one. It is the defining security issue of our time. That we, by funding the U.N. without holding it accountable, indirectly compensate and support the forces that have vowed our demise is nothing short of disgraceful. That the U.N. refuses to take the lead or even the determined side against terror provides a guide as to what America's path will most likely be in this fight. Our security cannot be entrusted to the U.N. Moreover, until reforms are instituted, we cannot view the world body as a competent partner in this, our most critical endeavor.

So if not security, with what can we trust the U.N.? The more basic and often more laudable work of the U.N. comes from its humanitarian undertakings. Yet, as we have seen time and time again from its entering into business and negotiations with the unsuitable, the U.N. has had its share of problems in this area as well. In light of the backstabbing and back-room maneuvering of member nations—and the inability of the U.N. to direct funds to their appropriate ends—can America count on the U.N. to provide a baseline stability for world affairs through humanitarian efforts? The prospects, unfortunately, have not been encouraging.

– 13 –

HUMANITARIAN ERROR

Humanitarian efforts at the U.N. can serve a dual purpose. On the one hand, they can keep people alive. The U.N. has been devoted to this cause since its inception. Moreover, the services can help to stabilize regions on the brink of anarchy and chaos. In the modern age of terrorism, the United States has a vested interest in seeing the U.N. succeed in providing a calming influence to world affairs. And we all have an interest in alleviating suffering wherever we can, given our unique position in the developed world. However, it has become a favorite pastime of tyrants to hold their people hostage as the powers of the world debate doing nothing or doing something. And far too often the something winds up in the pockets of those who are furthest from needing our help. To further complicate matters, there are many corporations and businesspeople involved whose intentions are often far from noble. The compounded factors of organizational, international, and financial disarray that the U.N. has allowed to evolve unchecked have left its humanitarian missions as compromised as its others. The United States funds these humanitarian efforts in troubled areas for their charitable and stabilizing effects. Yet as we've come to see in U.N. World, it's hard to get what you pay for.

By outsourcing its humanitarian contributions to the U.N., the United States loses not only authority over its money but also the credit it is due for its generosity. In a world too often delighted by the portrayal of America as a monster, we have to ask if the U.N. is doing its part to properly allocate our charity—and the recognition due us for our dedication to the causes and peoples we support. Considering the scams perpetrated on the Iraqi people, we may not want credit in any event.

The U.N. points to its World Health Organization campaign that has led to the eradication of smallpox, and notes that a WHO–UNICEF effort has eliminated polio "from the Americas," nations that just happen to have some of the most advanced government and private health-care systems on Earth. The U.N. takes credit for preventing SARS from exploding and for addressing the avian flu.

The U.N. also counts spending $30 billion a year in development in poor countries, $1 billion for disaster assistance, and another $5 billion for peacekeeping it says "has helped bring peace to many war-torn countries—for instance, Cambodia, Mozambique, El Salvador and Sierra Leone." East Timor and Eritrea should also be included. Yet there is little outside oversight of how the billions are distributed and to whom. And it must be noted that peacekeeping forces are deployed only after a political settlement is reached between hostile parties, showing up when a truce has supposedly already been achieved, which can take as long as six months.

The World Food Program, the world's largest humanitarian agency, distributes food to 104 million people, and the U.N. refugee agency helps seventeen million "displaced people" and asylum seekers. This perhaps is what the U.N. does best, but there is limited public scrutiny of who gets the contracts and whether the services are inflated.

Many companies were more than eager to enter into illicit agreements with the Iraqi regime when it came to humanitarian services, from willingly padding contracts to provide the 10 percent kickbacks demanded, to shipping inferior, low-quality items while charging an arm and a leg. After all, who would complain . . . the Iraqi people? Useless medicine, inedible food, and intentional distribution delays were common.

Worse yet, Senate investigators found the U.N.'s lack of quality control led to the importation of tainted blood that infected as many as 180 Iraqi children with HIV/AIDS.

Doctors claimed countless patients died or went untreated because of improper drugs or a complete lack of medicine.

The U.N. would acknowledge "difficulties" but continually praised their program, noting that the size of the individual food baskets did increase, providing a sufficient daily calorie level for the Iraqi population. The baskets were distributed by 44,358 government-approved corner stores.

The U.N.'s standard for the Iraqi foodstuffs was far below what the diplomats are accustomed to being served in the fourth-floor diplomatic dining room at U.N. headquarters. The white-jacketed waiters serve on pressed white tablecloths with U.N.-embossed silverware in a rarified, hushed, carpeted room where diners can appreciate the expansive view of the shimmering waters of Manhattan's East River. Chow down on an Oil for Food-provided food basket, however, sitting on the dirty banks of the Tigris in downtown Baghdad, and the U.N.'s standard for your meal was simply that it was "fit for human consumption."

That means, quipped Senator Coleman, "If you eat it and don't die, it passes the test." Shockingly, he was quoting the words U.N. officials used when describing to Senate investigators their quality standard for the trapped Iraqi populace.

The term *fit for human consumption* was coined by the U.N.

for the food bought by Iraqi oil. The definition left a large leeway that was fully exploited, explained Coleman: "Lesser quality goods were shipped into Iraq, allowing for the former regime and the complicit supplier to pocket the price difference between the lesser quality goods and the higher quality goods specified under the goods contract."

In other words, Hussein was actually running a global bait and switch. According to congressional testimony, the U.N. knew about it and let unapproved food enter Iraq.

Claude Hankes-Drielsma was an adviser to the Iraq Governing Council, which retained the accounting firm KMPG to conduct their own investigation. He says that when he asked the U.N. what measures were taken to ensure that the food met their minimal criteria, the U.N. told him to produce evidence that it didn't meet even those lame standards.

"I believe the U.N. was actually aware that on certain inspections, the food wasn't fit for humans," he said, adding that agency officials even confirmed it. Like prison inmates, the Iraqis had no choice.

While Benon Sevan's lawyer claims his client "confronted both the Iraqis and the members of the Security Council without fear or favor" about the program's problems, it seems the esteemed Sevan saved his most stinging public review for when it would matter the least. In November 2002, as the program's end neared with the prospect of an impending war, even Sevan had to finally admit the Security Council had been scammed.

"Pharmaceuticals and medical supplies are delivered with short shelf life," he told them. "High protein biscuits and therapeutic milk that fail quality control; items with essential components missing or defective; equipment delivered but not assembled; vehicles, machines, and spare parts delivered in a damaged condition or with wrong technical specification; foodstuffs, that while being safe for human consumption, are of an inferior quality to that contracted."

Of all his Security Council public statements, the above was the most detailed litany from Sevan of how the U.N. had failed the Iraqi people. It came on November 19, 2002, only four months to the day before the first bombs would fall on Baghdad. It was his last report issued under Hussein's regime. The diplomats should not have been surprised, had they actually looked at the small print in all those Oil for Food contracts. Incredibly, the company hired to inspect the humanitarian goods that kept the Iraqi nation going says the U.N. never even required that the food be fully examined for quality.

The company, the Swiss firm Cotecna, had a troubled and controversial role in this scandal, which brings us back to the dangers of U.N. inconsistency and the conflicted interests of its members and servants. This time, however, the questionable behavior was at the very top of the food chain. Cotecna first employed Kofi Annan's son Kojo in October 1995, hiring him for a London training program that the company hoped would lead to his posting in Africa. He was named assistant marketing manager of the Cotecna office in Lagos, Nigeria, while his father was a U.N. Undersecretary-General. He became a consultant to Cotecna in 1997 and was then placed on a "no-compete" clause in December 1998.

While Cotecna admits Kojo attended various U.N. meetings on behalf of the company in locations from Africa to U.N. headquarters in New York, it insists that Kojo's responsibilities had nothing to do with Oil for Food, and that he was not hired because he was his father's son. Yet it turned out that Kojo was on the payroll throughout the existence of the Oil for Food program and after it ended. In November 2004, the U.N. and the Secretary-General were forced to admit Kojo was actually paid up to just eight months earlier, in March of that year. Kofi conceded his son actually earned about $150,000, for a much longer period than had first been claimed. Critics called the payments a "slush fund," but the Messrs. Annan denied doing anything wrong. It was an embarrassing revelation that left Kojo's father insisting he never knew his son was still on the Cotecna payroll. He had "warm family relations with his son," he said. "But he is in a different field. He is an independent businessman. He is a grown man, and I don't get involved with his activities, and he doesn't get involved in mine."

Of course, it turned out that the fields and activities were a lot closer than Annan claimed. Four months after the Secretary-General's statement that seemed to distance himself from any involvement with his son and Cotecna, the Volcker Committee issued its second much anticipated report, and there was a bombshell. Kojo had actually been paid more than twice the amount first claimed—$484,492 by Cotecna, some of it funneled through four other companies run by the family of Cotecna's owners. Investigators say the diversion was done at Kojo's request, directing deposits to a Swiss bank account to supposedly fund a British football club of which he was the president. The Secretary-General's diary revealed he did indeed have several contacts with the top Cotecna executives, though Volcker's investigators concluded that there was not enough evidence to prove he improperly influenced the selection of Cotecna. The evidence was "not reasonably sufficient to show that the Secretary-General knew in 1998 that Cotecna was bidding" on the Oil for Food contract.

The report had harsh words for Kojo and his employer, however. It concluded that the son of the Secretary-General had engaged in deceitful behavior to hide his relationship with the company and had lied to his father, and that "significant questions" remained about his actions and "the integrity of his business and financial dealings with respect to the Oil for Food program." Cotecna, said investigators, lied to the public, the United Nations, and Volcker's committee about its relationship with Kojo, hid hundreds of thousands in dollars of payments to him by routing the cash through affiliate companies, and maintained that the company's owners, Ellie Massey and his son Robert, were not forthcoming about Kojo's continued hidden payments.

Cotecna responded by accusing Volcker's committee of making "false, misleading, and malicious" statements and presenting a "distorted and untrue picture of the company." They expressed "outrage" over the allegations of hidden payments.

Kofi Annan, however, thought he was off the hook. He declared Volcker's report meant he had received an "exoneration" that came as "a great relief," while expressing disappointment at the behavior of his son.

One of the two cochairmen of Volcker's committee, Mark Pieth, pointedly declared otherwise regarding the SG.

"We did not exonerate Kofi Annan," he said.

I asked Paul Volcker if he thought Annan was exonerated.

"I thought we criticized him rather severely. I would not call that an exoneration," he replied. "I would not have used that word."

Yet accusations that Volcker went easy on Kofi persisted. Two of his investigators, Robert Parton and Miranda Duncan, resigned in protest.

Kojo's former business partner, Pierre Mouselli, told investigators that Kofi knew his son was doing business in Iraq before Cotecna nabbed the contract. He claimed to have discussed it with the Secretary-General and his son during a private lunch together in 1998 during the Durban Conference on Racism. But the Volcker Committee did "not credit" Mouselli's claims, concluding that "no independent witnesses" could back up the assertion. Mouselli's lawyer later accused the Volcker Committee of being "manipulated" by Annan's lawyer, who happened to be Greg Craig, President Clinton's special White House counsel during the Monica Lewinsky investigation.

Craig, whose former boss was named a special U.N. envoy for tsunami relief, was working for Annan for free, according to the *New York Sun*. The paper reported that Mouselli's attorney, Adrian Gonzalez, thought Craig "was able to contact the committee to pressure them" to basically let Kofi escape being nailed on what he, his son, and Mouselli discussed during the lunch. Craig's alleged involvement occurred at the same time Clinton was taking a highly visible role at the United Nations, was being mentioned as a possible successor to Annan, and was being given his own office at a U.N. agency. Volcker admitted he had the testimony regarding the lunch, but Annan told his investigators that he did not remember it. Yet the date and place (room 812 at the Hilton hotel) were written on his schedule. Clearly some thought Annan was lying, covering up his knowledge that his son was trying to do deals with oil in Iraq. While professing to have not been "involved" in Kojo's activities, Kofi already was quite familiar with Cotecna and the Massey family, because the company had performed work for the U.N. since 1992. Annan and his wife actually had cocktails with Cotecna's founder and chairman Ellie Massey and his wife during the World Economic Forum in Davos in 1997. The next year Massey also visited the elder Annan in his U.N. office to propose running a U.N. lottery, though the Volcker investigators slyly state, "There are no notes or written record of what they discussed."

Kojo had been the one to arrange the meeting, according to an e-mail to Kofi from his assistant. "Kojo asked me to check with you if it is possible to arrange two appts. For Dr. Olusola Saraki (former Senator, Nigeria) and Mr. Ellie Massey (Chairman, Cotecna) for the week of 14 Sept. He said he will check with you too." Kofi's appointment schedule said "Kojo—Mr. Massey (private)." There is no evidence, says Volcker, that Kojo attended the meeting. However, during that time, "the second half of September and early October 1998, including on the day that the procurement department issued an RFP [request for proposal] for the Iraq inspection contract, Kojo Annan was in New York and stayed at the Secretary-General's residence." Kojo was attending the U.N.'s General Assembly meetings on Cotecna's dime to drum up business for the company.

Yet another meeting between Kojo's father and Cotecna's founder occurred after a January 1999 article appeared in the British newspaper the *Sunday Telegraph* that blew the cover on Kojo's Cotecna employment. The headline: "Fury at Annan Son's Link to £6 Million U.N. Deal."

Volcker investigators say that during a visit to Geneva, Massey approached the Secretary-General "to apologize for any embarrassment he may have caused him. Ellie Massey advised the Secretary-General that Kojo Annan had nothing to do with the contract."

Despite the revelations, and only a few months before the Oil for Food program scandal burst in the headlines, Kofi Annan continued to go to bat for Massey and Cotecna. In the summer of 2002, Massey asked the Secretary-General to intercede in his native Ghana to try to prevent Cotecna from losing a government contract. Annan, say investigators, did just that. He spoke about it to the ambassador from Ghana, who in turn passed on a letter from Massey that Annan had received to his government in Accra. The Secretary-General's support of Cotecna wasn't enough. The contract was abolished anyway. Kofi Annan denied that he helped Cotecna land the contract or did anything to "make ethical misjudgments" that undermined his "moral authority."

"I absolutely did not," he insisted during a September 13, 2005, news conference. "I did not do anything or attempt to influence the contract. And you have my word, I did not. I will never do anything of the sort."

He also derided the reporting of the Oil for Food scandal, admonishing one of the more aggressive correspondents, Benny Avni of the *New York Sun* when he asked a question about it.

"Your world is so small. You are lucky—I am envious," the Secretary-General said rather snidely. "You live and breath oil-for-food. . . . This has been dealt with and investigated. We are pressing ahead with what needs to be done, so I would urge you also to move on, my dear chap."

The answer, probably made in a moment of frustration, actually belittles the significance of the scandal, which represents the complete undermining of the international community by the U.N.'s failures and the abrogation of the very principles and ethics it is supposed to espouse. It seems as if the U.N. top command would have liked nothing better than for the investigators, whether journalistic, congressional, or prosecutorial, to simply "move on."

But the Annans' Cotecna connection—through socializing, payments in the hundreds of thousands of dollars, and a helpful word or two—were by far the least egregious acts committed in this sorry saga that involved Cotecna. U.N. judgment bordered on the criminal with the decision to send food to twenty-four million helpless people without confirming its quality.

It seemed remarkable and so illogical. The company hired to inspect humanitarian shipments into Iraq defends itself by saying it was never required to check food quality and didn't even examine all of the shipments.

Robert Massey, the chief executive officer of Cotecna and the son of founder Ellie, conceded, "It was not our job to . . . assess quality as we do in other contexts around the world." He also admitted, "We did not inspect all goods entering Iraq but only 986."

Nine hundred and eighty-six! That's it? There were thirty-eight thousand humanitarian contracts!

Cotecna says it was only required to verify that the goods bought were the goods delivered. Their inspectors did that by examining shipping bills and paperwork. While the inspectors would "visually examine" the material, they would only actually slit open the boxes and peer inside an estimated 10 percent of the time.

Cotecna did analyze food in labs for radioactivity, heavy metals, microbes, and pesticides, but medicines were ignored. The inspectors only looked at pharmaceutical samples, and by 2000, Cotecna claims, Sevan's program told them to stop doing even that.

Vernon Kulyk, a Jesse Ventura look-alike who had spent thirty years with Canadian customs, was a Cotecna inspector working on Oil for Food for three years. "Our mandate," he said, "was to make sure the goods were delivered, not to make sure that the government of Iraq was satisfied with the quality of the goods."

He described what they were supposed to do at their posts, but according to one former Cotecna inspector they did a lot more when they were not on the job. Arthur Ventham, a ruddy and rotund fifty-four-year-old Australian, had held senior positions with the Australian Customs Service for twenty-seven years. He signed on with Cotecna in Iraq to inspect trucks. At his first inspection spot, he recalled "the majority of the time was spent either on the Internet, watching DVDs . . . reading in your room, working out in the gymnasium," or spending time "in the bar."

He soon realized that "ad-hoc inspections . . . were not going to stop" illegal items from entering Iraq, and became so bored that he transferred to other inspection sites. He finally quit in disillusionment after ending up at the Iraqi port of Um Qasir, where he says his boss and a group of his fellow inspectors spent "the majority of the day in each other's rooms drinking vodka."

"I went to Iraq to try and do something for the people of that country as well as assisting an organization that I had a lot of respect for, namely the U.N.," he recalled. But his experience, he said, "was contrary to everything I had been taught . . . [in] university, the military, or customs."

It is tragic that the U.N. would wash its hands in regard to the quality of humanitarian items delivered under its much vaunted program. Cotecna wasn't checking, and clearly the U.N. wasn't either. Someone should have flipped through the original agreement between the U.N. Secretariat and Hussein that established the Oil for Food program. The ten-page Memorandum of Understanding set the guidelines for the way Oil for Food would be operated, as required by the Security Council resolution that created the program. Paragraph 27 is all you need to know about how the United Nations turned its back on its own rules:

> The independent inspection agents will confirm delivery to Iraq of shipments. . . . They will also have the authority to perform duties necessary for such confirmation, including: *quantity inspection by weight or count, quality inspection including visual inspection, sampling, and, when necessary, laboratory testing.* [Italics added.]

What is it about the words *quality inspection* the U.N. doesn't understand?

The words are on page 4.

But then the world body's standard was one notch above Alpo.

Even when asked, U.N. agencies denied they were responsible for the quality of the only goods some Iraqis were given. The Iraqi Kurds, living in their semiautonomous northern section of Iraq, complained that "The World Health Organization denies having responsibility for the quality or usability of medicines and medical equipment. . . . When evidence of quality control is asked for it is not given." The U.N., however, has since defended its record by pointing to a WHO study that "found only 0.4 percent of shipments of medicines unfit for use. Shockingly, when food was delivered and discovered not to be "fit for human consumption," the U.N. also apparently failed to act.

In 2001, supplies of contaminated wheat arrived. "A junior U.N. official suggested that the U.N. immediately issue public announcements warning the population and telling them. . . . This official's suggestion was overruled," claimed Howar Ziad, the representative of the Kurdistan Regional Government U.N. Liaison Office.

The oppressed Kurdish minority in the North were murdered, starved, and gassed by Hussein. They also charge they were abused at the hands of the U.N.

There were perhaps few populations as helpless as the Iraqi Kurds. Human Rights Watch documented Saddam's campaign of genocide, including the use of chemical weapons on women and children, the razing of thousands of Kurdish villages, and executions of more than a hundred thousand. Occupying an area similar in size to Vermont, the northern provinces of Iraq were in line for 13 percent of Oil for Food's revenues, or about $8.4 billion. They never saw it. Hussein swallowed up more than $2 billion of that amount, and the U.N. snagged another $1.6 billion it didn't spend, so the Kurds ended up with less than $5 billion and a lot of empty U.N. promises.

A new general hospital that was supposed to be built with Oil for Food money remained a dream. The Kurds say only 20 percent of the medical supplies were being delivered, and their pleas were ignored by an unfeeling U.N. bureaucracy. On September 3, 2001, the Kurdish health minister, Dr. Yadger Heshmet, laid it out in the starkest of terms. He alerted the U.N. that there was a "total lack of essential drugs and medical supplies that have nearly paralyzed the work of our hospitals." He informed Oil for Food officials that the severe shortages had "catastrophic consequences," especially with the lack of drugs for cancer, kidney problems, heart disease, and hypertension—routine medical supplies the nations on the Security Council take for granted.

Dr. Heshmet was sharp and concise: "We find no logic or satisfying statements from your offices. . . . There is no excuse in delaying the delivery of our essential health needs. Our people will not forgive those responsible for such delays."

It's not like the U.N. didn't know. Only four months earlier Dr. Heshmet held a face-to-face meeting with the Oil for Food executives to air the same complaints and says they promised to address the dire and dangerous medical shortages. The result?

"Nothing was done," reports the doctor. When he complained to Sevan's office in New York, he says there was no response. Meanwhile, in his addresses to the Security Council during this time, Sevan continued to hold Saddam responsible for the "very difficult conditions." He claimed, "Despite its shortcomings as well as complaints and criticisms," Oil for Food "continues to make a considerable difference in the daily lives of the average Iraqi."

Howar Ziad has another view.

He says Oil for Food "was corrupted by the U.N. Secretariat."

Former Oil for Food coordinator Michael Soussan laments the U.N.'s passivity. "We should have spoken out when the Iraqi government delayed or sabotaged our humanitarian program in Iraqi Kurdistan. . . . We should have spoken out when the government fed us bold-faced lies."

What condemnations there were turned into puffs of smoke, as if from a single Gauloise.

The overseers of Oil for Food continued to entertain absurd requests from Saddam's regime, such as allocating $20 million of Oil for Food proceeds to build an Olympic sports stadium, the pet project of Saddam's sadistic son, Uday. Then there was the $5 million submission for "animation equipment" for the Iraqi information ministry.

In other words, cartoon-making equipment for Baghdad Bob.

Only the war interrupted the approvals.

As late as six years into the program, Saddam's priorities can best be judged by the following: during one week of orders, the regime listed "22,000 tons of chewing gum machines, 12,000 tons of mobile phones, 36,000 dishwashers, and over 750,000 television sets." All this, while our Department of State noted desperately needed water, sanitation, and electrical projects were delayed because the 130 U.N. experts, ready to be deployed in Iraq, were cooling their heels waiting for Saddam to give them visas to enter his country. This was one result of the noble U.N.'s work so lauded by Annan and Sevan when Oil for Food closed shop in November 2003. The war had toppled Saddam's government, so the Security Council voted to drop sanctions now that the tyrant was no longer in power. More than $8 billion worth of food, medicine, and other supplies were transferred to an Iraq Redevelopment Fund under the Coalition Provisional Authority. Much of that was later said to have vanished.

On Wednesday, November 19, 2003, exactly one year to the day after Sevan detailed some of the program's specific failures to the Security Council, he appeared before them for the last time. The war had been going on for eight months as Sevan took his seat at the end of the large, familiar, curved table in the Security Council. It was the table where Colin Powell had made his disputed presentation about Saddam's stockpiles of weapons of mass destruction in

February; the table Soviet leader Nikita Khrushchev pounded on with his shoe while shouting at the American ambassador, "We will bury you!"; the table where Adlai Stevenson had rebutted Soviet denials of placing missiles in Cuba; the table where Jeane Kirkpatrick had presented the secretly recorded audio intercepts of the Soviet Mig fighter pilot who fired the missile that destroyed Korean Airlines flight 007.

Now that same table belonged to a man who would be disgraced in the coming months, while the United Nations itself would come under unprecedented scrutiny leading to criminal investigations and an upheaval at its highest levels.

"Irrespective of the political and other constraints, the program made a real difference in the lives of the average Iraqi citizen," Sevan declared. "As long as sanctions remained in place, there was no alternative."

Kofi Annan praised but also qualified the program's accomplishments, noting that Oil for Food "has been required to meet an almost impossible series of challenges." Sevan, he said, had served the U.N. "beyond the call of duty."

Annan ended by promising, "We are closing the Oil for Food program, but we remain determined to continue helping Iraq's long-suffering people in whatever ways are still open to us."

Perhaps many Iraqis would hope not.

They might remember that only five years earlier Annan had shaken Saddam's hand as the two sat puffing cigars in one of Saddam's palaces paid for with Oil for Food money.

The story is a telling one of the current crisis of confidence that faces the U.N., a crisis rooted in erroneous judgment and the faulty decisions that ensued. In February 1998, Annan embarked on a much criticized personal visit to Hussein, to try to convince him to resume cooperation with the U.N. weapons inspectors—as if the dictator needed to be given the respect and accommodation of such a plea. Hussein had arbitrarily barred the inspectors because the sanctions had not yet ended, and President Clinton was threatening to bomb if Iraq did not accede.

"About an hour into the meeting," Annan told the Yale U.N. Oral History Project, "President Saddam Hussein excused himself and said he had to go and pray. And so he left and went and prayed and came back, and that was the first time I've been in a meeting where someone has left me to go and pray and then come back, so that was unusual. . . . He did come back in to continue the discussions, and then as things calmed down and as the talks continued and they began to be more relaxed—a bit more relaxed, he offered me a cigar. He took one. So we continued our discussions in a very direct and professional manner."

"Like a peace pipe," observed the interviewer.

"A peace pipe, yes," agreed Annan.

Hussein agreed to resume inspections.

But some peace pipe.

The Secretary-General had been bamboozled by a shyster, just like any three-card–monte victim. When Annan returned to U.N. headquarters, he was received in delirious triumph. Hundreds of the building's staff packed the historic lobby and, when the SG emerged from his car, they erupted in euphoric, sustained applause. Finally it was one of their own who could claim victory, not a U.S. president, but a product of the U.N. and diplomacy itself. They swarmed around him, parting as he slowly moved toward the elevators, the crowd forming an aisle for him to pass as he accepted the handshakes and smiles of the beleaguered bureaucrats who for so long had been beaten down by Saddam's and the U.N.'s critics. It was a moment of hope and success. But it was not to last. Although Mr. Annan later told me he did not regret the trip because he had convinced Saddam to resume cooperating with the United Nations, the tyrant soon returned to form and broke the agreement. Within six months the deal was dead, the inspectors kicked out yet again, and the Clinton administration responded by launching air strikes on Baghdad that December. No U.N. inspector walked back into Iraq until President Bush threatened to take military action and the Security Council passed resolution 1441 in November 2002.

Yet after shaking Saddam's hand, Annan famously declared the prophetic words that would haunt him and his organization:

"He's a man I can do business with."

Did he ever.

Since the scandals, the U.N. has made efforts to be more open and public about its humanitarian contracts, even posting the procurement bids and results on a special Web site. But if the organization has trouble reading Saddam Hussein, how can it gauge the intentions and the interests of any leader of the world, any corporation, any diplomat, or any civil servant? Can anyone be surprised that the world body has been played, at one time or another, by nearly every kind of agent with which it has interacted? Looking at the recent history of the organization, the onus will soon be on the representatives of this nation who willingly entwine American interests with U.N. activity without defined conditions of interaction and a strict code of adherence to them.

So here we are today looking back at the shattered landscape of the past few years in U.N. World. We have seen a collapse of confidence in the world body, with compromise, negligence, and fraud at the root of the problems. The United Nations has proven that it does not have the backbone to stand against tyrants, that its members abuse its systems for short-term gain, that it is careless with the money it's given, that its employees and contractors cannot be wholly trusted to execute its lofty ambitions, and that even its humanitarian efforts are undermined and shortchanged as a result. At long last, the attention of U.N. officials, journalists, and American representatives is being directed to the U.N. with skepticism, in the hopes that a thorough examination of the organization will yield possibilities for the future.

Yet at this time, when the U.N. is rightfully under the microscope, when it is most apparent that reform will be needed to rebuild its reputation, when frustration has pushed many Americans to the brink—what does the U.N. do?

Well, it asks for more money. Of course.

– 14 –

MORE MONEY, PLEASE

The U.N. chief of staff was dispatched to Capitol Hill with one request: get money.

"From where I sit, the United Nations is stretched too thin, in both material and human resources, to be able to do the job that people and governments around the world want it to do," Mark Malloch Brown told the House International Relations Committee.

What the U.N. wants, in other words, and believes the world wants it to do is simply to eradicate or greatly reduce poverty and life-threatening diseases, prevent war, ease strife, stop hunger, rectify injustice, and restore order to failed states. Though it has been able to partially achieve a few of those goals in some areas of the world, to fulfill its vision the organization claims it needs far more funding and far more cooperation than member governments have ever provided. "The organization still has a long way to go," Annan's top aide admitted. "It started life running conferences and writing reports and being a group of diplomats doing diplomatic things.

It's now running some very big complex global operations and needs the management systems and people to run these new kinds of challenges more effectively, frankly, than it has done in some cases."

Is the answer a big blank check? Or is it more carefully considered and better scrutinized allocations of the present budget? Is it possible that, with proper management, the U.N. could do more with less?

The 2005 U.N. assessment for the United States stood at $2.2 billion, and that figure is pushed skyward by funding for U.N.-related development banks, resulting in a total of $3.7 billion. The United Nations Association of the United States of America (UNA–USA) analyzed our share of the U.N. expenses at $362 million for the regular operating budget, $420 million for the specialized agencies such as the U.N.'s World Health Organization or the IAEA (International Atomic Energy Agency), $31 million for the War Crimes Tribunals, $650 million for peacekeeping operations, $700 million to organizations such as UNDP (the United Nations Development Program) and UNICEF (the United Nations International Children's Fund). The contribution to the U.N.'s regular budget was expected to increase by about 20 percent, to a $438.9 million share of a $1.8 billion budget. Americans pay more to run the U.N.'s internal bureaucracy than to fund the executive branch offices of the president and vice president.

"Our annual contributions to the U.N. system—comprising about one-tenth of one percent of the federal budget—enable the United States to partner with other countries to jointly address global problems," explains the U.N.-supporting United Nations Association of the United States of America. "Working through the United Nations allows the United States to share with other countries the costs of promoting American ideals and of advancing vital U.S. national security interests," they say. Failure to pay dues such as those for peacekeeping "would damage U.S. credibility and influence within the United Nations and specifically the Security Council."

(Note to UNA–USA: Read the preceding chapters of this book to learn how we are really treated in the Security Council.)

We happen to pay far more than the three permanent Security Council members who have so criticized and opposed us—combined. France's share of the regular U.N. budget is less than one-fourth of ours, at $107 million or 6 percent; China comes in at a paltry one-third of France's for $37 million, or 2 percent of the share; Russia barely pays the taxicab fare for its diplomats to Manhattan from JFK, weighing in at $15 million, or just 1.2 percent of the U.N.'s operating budget. Those three nations that carry so much clout, that hardly pay the expenses to outfit a globe-trotting diplomat with Gucci loafers and a Louis Vuitton briefcase, fall short of the efforts provided by six U.N. dues-paying members that did support the invasion of Iraq. Japan and the United Kingdom pay more than France; they, along with Italy and Spain, fork over more than China; while Japan, the UK, Italy, and Spain, in addition to the Netherlands and Australia, provide more than veto-wielding Russia. The poorest nations, some of which were part of the Iraqi war coalition, only pay a bottom-line $17,795 in annual U.N. dues, which gives them one General Assembly vote, the possibility to serve a two-year term on the Security Council, and the honor of flying their flag out in front of the building.

With only a select few countries covering the tab, it's no wonder the U.N.'s mantra remains "more money, please." And it is a sales pitch aimed at the people who already pay the overwhelming amount—U.S. taxpayers. Malloch Brown sounded like the voice on a telemarketing call.

"If there is something that we agree the U.N. needs to do, let's fund it to do it right," Malloch Brown requested. In other words, "You are paying now, but not nearly enough, which is why the U.N. is doing it wrong."

"Peacekeeping is a classic example of the cost of trying to do it on the cheap," Malloch Brown pointed out. "The U.N. is running eighteen peacekeeping operations around the world at a cost of $4.5

billion. Just half a percent of world defense expenditures. The cost of doing it on the cheap is pretty clear. . . . We can't afford to put enough military police into these operations to make sure the troops stay off the streets and out of the bars when they are off duty. We don't invest enough in rest and relaxation facilities, let alone rotating troops out frequently enough to make sure we have the incentives as well as the discipline to prevent the behaviors." To wit, alleged rapes and sexual exploitation.

"We have a lot to get fixed, but cutting budgets is not the solution for the priorities."

That's like saying peacekeepers are raping and having sex with twelve-year-old girls because the U.S. Congress doesn't give us enough money to subscribe to satellite TV, buy pool tables, and pay for airline tickets so the guys can get back to their girlfriends. If you cut our budget, there's no telling what they will do!

Malloch Brown admitted, "The financial burden of peacekeeping falls disproportionately on the United States and other western countries; the physical burden, the troops are increasingly just from developing countries. Of seventy thousand troops serving around the world only four are American. . . . that is a pity." More money, please. And while you are at it, throw in some troops.

The cornerstone of Kofi Annan's legacy, he hopes, will not be failures and scandals, but his reform proposals designed to return his beloved U.N. to the stature he believes it was intended to carry. He has proposed a wide-ranging and financially broad goal of implementing U.N. mandates designed to return the world body to the center of international policy and to finally reform its misguided practices. The foundation is a plan he calls "In Larger Freedom, Toward Development, Security, and Human Rights for All," which lays out the U.N.'s goals. They include hiking the amount of donations from the wealthier nations to the third world; establishing "gender equality" along with environmental, health, education, and scientific proposals; eliminating taxes on products imported from poorer nations; and forgiving third world debt.

"Enlarger Fiefdom," is what Michigan Congressman Thaddeus McCotter brands it. A Republican member of the International Relations Committee, he has been particularly astute and skeptical about the U.N.'s pronouncements.

"The more cynical amongst us would be tempted to remember that when a political machine is caught in corruption, the only sin the political machine concedes is being caught," he told Malloch Brown during one hearing. "The cynical would think the spark for U.N. reform, internally at the U.N. absent the outside influence of individuals who are pesky, like say the United States Congress, seems to be a bit strangely timed to the uncovering of the scandals that are occurring at the U.N."

The U.N. hoped the life preserver to pluck it out of the mire of scandal and embarrassment would be the touted reform plan, developed from what was known as the millennium goals, an overreaching agenda that sparked a raging and irresolvable political debate inside the building. The platform included the noble goals of halving world poverty, hunger, HIV/AIDS cases, and the number of people without sustainable access to safe drinking water and basic sanitation by 2015; ensuring that every child on Earth will complete a full course of primary schooling; promoting gender equality and empowering women; reducing child mortality by two-thirds; and developing a global partnership for development such as addressing debt, providing decent and productive work for youth, as well as providing access to affordable, essential drugs in developing countries, and making information and communications technology available—admirable goals that sound as if they can only be achieved through the creation of a worldwide welfare department.

The debate about the U.N.'s role echoes the domestic political confrontations of 1980s America that resulted in the Reagan Revolution. A generation after Ronald Reagan's conservative agenda took command of the federal government—allowing even the Democratic Party to recapture the presidency for two terms under Bill Clinton's relatively conservative policies—the very same arguments have now taken the international stage. Except some members of the American delegation, those who advocate for "big government," who see the myriad of U.N.-run programs as the only salvation for the globe's most unfortunate citizens, are in command.

The philosophical foundation of the U.N. presupposes that struggling economies can only be salvaged and then improved by U.N. funding, the doling out of many more billions on top of what has already been delivered over many years. Yet like the argument against American welfare, it seems the cycle of dependency, true with nations as with individuals, has only magnified the problems. The heart of the "development" argument that seeks to pour billions into programs and forgive billions more in debt has resulted in success in parts of Asia and Latin America. But the challenge is to replicate that progress in Africa and the Middle East. Some of the proposals are surprisingly simple and attainable. Mosquito nets that cost less than fifty cents each could save hundreds of thousands of lives by protecting against malaria-bearing insects. The broader challenge of raising African economies, hobbled by corruption and waste, proves far more complex.

The ideological battles of the Reagan years are being played out in the U.N. hallways. Reagan may have tried to declare the end of "big government," but at the U.N. it is only just beginning. The old battle lines are the same: it's the many U.N. advocates who say the forum should be the all-encompassing central depository intended to solve the world's ills against the critics who say it is up to individual member states to save themselves. As government handouts collide with individual responsibility, the American debate pits the proposals for mass social programs versus the power of the individuals. It is the classic liberal-versus-conservative ideological conflict. But at the U.N. they were all liberals, while the conservatives were sitting across the street at the U.S. mission, controlling the purse strings in Congress or in the White House, taking a much more measured approach.

The U.N. was on Capitol Hill begging for more funding just as others were urging it to cut the fat, much like the era when Reagan had promised to take a hatchet to the bloated federal budget. Not only were the arguments the same, but in some cases so were the players. Former Republican House Speaker Newt Gingrich and former Democratic Senate Majority Leader George Mitchell led a bipartisan task force on the United Nations that recommended a massive reduction in the U.N. headquarters' workforce, urging that the priority should be "management capability. . . . Management systems common throughout the world, in both public and private institutions, are often lacking at the U.N." They concluded, "The United Nations needs reform and reinvigoration. Otherwise, the organization risks declining credibility, and its own future will be at risk. . . . The United Nations shares the blame for inaction [because it] failed to undertake anything approaching the sweeping reforms needed for effective operation of the institution." Gingrich and Mitchell called for a new standard of personal ethics and the application of "new business models for delivering assistance," such as simplifying "the funding of U.N. programs" while creating what it called "third party and independent mechanisms for auditing, monitoring, and evaluation" of where all the newly demanded money would go.

The millennium goals seemed to take a page from the conservative agenda on individual responsibility, declaring that "each developing country has primary responsibility for its own development" through such measures as "combating corruption." But such declarations are far easier to make than to actually achieve. U.N. officials said supporting development, as called for in the millennium goals, are actually similar to the Reagan or Margaret Thatcher philosophy on welfare. They saw it not as a handout, but as hand-up. The U.N. goal was "to create the environment so that private investment can prosper, and then you can walk away." Or so the U.N. Development spokesman, William Orme, described the political thinking of the world body.

Yet the political philosophy at the U.N. remains steadfastly liberal, and it is from that viewpoint that new proposals are created. The broad stereotype of U.N. politics depicts the heathen Republicans leading the barbaric charge on the principled Democrats who fight to defend the U.N. at all costs. During the U.N.'s travails, Annan was receiving personal counsel from a cabal of Democratic advisers. *The New York Times* reported that in December 2004, his supporters held a save-Kofi-and-rescue-the-U.N. powwow at the Manhattan apartment of Richard Holbrooke, the Democratic international policy sage who has served as President Clinton's U.N. ambassador and had been rumored to be in line for secretary of state had Senator John Kerry won. Among the other advisers were former Democratic Colorado Senator Tim Wirth, president of the United Nations Foundation, and Kathy Buskin, the foundation's executive vice president and chief operating officer. She, prior to a distinguished corporate career, had served as Democratic Senator Gary Hart's Senate and presidential campaign press secretary in 1984, four years before the senator's second presidential attempt culminated in the notorious Donna Rice monkey-business-lap-sitting photograph. Yet another Annan adviser was Robert Orr, named assistant Secretary-General for strategic planning just four months earlier, who had served with Mr. Holbrooke as his deputy and was the global affairs director of the National Security Council during the Clinton administration.

One noted Republican was actually installed to shake up the place. Wall Street investment banker Christopher Burnham, a seasoned executive who was once state treasurer of Connecticut, came on board as part of Annan's reform push as the new Undersecretary General for Management. But at least with respect to ideology, he's decidedly in the minority.

One Annan aide who was apparently absent from the Holbrooke gathering was Columbia professor Jeffrey Sachs, who serves as a special assistant to the Secretary-General and as his director of the millennium project. A respected international economist, Dr. Sachs has also been highly critical of President Bush and his policies, both international and economic. He has called the U.S. government "fools and liars" and the Bush administration "thuggish," declared that the United States can be "a force for great ill," called for "a Declaration of Independence from the U.S.," and blamed George Bush, not the U.N. or its Security Council, for world failures, even writing an op-ed piece in the *Los Angeles Times* titled "Africa's Suffering Is Bush's Shame." Is the United States now the *only* U.N. member?

In the summer of 2005, allegations surfaced that Justin Leites, described as "a senior official" in Mark Malloch Brown's United Nations Development Program (UNDP) who had supposedly violated U.N. rules by working for John Kerry's presidential campaign while on the U.N. payroll. The *New York Sun* reported that twelve UNDP staff members filed an official complaint, but the U.N. claimed no staff rules were broken by Leites in using his leave time to run a Kerry–Edwards campaign operation in Maine.

The liberal, big-spending, massive-government-style program philosophy provides the centerpiece for U.N. thinking—ideals that seem to suit Chief of Staff Malloch Brown, the organization's most ardent public defender, quite fine. He is a veteran international aid official who attempted to run for a seat in the British Parliament as a candidate of the Social Democratic Party in the 1983 elections. The Social Democrats had split from the Labour party because of its far leftist views, which included abolishing the House of Lords and canceling Britain's nuclear deterrent, extreme positions even a liberal-minded young politician could not accept. The Social Democratic Party (SDP) joined with the Liberal party and formed a rival to Labour known as the Alliance, which, while garnering 25 percent of the vote, eventually disbanded and was folded into the existing Liberal Democrats in 1988, now the nation's third largest party behind the Conservatives and Labour. The Liberal Democrats' current positions include having "strongly opposed" Tony Blair's decision to join the United States in the coalition, calling it "the biggest mistake" the Blair government has made. Every Liberal

Democrat member of Parliament voted against the war and strongly supported a role for the U.N. in Iraq. Perhaps these views reflect those of former SDP aspirant Malloch Brown, but it is just as well that he returned to U.N. service after his abortive foray into elective politics, because in 1983 Margaret Thatcher and the Conservatives were reelected by a landslide.

In keeping with the current Liberal Democrat view of a strong U.N., Malloch Brown has called the millennium proposals "the single biggest piece of intellectual work undertaken at the U.N. in the last twenty or so years." He labeled it a "grand bargain," perhaps mindful that a key provision would cost the United States many more multibillions when the U.N. came around with the tin cup. The major financial goal of the millennium plan is the requirement that wealthy nations commit to spending 0.7 percent of their gross national product for development in the third world by channeling the billions through the U.N. system. Over years, the potential for graft and abuse could dwarf what Saddam achieved by perverting the Oil for Food program.

"It's a blatant money and power grab," declares Melanie Morgan, one of the leaders of the conservative group, Move America Forward. Striking a nerve with the American people, that group was flooded with five million e-mails and hits on its Web site, and raised more than $1 million when it proposed a goal of sending the U.N. packing. They insist their mission is not to dismantle or shut the organization down, but just to relocate the home office elsewhere, such as Geneva or Paris—where the U.N. bureaucrats could continue to enjoy their luxuries absent the cacophony of American critics, cracks Ms. Morgan. Along with Howard Kaloogian, a former Republican California assemblyman who was also behind the recall of former California Governor Gray Davis, the pair set their sights on the foreign diplomats and their treatment of their host country.

"The bureaucracy at the U.N. is unaccountable," says Kaloogian. "It's a gathering place for the third world dictators and tyrants to get together and agree with each other that they should remain in

power. If America's goal is to change the world and bring freedom to millions of others, then those tyrants are going to oppose
that message. That is why we struck a chord with the American
people."

"The United Nations has abused our hospitality, committed
crimes on our soil, and then asks us to repeatedly bail them out
when they misspend our money," adds Ms. Morgan. "I'm sick and
tired of the same forces, the same countries, and the same leadership that has demonized us, the United States and the American
people, who are some of the biggest donors in the world, portrayed
as arrogant colonialists. It's been a concerted effort to demonize the
American character," she declares, by an organization that "creates
the problems and then blames them on us."

They believe the U.N. millennium proposals will just bring
more of the same. "It's a power beg," quipped Congressman Mc-
Cotter. "They can't make us give them the money. It makes the
hypocrisy painfully clear that people who line their own pockets or
squander other people's money are then asking other people to
spend more money. If the U.N. bureaucracy doesn't recognize the
worthy goals which they were employed to pursue, how can they
then ask other people to care more about them and contribute more
toward them?"

The United States has been roundly and continually criticized
for not supporting the 0.7 percent target when a handful of other
nations, such as Sweden and Norway, were already providing that
amount by 2005. The U.S. GNP as of 2004 stood at nearly $11 tril-
lion, more than Japan, Germany, the United Kingdom, France, and
China combined. The U.N. has estimated that the U.S. share of the
U.N. plan would add approximately $60 billion a year to our U.N.
tab, "approximately what it spent on Iraq [in 2004]," notes millennium director Jeffrey Sachs. The Bush administration estimated
that the total demanded by the U.N. would actually top $91 billion,
though President Bush has committed to the goals.

"We couldn't spend $91 billion if we wanted to," observed the director of the United States Agency for International Development, Andrew Natsios, during a U.N. visit on the proposals. He told reporters, "No matter what we do, we will never reach the 0.7 percent," saying that the U.S. government does not put stock in "any magic numbers," which would only result in a meaningless "check writing exercise." Critics of the United States point out that our percentage of the burden has usually been the lowest of any industrialized nation. But the U.N.'s own figures show that, in 2004, the United States funneled nearly $19 billion in official development assistance, more than France, the UK, and Russia combined. The 2005 amount was set to soar even higher, to $24 billion. That means we help pay for Russia's veto of our proposals in the Security Council. Russia happened to be the second largest recipient after Egypt of U.S. development aid, taking in $808 million in 2003.

According to a study by Dr. Carol Adelman of the Hudson Institute, Americans accounted for $130 billion in foreign aid and investment to developing countries. We gave at least $62.1 billion annually in private donations alone, in addition to U.S. government foreign assistance at about $18 billion. That means $80 billion in private and official aid is already flowing beyond our borders—just to the developing nations—each year, the largest amount of any nation. Yet former President Jimmy Carter in 1999 described his fellow citizens as being a part of "the stingiest nation of all," during a speech reported on by *The Christian Science Monitor*. That parsimonious view of American giving was famously repeated in the wake of the 2004 tsunami disaster by U.N. Relief Coordinator Jan Egeland, who criticized the United States and the other wealthy nations of also being "stingy" in their response.

The 0.7 percent slice, in the eyes of the U.N., is designed to correct the perceived imbalance. Perhaps there is no proof of the U.N.'s ability to exploit good intentions that is more stark than the double standard that accompanied the debut of the millennium declaration in 2000, so proudly announced and endorsed by all the U.N. members at the gathering of the General Assembly in

September of that year. In Malloch Brown's words, all agreed to "an open call for peace and security, disarmament, human rights, democracy and good governance, free markets and truly free and fair trade, and the opportunity to unite around a common vision to build a better world for all people."

Among those supposedly supporting those very worthy goals were Iraq's Saddam and every other dictator whose stooge sits in a General Assembly seat. Among the nations whose officials endorsed those noble proposals were the presidents of Eritrea and Somalia, both wracked by conflict; the minister of foreign affairs of the Congo, whose young female citizens lived so desperately that they would later serve as sex toys for U.N. peacekeepers; and the leader of the Islamic Conference, whose members can provide a stellar example of respecting women's rights. The summit also heard from Libya's representative, who denounced the International Criminal Court. (Four years later Libya would settle its bombing of Pan Am flight 103 and renounce its WMD program through the efforts of the Bush administration and not the U.N. The Libyan official also branded the World Bank and other U.N.-related development efforts as "forms of terrorism." Among the other notables speaking at the birth of the millennium goals was none other than Saddam's Tariq Aziz, who told the assembled dignitaries that the U.N. "had become a tool in the fundamental violation of human rights." He used the opportunity to claim the United States, "in the service of its own interests and hostile policies, hijacked the Security Council." Perhaps no one told him how his government had been so ably winning inside the 661 Committee.

"A tiny dictatorship destitute in its economy is not the equivalent of the United States of America either in voting strength or in the weight its views ought to carry," observed Democratic Congressman Tom Lantos of California during congressional U.N. hearings. But it is precisely those tiny and not so tiny dictatorships that seek the cover of the U.N. seal to participate in the proposals and enrich their bureaucracies while doing so. Critics see the 0.7

percent proposal as the U.N. establishing a "global tax" that will be immune from American responsibility and control; Kofi Annan says it is a necessary and achievable measure to spur development in the third world. While introducing the millennium proposals, he warned the delegates that unless they acted on the problems facing mankind, "The United Nations will have little or no role to play in the twenty-first century." He called the millennium proposals "a defining moment for world leaders and the United Nations." He said, "You may think I am a dreamer, as some have called me. But without the dream you do not get anything done. . . . It is realistic. It is not utopian. The only thing lacking is the will."

And a lot more money, please.

"I've not seen anything that would lead me to think that more expenditures of taxpayers' dollars will lead to better results at the U.N.—quite the opposite," observed Congressman McCotter. "What will the U.N. do other than grow itself?" asks Kaloogian. The U.N. is an "eternal government program," he says. "What will it do with the money? Will it just line the pockets of people like it did of Saddam Hussein? How many current programs that we consider humanitarian aid are now, today, propping up the dictatorships in third world countries that would otherwise topple? If we want to help the world's poor, we can contribute to missions and give to the charities of our choice, and we do, massively. The American people are not against the idea of helping the world's poor. But I am unconvinced that the U.N. would actually do that."

It is a probability worth raising.

The Hudson Institute estimated that from 1979 to 2005, about $520 billion, more than half a trillion dollars, in Overseas Development Aid (ODA) had poured into the deserving countries of Africa, with the result being "few if any economic growth effects" from all that money. Indeed, some of the seemingly intractable problems of poverty and disease only worsened, along with the continuing genocide the U.N. was unable to stop. Dr. Carol Adelman, the Hudson Institute senior fellow, notes this staggering amount does not include private investments or charitable contributions, or oil revenue, such as the $300 billion earned by Nigeria. "It's absurd to go for the extra money," says Adelman.

"Where did this money go?" she asks. "Why is Africa in such abject poverty? What worked, and what didn't work in foreign investment and assistance? These are the questions that need to be answered before the developed world pours more money into Africa."

David Brooks in *The New York Times* estimated that over the last half of the twentieth century, $2.3 trillion was actually spent to "address global poverty without producing anything like the results we would have hoped for." He says the architect of the U.N. plan, Millennium Director Sachs, "tends to regard anyone who disagrees with him as immoral, is contemptuous of the Bush administration. The Bush folks, he argues, have failed the poor." But it turned out that the president those at the U.N. love to hate actually spent more on African aid than his predecessor, Clinton, despite the symbolism of his 1998 visit to the infamous Door of No Return on the Senegalese island of Goree, from which two million African slaves had been shipped off to America. Brooks argues that "human factors like corruption, greed, institutions, governance, conflict, and traditions have contributed importantly to Africa's suffering," but that the master planners at the U.N. downplay or dismiss those realities.

The U.N. insists it needs to spend more.

"The point-seven percent is exactly like it sounds," counters the spokesman for the main U.N. development program, William Orme of UNDP. "It's less than one percent of every dollar earned by wealthy countries, and even half a cent would be a doubling of what Americans are doing now," he says, noting that the U.S. figure in 2005 stood at about 0.17 percent. "It's a myth that there have been billions and billions spent on poor people in the poorest countries . . . look at our aid. The largest chunk of our aid has gone to Israel and Egypt." U.N. statistics show aid to Africa actually declined during the 1990s. Orme says, "There has to be not just more money but, more importantly, smarter money, more focused money, aimed at the neediest segment of the world population."

Yet Adelman says that will only mean that most of the money will end up "going into public budgets so that government bureaucrats can engineer solutions." She notes that much of it will go to countries "with customs officials who want bribes, leaders who favor their own tribes or withhold food from rival tribes or religious groups," and regimes that terrorize or exploit their own people while being feted by the U.N.'s development aid. Case in point: Zimbabwe—which lands at the bottom of nearly every U.N. index of prosperity, human rights, and corruption under the despotic Robert Mugabe—was slated to receive $8 million in development funds.

"You do have to question the motives of the U.N. and the people calling for this because this is money that will fuel their programs," notes Adelman. "You really run the risk that we had with the Oil for Food program."

Yet the 0.7 percent standard, while a new challenge, is "an old, outdated idea," which emanates from the 1950s, she says. "It's related to nothing. It's just a percent pulled out of the sky. You should be figuring out how much to give a country based on how well they can spend it, what it's going for, what the results have been, whether they are achieving results with the foreign aid you are giving them. Not just pick out a number and say, 'This is what you have to give to the developing world.'"

The formula concocted by the U.N. also penalized the United States, because it does not even consider the largest source of our donations, which is private giving. The U.N. has declared that government assistance should be the only standard upon which wealthy nations are to be judged.

"If you are going to be fair . . . then you have to include all of the money Americans give, not just the tax money," observes Woodward. "Americans are very generous, but we don't always give through government because we are skeptical of government."

He and others think the 0.7 percent is a false, misleading, and useless standard because the enormous amount of our private giving is not counted.

"What's the rationale for not including private contributions?" asks McCotter. "If you are talking about what countries contribute, it should include everything. They are basing it on the gross national product, and part of the gross national product winds up being filtered through the people who've earned it to the charitable organizations. So why is there this distinction between private giving and public giving? The only explanation would be to maximize how much more money they can milk from American taxpayers. We're not being credited for being charitable! It's incumbent upon the U.N. to explain why, if the American people are more charitable and giving than other nations, then why is that being held against us?"

Despite the seeming inequity aimed at the United States, the Bush administration continually increased our donations, even accelerating development assistance for three years. Yet a key point for the administration, as for the U.N., is preventing the world body from turning into a worldwide welfare department.

"Increases must be matched by increases in effectiveness and sustainability," warned the United States Agency for International Development head, Andrew Natsios. The United States has clearly tired of throwing tons of money down a black hole, and has linked the democratic process and accountability to our disbursements.

"Countries that have proven their commitment to change—that govern justly, invest in their people, and maintain policies and institutions that support market-led growth—will receive billions of dollars," he said. The intent was clear: if you continue to skim and scam, you won't get the money. It was a message the U.N. has reconfirmed, for what it's worth. "Developing countries should recommit themselves to taking primary responsibility for their own development," the guidelines claim, a task easier asked than done. Kaloogian is not impressed by the U.N.'s approach.

"It doesn't change," he says.

"The goal is not to divvy up the pie differently. The goal is to make the pie grow bigger so that other people have prosperity. The U.N. doesn't get that. The U.N. is designed to promote stability, which means the status quo. The people who are in power, whether they are corrupt and dictatorial and tyrannical, they should stay in power—that is the basic assumption of the U.N. If we really want to help people, we will change that equation. We should give them something of true value, and that would be their freedom and to help change their system of government to bring prosperity to their nation. So the U.N.'s whole premise is all wrong."

More money flooding into the U.N. system would, in the view of others, only feed an already corrupt political machine.

"The question in the minds of many people is going to be are we to continue to pay dues to an organization that has continued to engage in a practice of corruption that has betrayed its mission? I think what we have to look at also is the deplorable venality of the bureaucracy that runs it," noted Congressman McCotter. He realizes that no number of well-meaning pronouncements can eliminate not only graft, but the continual attempts for the U.N. to expand its purview.

"It's their ideology," Adelman says of the U.N. She states that some in the U.N. "work against not the United States, because we are the largest exporter and largest innovator, but it's working against the interests of the developing countries." Yet the balance between funding too little and too much—and ensuring that the billions are properly spent—may be beyond the United Nations' ability. When human lives are at stake, does it matter if despotic governments benefit, as long as their people do too?

"It's really important to reach the 0.7 percent," says Ann-Louise Colgan of the Washington, D.C., advocacy group Africa Action. "When you are dealing with HIV and malaria, thousands of people are dying preventable deaths. It's unconscionable not to . . . get the problems under control." She says the real scandal of international aid programs is that for all the money earmarked to Africa, more returns to the wealthier nations through the repayment of government debt service. "When people talk about money thrown down the 'rat hole,' it's not true," Colgan insists. "The money is simply being turned about and paid back to the donors." She points out that the U.N. estimates it would cost $10 billion to get AIDS under control in Africa, but those same nations spend $15 billion—$5 billion more than what they spend on AIDS—in debt repayments annually, a stark imbalance that can be erased by wealthy governments canceling the Africans' debt. But sadly, that would still be far from enough to address the chronic poverty U.N. planners say can only be solved through even more billions in development and humanitarian aid. "The U.N. estimates that African countries are 150 years away from the current goals of reducing extreme poverty by half," says Colgan.

The Bush administration says it has tripled American aid to Africa, a claim critics dispute. Bush doubled the amount of U.S. funding to fight malaria, an illness that can be easily prevented even though estimates say nearly three thousand people in sub-Saharan Africa die from the disease each day, most of them children. How much do you give to help struggling African economies, or how much would you be willing to give? That is the fundamental dilemma when the U.N. comes calling asking for more money, please. Money may ease the suffering, but money alone clearly will not solve the crises. It is up to stable, empowered, and incorruptible African governments to have the self-determination and ability to face their own problems, with the world's assistance. More money may help in the short run, but will likely not last to the next time the bureaucrats appear and ask for "more money, please." And they will.

The resistance by the United States to reach the mandated 0.7 percent has been turned against us, no matter how principled the analysis. But it took the U.N. scandals to legitimize criticism of the institution, as responsible people began to finally ask the reasonable questions about its programs and purposes. Until recently, many U.N. critics were portrayed as extremist loonies. In 1996,

Madeleine Albright enhanced that caricature when she appeared at Yale University and gave the George Herbert Walker, Jr., Lecture (named for a cousin of former President George H. W. Bush). "The truth is that the U.N. is not a threat to our sovereignty," stated Albright. "It cannot tax us, or bind us to do anything against our will. And despite the fantasies of some, it is not going to descend upon us in black helicopters in the middle of the night and steal our lawn furniture." Her jocularity notwithstanding, the U.N. does want to tax us as part of the millennium plan. (And the Secretary-General does have that large, very private back lawn behind the official U.N. mansion for any flinched chaise lounges.)

To its critics, Albright continued, "The U.N. is a four-letter word. Either they are afraid the organization could become a world-like government—which is nonsense; or they dislike it because there are so many foreigners in it, which really can't be helped." Perhaps in the not too distant future a succeeding secretary of state will take to the Yale podium and give the George Walker Bush lecture, declaring that U.N. critics were percipient, the troubled organization was finally reformed, and its members passed a resolution thanking Americans for both their overwhelming financial generosity to the world's needy and their support of the world body despite its historic flaws. Don't bet on it.

Whether an advocate or a critic of the U.N., one must accept that the U.N. is looking to grow. Wide-ranging jurisdictional entities have been established to monitor a variety of human activities, and the 0.7 percent assessment is but one of many such efforts. The critics say that some of these U.N. agencies and measures challenge American sovereignty.

The political stalemate over the International Criminal Court was finally resolved only when the Bush administration ensured that American personnel would not be subject to its jurisdiction and charged as "war criminals." The United States walked away from UNESCO (the United Nations Education, Scientific, and Cultural

Organization) in 1985 in protest of its extremist anti-Western ideology and mismanagement. Washington only agreed to return in 2003 when it became clear that the sins of the past had supposedly been expiated. Even earlier, Washington dropped out of ILO (the International Labor Organization) for a short time. American delegates stalked out of the 2001 Conference on Racism in South Africa that disintegrated into an anti-American and anti-Israeli series of rants. When the imposition of international agendas collides with U.S. vital interests, American officials or policymakers do not hesitate to object.

The Law of the Sea Treaty is one such example. It was rejected by President Reagan in 1983 as an infringement on American sovereignty with its specific Common Heritage of Mankind declaration creating an International Seabed Authority to regulate underwater natural resources. This U.N. authority would regulate seven-tenths of the world's surface. As with so many other U.N. authorities, violations would only be adjudicated in a U.N. court, leaving our fate in the hands of the international bureaucrats that many perceive as being biased against the United States.

Some provisions, say critics, would restrict our ability to defend our nation, such as the banning of such vital military operations as intelligence gathering by means of submarines. That would actually be regulated under the treaty. The Department of State rejects that view of the treaty. The official position is that the objections raised by the Reagan administration have now been correctly amended by the Clinton administration, but not yet ratified by the Senate. Ed Meese, attorney general under Reagan, wrote a harsh condemnation of the Law of the Sea for HumanEventsonline.com, arguing that his old boss would "still oppose it," branding it "a bad idea whose time should never come up, at least for the United States and for those who believe in economic liberty and national security." He calls it "an unconscionable" idea that would "entail history's biggest transfer of wealth and surrender of sovereignty."

Frank Gaffney, Jr., a former Reagan administration assistant secretary for defense and current president of the Center for Security

Policy, has claimed that "the ill-concealed hostility of an overwhelming majority of the participating nations to American economic and military power" would be codified by the treaty and used by the U.N. America haters "to constrain our sovereignty and strengthen and redistribute the industrial world's wealth—ours—to undeveloped states." He and other critics fear that the U.N. would be requiring the United States to "submit to a supranational agency that has all the trappings of a world government" that would be "dictating to us our use of and access" to the oceans, Antarctica, and eventually even Space. Most disturbingly, he has pointed out that the treaty does not even include the provision that ships can be boarded and searched for weapons of mass destruction or terrorist-related activities.

Yet this is exactly the path pursued by the Bush administration through his proliferation security initiative (PSI). The PSI has already completed several sea-borne exercises, in which mock cargo ships carrying weapons of mass destruction have been boarded. It was the PSI that enabled the German freighter carrying WMD-related material bound for Libya to be diverted to an Italian port. And that was the impetus that prompted Qaddafi to turn to the West and surrender his nuclear, chemical, and biological intentions.

U.N. critics see the Law of the Sea as an unnecessary adjunct, especially since the United States would be required to foot the bill for one-quarter of the Law of the Sea funding. "At stake," warned Congressman Roy Blunt of Missouri at hearings in 2004, "is everything from access to the deep seabed mineral resources of our coastal regions to our ongoing ability to guarantee the security of our shipping routes."

Others disagree. The Law of the Sea "supports our war on terrorism by providing important stability for navigational freedoms and oversight," according to the Department of State legal adviser William H. Taft IV. He also rejects the arguments that it would force the United States to surrender to a global authority that could impose taxes, pointing out that the International Seabed Authority only addresses the issue of undersea mining and has no other role and had no general regulatory authority over the use of the oceans.

Yet the thought of another sweeping U.N. program has inspired caution in others. Gaffney warned of the possibility that a U.N. superagency responsible for the regulation of natural resources would turn into an even bigger version of the Oil for Food scandal. He said the U.N. bureaucracy could "similarly abuse . . . billions of dollars worth of ocean-related commerce." Baker Spring, research fellow in national security policy at the Heritage Foundation, adds that the treaty "establishes institutions with executive and judicial powers that in some instances are compulsory . . . [and] supersedes the sovereign power of participating states."

Handing international powers to unaccountable governing boards may be a U.N. specialty, but Admiral Michael Mullen, who was vice chief of naval operations, called the treaty "a top national security priority" because it "codifies the right to transit through essential international straits and archipelagic waters. It reaffirms the sovereign immunity of our warships and other public vessels." He claimed that the treaty did not prohibit naval operations such as "the boarding and search of ships and our maritime intelligence activities."

Perhaps few U.N. proposals garnered as much conflicting passion as the treaty, and in the post-Iraq vote détente between the U.N. and the United States, the Bush administration pushed for Senate ratification of the treaty despite the critics' misgivings. It has the support of the military, the White House, Secretary of State Condoleezza Rice, and the Senate Foreign Relations Committee, which on February 25, 2004, unanimously voted (nineteen to zero) to send the resolution to a full floor vote in the Senate. Supporters point out that it will provide free access for our navy to all waters, prohibit dumping of industrial waste off the continental shelf, and provide for replenishment of dwindling fish stocks.

"We can control the vast riches up to two hundred miles off our shores," trumpeted Indiana Senator Richard Lugar during the

Senate hearings. "Including huge schools of fish in the ocean and the oil and gas underneath it."

Yet despite the support of leading Republicans and Democrats, the treaty has yet to be ratified by the Senate. That decision languishes on Capitol Hill, with many fearing the possible downside of the U.N.'s good intentions.

The U.N. has ambitious plans for the future, but it is clear that they will not be realized unless the institution changes soon. The United States is leading the cavalry in the movement to reform the U.N. As a direct result of both the Volcker Committee's revelatory and damning report, and the ensuing hearings on Capitol Hill, Kofi Annan proposed concrete measures to help hold the U.N. to ethical standards. Among these measures are:

- Expanding the investigative arm of the U.N.
- Creating an independent auditing and oversight board.
- Strengthening rules against fraud and corruption.
- Protecting whistle blowers.
- Preventing sexual harassment and sexual exploitation.
- Establishing a code of ethics and an ethics board.

In addition, the U.N. Democracy Fund has been established to help spread democratic values among U.N. members. The creation of the fund was announced with great fanfare in the summer of 2005. A total of 141 member states "embraced" the idea, which in U.N. parlance admittedly means very little. Out of the 141 nations, only 26 agreed to actively support it.

The General Assembly trumpeted other reforms in 2006: the creation of a Peacebuilding Commission to oversee post conflict areas, the Human Rights Council (which most critics saw as being just as discredited as the old Human Rights Commission it replaced), a new Ethics office and revamped financial disclosure rules, but the measures clearly fell short. U.S. Ambassador John Bolton criticized them as "insufficient." The United States, Australia, and Japan, which alone account for 43 percent of the U.N. funding, denounced the efforts as far from enough. While the General Assembly President hailed the reforms as "remarkable," fixing the internal U.N. system such as the audit, management, and investigative departments were delayed. "It appears that the reform of the United Nations has been left in the dust," commented Senator Norm Coleman.

The fact remains that many of the U.N.'s member nations see little upside to supporting measures that would disturb the comfortable status quo. That they do not realize that serious reform is essential to their organization's survival says much about their provincial world views. Fixing what's broken will be an uphill battle.

With the U.N. now viewed in a more realistic and sobering light, the skeptics have gained the upper hand for the time being. Blind faith has been replaced by much-needed critical questioning. No longer can the U.N. be assumed to be doing what's right. It has squandered its goodwill. It is up to us and to our true international partners to hold the U.N. to the ideals upon which it was founded and to rally nations to unite against terrorism, to unite against nuclear proliferation, and to unite against all threats to global security. The U.N. should accept nothing less from itself than scrupulous conduct and an active and relevant contribution to the international community.

If this is not possible, and if the United Nations continues to be little more than a façade, then whenever America stakes out positions and our diplomats settle in behind the Formica sign that reads THE UNITED STATES, our security will be threatened, the world will be failed again, and real answers to that day's biggest problems will have to be sought elsewhere.

EPILOGUE

The U.N. must be strong and efficient, free of corruption, and accountable to the people it serves. . . . The U.N. must stand for integrity—and live by the high standards it sets for others. . . . If member countries want the U.N. to be respected and effective, they should begin by making sure it is worthy of respect.

—*President George W. Bush*
U.N. World Summit
September 14, 2005

MEMO TO UN:

Read the Charter.

Chapter 1 states,

The purposes of the United Nations are: to maintain international peace and security, and to that end: to take effective

collective measures for the prevention or removal of threats
to the peace and for the suppression of acts of aggression or
other breaches of peace.

On June 8, 2004, the Security Council unanimously welcomed
and recognized the newly elected democratic government of Iraq.
In doing so, it noted "the importance of international support" and
"that the multinational force shall have the authority to take all necessary measures to contribute to the maintenance of security and
stability in Iraq." Resolution 1546 granted legitimacy to the Iraqi
government and its efforts against the insurgents. So where are
France, Russia, and China?

The official stamp of approval has been given, yet the failures of
the Security Council are exposed for all to see by the refusal of those
three American rivals to immediately dispatch one hundred thousand troops to help Iraq achieve full stability. There is no more blatant example of the moral and political irrelevance of what the U.N.
stands for than the continued double-cross of the Iraqi people.
Those three nations profited from Saddam, and now turn their backs
on the Iraqi people.

"The United Nations has no choice except to use the collective
strength of its members to curb aggression," said President Harry
Truman to the General Assembly on October 24, 1950. He was talking about Korea. He could have been talking about Iraq. Or the
threat of terrorism. Or Iran. Or North Korea. This is the time for
the United Nations to take action, yet it again does not do enough.

On the sixtieth anniversary of its founding, on June 25, 2005, a
U.S. ambassador reminded the U.N. of its purpose. Back in 1945,
this tall, distinguished figure seemed an unlikely choice to be addressing the diplomatic corps, let alone as an American. His name
was Sichan Siv, and his words laid out the Bush administration's
U.N. strategy.

"We want the U.N. to live up to its founders' vision," he said.
"The U.N. advances peace and prosperity when it works against

terrorism and the proliferation of weapons of mass destruction, as well as when it promotes democracy and freedom, protects refugees, and combats human trafficking." He told them that the U.N. "must be effective . . . fit for member states to uphold their core values," and that "America wants good stewardship of U.N. resources. . . . We must focus on its management and finances to ensure the highest standards of integrity and efficiency."

But Ambassador Siv saved his most important message for last.

He told the delegates that as a child in Cambodia, he had waved a flag to welcome Secretary-General Dag Hammarskjöld. "Many of us were inoculated by UNICEF," he recalled. But after playing a role in maintaining peace and security in his homeland, the U.N. turned from the symbol of hope to a caldron of uselessness when the Khmer Rouge terror began in 1975. It was a presage of the repeated failures to come.

"I lost my mother, older sister, and brother, and their families," recounted the ambassador. "Fifteen people altogether were clubbed to death. Having said, 'never again,' at the end of World War II, the U.N. was powerless to stop the genocide. Only five countries spoke out against these worst violations of human rights: Australia, Canada, Norway, United Kingdom, and the United States. In 1976, I escaped the forced labor camps to Thailand, where I was under the care of the U.N. High Commissioner for Refugees. Then I was able to come to America and start my new life as a free man. With two dollars in my pocket and a heart full of hope, I was on my way to reap the benefits from this Promised Land. Now, I have the enormous privilege to represent the United States at the United Nations. Each time I walk in, my colleagues look at me. Through me, they see America. They see its promise. They see its opportunity. They listen in complete silence when I pronounce: 'On behalf of the President, the people, and the Government of the United States . . .' That is my proudest moment!"

Siv is an American—and U.N.—success story.

As a Cambodian refugee he settled in Wallingford, Connecticut, and was sworn in as an American citizen in the summer of America's bicentennial in 1976. He went on to earn a master's degree in international affairs at Columbia University and served the first President Bush as a deputy assistant to the president and deputy assistant secretary of state. Are the children now in U.N. refugee camps longing to come to America? Or have they been indoctrinated to kill us? Will the nations that seek compromise with terror prevail? Or can the building on the East River again truly represent nations united in the service of man?

There is a large painting that looms over the Security Council chamber. It hangs behind the semicircular table, a giant reminder of the intent of those who gather there. In the center, rising from the ashes of the world war that created the U.N., is a phoenix. It is meant to symbolize the birth of a new world—let it now stand for the birth of a new U.N. as well.

ACKNOWLEDGMENTS

As a television newsman writing his first book, I found the prospect of committing my words to print—and thus to a certain permanence—both exciting and admittedly more than a little intimidating. Writing this book was, however, an eminently rewarding experience and I have many to thank for their encouragement.

Roger Ailes, my boss at Fox News, has revolutionized American journalism by making it acceptable to question long-held assumptions. His leadership has created a more balanced public discourse, and for that I believe my profession owes him a debt of gratitude. I thank him for his vision and support.

John Moody, executive vice president for editorial at Fox News, has been a judicious hand at the editorial helm, eminently honorable as he lassos the rhinoceros every day. I am privileged to have his stewardship.

Bill Shine, senior vice president of programming at Fox News, keeps the apparatus humming along with equanimity and humor.

Dianne Brandi of Brandi & Silvestri, LLC, navigated the legal waters along with Lesley West.

I am especially glad Sentinel's founder and publisher, Adrian Zackheim, and my editor, Bernadette Malone, took a chance on a television newsman whose writing usually does not extend beyond a two-minute news piece. Bernadette's editorial guidance and counsel were perceptive, incisive, and on the mark. Thank you. Will Weisser was masterful at spreading the word.

Eric Lupfer at the William Morris Agency is far more than a book agent. I thank him for his input, shaping and reshaping the material as he babysat multiple manuscripts, and for being a one-man IT department.

Mel Berger at the William Morris Agency was perceptive enough to express interest in a burgeoning scandal that had yet to be recognized by the mainstream media as a legitimate story. Thank you.

John Gibson gets the *Big Story,* and I am grateful to my Fox News colleague for his faith and confidence.

Kendall Hagan, Fox News producer, has been a wonderful long-time news partner of the utmost professionalism and fairness. Thanks for putting up with me.

Jonathan Wachtel, U.N. producer and buddy, has deftly translated the mysteries of U.N. World for the American public while mixing amid the internationalists.

My Fox News U.N. beat colleagues deserve a salute: Bow-Tied Executive Editor George Russell, Bureau Chief Refet Kaplan, U.N. Producer Per Carlson (who will one day pick those Swedish berries with Hans Blix), Specials Producer Brian Gaffney, Ed Barnes, Grace Cutler, State Department Producer Teri Schultz, Executive Producer Holly Cerelli, and my on-air compatriots David Asman, Jonathan Hunt, and David Lee Miller. The indomitable Fox News camera and satellite truck crews are the best; you know who you are!

Special kudos to Claudia Rosett of The Foundation for the Defense of Democracies for sniffing out a story before anyone else and persevering against the doubters, embodying the finest traditions of American investigative journalism.

Thanks to Aaron Klein, Jerusalem bureau chief of *World Net Daily,* for his contributions to the chapter on terrorism. He is a spirited and industrious reporter for whom the future is unlimited. Dr. Nicole Brackman filled in the historic perspectives on the interplay of the great powers that predated Oil for Food.

At the U.N., I wish to acknowledge the Secretary-General's spokesmen, the now retired Fred Eckhard and his able successor, Stephane Dujarric, who have handled the recent pressures with patience and professionalism.

For their advice and support I want to cite John Batchelor, Liz Trotta, and Steve Dunleavy. Claudia Dowling, your contributions were astute and enormously appreciated. Now you can actually enjoy Block Island.

A special thanks goes to the numerous ambassadors, delegation officials, and U.N. employees who shared their time and thoughts freely, willing to speak the truth. I applaud their candor about the institution they serve and I am grateful for their trust.

I also thank the investigators and staffs of the Senate Permanent Subcommittee on Investigations; several House committees (notably International Relations; Oversight and Investigations Subcommittee; Banking and Commerce; and the Subcommittee on National Security, Emerging Threats, and International Relations), the Independent Inquiry Committee into The United Nations Oil for Food Program, the United States Mission to the United Nations, the U.S. Department of the Treasury Office of Public Affairs, the U.S. Attorney for the Southern District of New York, and the Manhattan District Attorney's Office.

Indescribable gratitude to Lisa for her editorial advice and limitless patience.

A tip of the hat to the greats: Runyon, Royko, Breslin, Kempton, McAllary, Hamill, and all of the others who encouraged their journalistic heirs to keep fighting City Hall.

APPENDIX

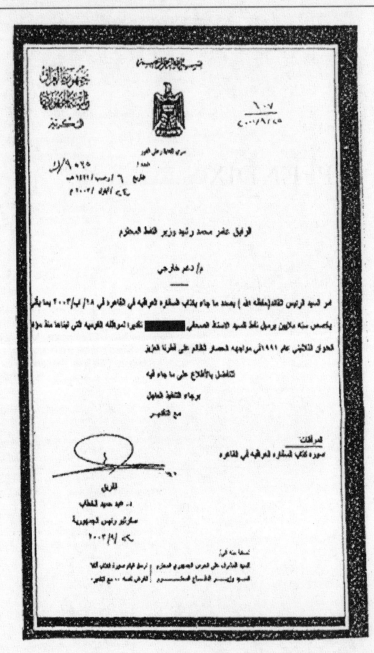

The U.N. so badly bungled the Oil for Food program that many Iraqis went hungry as Saddam grew stronger and richer. Vouchers for Iraq's oil, such as this one addressed to an Arab journalist, were used by Saddam Hussein to

Oil Coupons

Coupon No. 1

In the Name of Allah the Most Merciful

The Republic of Iraq
Presidency of the Republic
The Secretary

Top Secret and most urgent

Number 9525/K
Date 6 Rajab, 1422
24 September, 2002

Comrade 'Amer Muhammad Rashid Minister of Petroleum

External Support

The President leader (may Allah preserve him) has ordered in connection with a letter from the Iraqi embassy in Cairo of 18 August, 2002 as follows: six million barrels of petroleum will be allocated to Mr. Ustadh [honorific title for professors, lawyers and journalists] journalist ███████████ in appreciation of his nationalist positions which he has adopted since the thirty-nation aggression [the Iraqi designation for the coalition which expelled the Iraqi army from Kuwait] in the year 1991 in confronting the unjust blockade of our dear country.

Please be informed of the content
And for urgent execution
With appreciation

Attachment
A copy of the letter [from] the Iraqi embassy in Cairo

Al-Fariq [Lt.General]
D. Abd Hamid Al-Khattab

Secretary of the President of the Republic
24/9/2002

Copies to
The [person] I charge of the Republican Guard
Mr. Minister of Defense

bribe officials from other countries, members of the media, and other opinion makers into supporting his regime.

CRUDE OIL ALLOCATIONS DURING 12TH PHASE OF MOU

- TOTAL QUANTITIES LIFTED ABOUT 193 MM BBLS
- ESTIMATED PROFIT MARGIN IS US $0.20 PER BBL

SER. NO.	CONTRACT NO.	ALLOCATION HOLDER	CONTRACTED COMPANY	ALLOCATED QTY. MM BBLS	LIFTED QTY. MM BBLS
1	M/12/01	MACHINO IMPORT (RUSSIAN)	MACHINO IMPORT (RUSSIAN)	10.000	8.800
2	M/12/02	MR. MOHAMMED SALAH (EGYPTIAN)	ARAB TRADING DEVELOPMENT CO. (EGYPTIAN)	2.000	NOT PERFORMED
3	M/12/03	ZAN GAS (RUSSIAN)	ZAN GAS (RUSSIAN)	2.000	NOT PERFORMED
4	M/12/04	MR ROBERTO FRIMIGONI (ITALIAN)	COGEP (ITALIAN)	1.500	0.463
5	M/12/05	MR AGABABOV (RUSSIAN)	ROSNEFT GAS EXPORT (RUSSIAN)	2.500	2.354
6	M/12/06	ZHUHAI ZHEN RONG CO. (CHINESE)	ZHUHAI ZHEN RONG CO. (CHINESE)	1.500	1.439
7	M/12/07	MR AHMED AL BASHEER (JORDANIAN)	ALRASHEED FOR INTL COOPERATION (JORDANIAN)	1.000	NOT PERFORMED
8	M/12/08	NORENCO (CHINESE)	CHINA WAMBAO (CHINESE)	3.000	0.959
9	M/12/09	MR MOHAMMES SALIH HORANI (JORDANIAN)	JALOL CO. (JORDANIAN)	1.000	NOT PERFORMED
10	M/12/10	MRS MEGAWATI (INDONESIAN)	B T MEDCO (INDONESIAN)	2.000	NOT PERFORMED
11	M/12/11	MR ABDUL MAJID AL ATTAR (ALGERIAN)	ENERGY INVESTMENT (ALGERIAN)	2.000	1.827
12	M/12/12	ALSHANFARI GROUP OF COMPANIES (OMAN)	ALSHANFARI GROUP OF COMPANIES (OMAN)	1.000	1.036
13	M/12/13	BEL METAL ENERGO CO (BELARUS)	BEL METAL ENERGO CO. (BELARUS)	1.500	NOT PERFORMED
14	M/12/14	MR GEORGE GALLOWAY	MIDDLE EAST SEMI CONDUCTORS CO. (JORDANIAN)	3.000	1.400
15	M/12/15	MR SHAFRANIK (RUSSIAN)	SOYUZ NEFTGAS (RUSSIAN)	5.000	1.912
16	M/12/16	MR FAWWAZ ZURAYQAT	MIDDLE EAST SEMI CONDUCTORS CO. (JORDANIAN)	1.000	NOT PERFORMED

Even at the U.N., few are as savagely critical of the United States as Scottish member of parliament George Galloway. His name appears at #14

#	Code	Name	Company		
17	M/12/17	MR TATRINCO - (RUSSIAN)	RUSSIAN ENGINEERING CO.	1.000	1.128
18	M/12/18	AWAD AMMORA (SYRIAN)	AWAD AMMORA & PARTNERS CO. (SYRIAN)	8.200	8.254
19	M/12/19	US Person	MEDNAFTA (CYPRUS)	4.000	2.054
20	M/12/20	MR ABU AL ABBAS	AWAD AMMORA & PARTNERS CO. (SYRIAN)	3.000	2.923
21	M/12/21	STROY TRANSGAS (RUSSIAN)	KALMNEFTGAS (RUSSIAN)	2.000	NOT PERFORMED
22	M/12/22	AVINOIL (GREEK)	AVINOIL (GREEK)	2.000	0.894
23	M/12/23	MR SOKOLOV - IRAQI UKRAINIAN HOUSE	HIU LTD (UKRAINIAN)	3.000	1.000
24	M/12/24	PETROVIETNAM	PETROVIETNAM	2.000	1.969
25	M/12/25	PRESIDENT OF KALMEYKYIA REPUBLIC (RUSSIAN)	KALMNEFTGAS (RUSSIAN)	1.500	1.563
26	M/12/26	CHINA OIL (CHINESE)	CHINA OIL (CHINESE)	3.000	2.969
27	M/12/27	RUSSIAN COMMUNIST PARTY	ACTEC CO. (RUSSIAN)	12.000	NOT PERFORMED
28	M/12/28	MR BASHAR NOURI (SYRIAN)	NOURI FOR TRADING (SYRIAN)	1.500	1.495
29	M/12/29	ZARNEST SERVICE (RUSSIAN)	ZARNEST SERVICE (RUSSIAN)	5.500	5.675
30	M/12/30	MR JOAN (CHINESE)	CHASE STAR (HONG KONG)	2.000	1.542
31	M/12/31	COMMUNIST PARTY (BELARUS)	OIL COMPANY SIBERIA (RUSSIAN)	1.500	0.500
32	M/12/32	AL DOLAYMI GROUP (QATAR)	NATIONAL OIL WELL (QATAR)	2.000	2.016
33	M/12/33	SLOVAKIAN COMMUNIST PARTY	ACTEC CO. (RUSSIAN)	1.000	NOT PERFORMED
34	M/12/34	MRS TUJAN AL FAYSAL (JORADIAN)	MIDDLE EAST SEMI CONDUCTORS CO (JORDANIAN)	2.000	
35	M/12/35	ALCON PETROLEUM (LIETENSTIEN)	ALCON PETROLEUM (LIETENSTIEN)	6.000	6.026
36	M/12/36	ALHODA INTL. CO. (UAE)	ALHODA INTL. CO. (UAE)	9.450	9.481
37	M/12/37	MR STROYEV (RUSSIAN)	URAL INVEST OIL CORP. (RUSSIAN)	1.600	NOT PERFORMED
38	M/12/38	SINOCHEM (CHINESE)	SINOCHEM (CHINESE)	18.600	18.714

on this page of the 270-name oil-allocation list, provided by the CIA Iraq Survey Group.

Revenues from the U.N.'s Oil for Food program funded terrorism, investigators concluded. This $25,000 check from the Saddam Hussein's Grant Program went to the mother of a Hamas suicide bomber who killed eleven and wounded sixteen when he blew himself up in Jerusalem in 2002.

The U.N. knew Osama bin Laden was a terrorist who meant to harm the United States, but did little more in 1998 than call for the Taliban to turn him over or face restrictions on air travel and funds transfer. (Note that China urged the U.N. to go easy, despite the imminent threat to the United States.)

°15 October 1999

PRESS RELEASE
SC/6739

SECURITY COUNCIL DEMANDS THAT TALIBAN TURN OVER USAMA BIN LADEN TO APPROPRIATE AUTHORITIES

19991015

Resolution 1267 (1999), Adopted Unanimously, Sets Out Measures To be Imposed if Demand Not Met by 14 November

Acting under Chapter VII of the United Nations Charter, the Security Council this afternoon demanded that the Afghan faction, known as the Taliban, turn over Usama bin Laden to appropriate authorities in a country where he would be brought to justice. In that context, it decided that on 14 November all States shall freeze funds and prohibit the take-off and landing of

Taliban-owned aircraft unless or until the Taliban complies with that demand.

Mr. bin Laden and his associates were indicted by the United States for, among other things, his role in the 7 August 1998 bombings of United States embassies in Kenya and the United Republic of Tanzania, and for conspiring to kill United States nationals. The Council's action noted this, as well as the United States' request to the Taliban to surrender Mr. Bin Laden and his associates for trial.

By unanimously adopting resolution 1267 (1999)—submitted by Canada, Netherlands, Russian Federation, Slovenia, United Kingdom and the United States—the Council decided that, should the condition not be met within the stated time frame, all States shall deny permission for any aircraft to take off from or land in their territory if it was owned, leased or operated by or on behalf of the Taliban. Further, all States shall freeze funds and other financial resources, including those derived or generated from property or undertakings directly or indirectly owned or controlled by the Taliban, and ensure that neither those funds or financial resources, nor any others, are made available by their nationals or any persons within their territory to or for the benefit of the Taliban.

The Council further decided that exceptions could be made to these stipulations should a Committee, established by this same resolution, grant exceptions for humanitarian reasons, including religious obligations. The Committee, consisting of all Council members, will report to the Council with observations and recommendations on matters, including requests for exemptions to these measures and granting an exemption in respect of the payment by the International Air Transport Association (IATA) to Afghanistan's aeronautical authority, on behalf of international airlines for air traffic-control services.

The Committee will also report on the impact of the measures to be imposed through the resolution, including the humanitarian implications. It will consider alleged violations of the resolution's measures, ask States to provide information on implementing them, report to the Council thereon and recommend responses.

Security Council - 1a - Press Release SC/6739
4051st Meeting (PM) 15 October 1999

Also through resolution 1267 (1999), the Council insisted that the Taliban, which also calls itself the Islamic Emirate of Afghanistan, comply promptly with previous Council resolutions. In particular, it must cease providing sanctuary and training for international terrorists and their organizations, take effective measures to ensure that the territory under its control was not used for terrorist installations and camps or for the preparation or organization of terrorist acts against other States or their citizens, and cooperate with efforts to bring indicted terrorists to justice.

The Council called upon States to act strictly in accordance with the provisions of the resolution, notwithstanding any rights or obligations derived from an international agreement, contract, license or permit entered into or granted prior to the date of the current text. It also called on them to cooperate fully with its Committee, and to bring proceedings against and impose penalties against any person or entity that violated the resolution.

Statements were made by the representatives of Afghanistan, United States, Malaysia, Bahrain, China and Canada.

The meeting, which was called to order at 12:14 p.m., was adjourned at 12:40 p.m.

Council Work Programme

The Security Council met this afternoon to consider the situation in Afghanistan.

Draft Resolution

The Council had before it a draft resolution (document S/1999/1054) sponsored by Canada, Netherlands, Russian Federation, Slovenia, United Kingdom and the United States, which reads as follows:

"The Security Council,

"Reaffirming its previous resolutions, in particular resolutions 1189 (1998) of 13 August 1998, 1193 (1998) of 28 August 1998 and 1214 (1998) of 8 December 1998, and the statements of its President on the situation in Afghanistan,

"Reaffirming its strong commitment to the sovereignty, independence, territorial integrity and national unity of Afghanistan, and its respect for Afghanistan's cultural and historical heritage,

"Reiterating its deep concern over the continuing violations of international humanitarian law and of human rights, particularly discrimination against women and girls, and over the significant rise in the illicit production of opium, and stressing that the capture by the Taliban of the Consulate-General of the Islamic Republic of Iran and the murder of Iranian diplomats and a journalist in Mazar-e-Sharif constituted flagrant violations of established international law,

"Recalling the relevant international counter-terrorism conventions and in particular the obligations of parties to those conventions to extradite or prosecute terrorists,

"Strongly condemning the continuing use of Afghan territory, especially areas controlled by the Taliban, for the sheltering and training of terrorists and planning of terrorist acts, and reaffirming its conviction that the suppression of international terrorism is essential for the maintenance of international peace and security,

"Deploring the fact that the Taliban continues to provide safe haven to Usama bin Laden and to allow him and others associated with him to operate a network of terrorist training camps from Taliban-controlled territory and to use Afghanistan as a base from which to sponsor international terrorist operations,

"Noting the indictment of Usama bin Laden and his associates by the United States of America for, inter alia, the 7 August 1998 bombings of the United States embassies in Nairobi, Kenya, and Dar es Salaam, Tanzania and for conspiring to kill American nationals outside the United States, and noting also the request of the United States of America to the Taliban to surrender them for trial (S/1999/1021),

"Determining that the failure of the Taliban authorities to respond to the demands in paragraph 13 of resolution 1214 (1998) constitutes a threat to international peace and security,

"Stressing its determination to ensure respect for its resolutions, "Acting under Chapter VII of the Charter of the United Nations,

"1. Insists that the Afghan faction known as the Taliban, which also calls itself the Islamic Emirate of Afghanistan, comply promptly with its previous resolutions and in particular cease the provision of sanctuary and training for international terrorists and their organizations, take appropriate effective measures to ensure that the territory under its control is not used for terrorist installations and camps, or for the preparation or organization of terrorist acts against other States or their citizens, and cooperate with efforts to bring indicted terrorists to justice;

"2. Demands that the Taliban turn over Usama bin Laden without further delay to appropriate authorities in a country where he has been indicted, or to appropriate authorities in a country where he will be returned to such a country, or to appropriate authorities in a country where he will be arrested and effectively brought to justice;

"3. Decides that on 14 November 1999 all States shall impose the measures set out in paragraph 4 below, unless the Council has previously decided, on the basis of a report of the Secretary-General, that the Taliban has fully complied with the obligation set out in paragraph 2 above;

"4. Decides further that, in order to enforce paragraph 2 above, all States shall:

"(a) Deny permission for any aircraft to take off from or land in their territory if it is owned, leased or operated by or on behalf of the Taliban as designated by the Committee established by paragraph 6 below, unless the particular flight has been approved in advance by the Committee on the grounds of humanitarian need, including religious obligation such as the performance of the Hajj;

"(b) Freeze funds and other financial resources, including funds derived or generated from property owned or controlled directly or indirectly by the Taliban, or by any undertaking owned or controlled by the Taliban, as designated by the Committee established by paragraph 6 below, and ensure that neither they nor any other funds or financial resources so designated are made available, by their nationals or by any persons within their territory, to or for the benefit of the Taliban or any undertaking owned or controlled, directly or indirectly, by the Taliban, except as may be authorized by the Committee on a case-by-case basis on the grounds of humanitarian need;

"5. Urges all States to cooperate with efforts to fulfil the demand in paragraph 2 above, and to consider further measures against Usama bin Laden and his associates;

"6. Decides to establish, in accordance with rule 28 of its provisional rules of procedure, a Committee of the Security Council consisting of all the members of the Council to undertake the following tasks and to report on its work to the Council with its observations and recommendations:

"(a) To seek from all States further information regarding the action taken by them with a view to effectively implementing the measures imposed by paragraph 4 above;

"(b) To consider information brought to its attention by States concerning violations of the measures imposed by paragraph 4 above and to recommend appropriate measures in response thereto;

"(c) To make periodic reports to the Council on the impact, including the humanitarian implications, of the measures imposed by paragraph 4 above;

"(d) To make periodic reports to the Council on information submitted to it regarding alleged violations of the measures imposed by paragraph 4 above, identifying where possible persons or entities reported to be engaged in such violations;

"(e) To designate the aircraft and funds or other financial resources referred to in paragraph 4 above in order to facilitate the implementation of the measures imposed by that paragraph;

"(f) To consider requests for exemptions from the measures imposed by paragraph 4 above as provided in that paragraph, and to decide on the granting of an exemption to these measures in respect of the payment by the International Air Transport Association (IATA) to the aeronautical authority of Afghanistan on behalf of international airlines for air traffic control services;

"(g) To examine the reports submitted pursuant to paragraph 9 below;

"7. Calls upon all States to act strictly in accordance with the provisions of this resolution, notwithstanding the existence of any rights or obligations conferred or imposed by any international agreement or any contract entered into or any licence or permit granted prior to the date of coming into force of the measures imposed by paragraph 4 above;

"8. Calls upon States to bring proceedings against persons and entities within their jurisdiction that violate the measures imposed by paragraph 4 above and to impose appropriate penalties;

"9. Calls upon all States to cooperate fully with the Committee established by paragraph 6 above in the fulfilment of its tasks, including supplying such information as may be required by the Committee in pursuance of this resolution;

"10. Requests all States to report to the Committee established by paragraph 6 above within 30 days of the coming into force of the measures imposed by paragraph 4 above on the steps they have taken with a view to effectively implementing paragraph 4 above;

"11. Requests the Secretary-General to provide all necessary assistance to the Committee established by paragraph 6 above and to make the necessary arrangements in the Secretariat for this purpose;

"12. Requests the Committee established by paragraph 6 above to determine appropriate arrangements, on the basis of recommendations of the Secretariat, with competent international organizations, neighbouring and other States, and parties concerned with a view to improving the monitoring of the implementation of the measures imposed by paragraph 4 above;

"13. Requests the Secretariat to submit for consideration by the Committee established by paragraph 6 above information received from Governments and public sources on possible violations of the measures imposed by paragraph 4 above;

"14. Decides to terminate the measures imposed by paragraph 4 above once the Secretary-General reports to the Security Council that the Taliban has fulfilled the obligation set out in paragraph 2 above;

"15. Expresses its readiness to consider the imposition of further measures, in accordance with its responsibility under the Charter of the United Nations, with the aim of achieving the full implementation of this resolution;

"16. Decides to remain actively seized of the matter."

Statements

RAAVAN A.G. FARHADI (Afghanistan) said his Government supported the draft resolution before the Council. The measures in that text signalled to the Taliban and their Pakistani mentors that the international community was concerned with the policy of Pakistan and the Taliban, which posed an immediate threat to international peace and security. The text's political message was strong: the foreign supporters of the Taliban should take necessary measures to dissociate themselves from the "Talibanization" of the region. The text directly affected the Taliban's financial resources, which came primarily from drug trafficking. It would not have any effect on the Afghan nation itself. The clause on exceptions ensured the delivery of humanitarian assistance to the Afghani people. He expected that the Council would use every mechanism at its disposal for the meticulous and strict application of all measures.

He considered the adoption of today's text a means of persuading the Taliban and their mentors to abandon policies which were harmful to the peace and security of the region, of which Pakistan was part. The Taliban must be convinced that there was no military solution.

NANCY SODERBERG (United States) said that, with the passage of the draft resolution before the Council, the United Nations would take a courageous step to combat international terrorism. It would send a direct message to Usama bin Laden and terrorists everywhere—"you cannot run, you cannot hide, you will be brought to justice". She said her Government attached the highest priority to disrupting Usama bin Laden's terrorist organization and bringing bin Laden to justice.

She said the Taliban continued to provide bin Laden with safe haven and security, allowing him the freedom to operate despite repeated efforts by the United States to persuade the Taliban to turn over or expel him and his associates to responsible authorities in a country where he could be brought to justice. The draft resolution gave the Taliban a choice: it had 30 days to turn over bin Laden or sanctions would begin. She hoped the Taliban would cooperate in bringing bin Laden to justice with that time frame. The choice between cooperation and confrontation rested with the Taliban.

The sanctions were limited and targeted very specifically to limit the resources of Taliban authorities and would, in no way, harm the people of Afghanistan, she said. The Council would work with the sanctions committee to implement the resolution in a way that did not hinder the provision of humanitarian assistance to the Afghan people. HASMY AGAM (Malaysia) said while strong measures to combat international terrorism were needed, his delegation was concerned about the impact on the innocent, ordinary people of Afghanistan. Sanctions should be a last resort before the use of force, when all other measures had been utilized and failed. They should be used as an instrument of coercion with great caution, because of their unintended grave consequences to the innocent population. The effectiveness and humanitarian impact should be assessed at all stages.

Sanctions directed at the Taliban would affect the general population in virtually every aspect of their lives, he continued. There should have been a more careful and exhaustive analysis of the likely impact of the proposed sanctions, as well as a phased approach in handling the situation. The Council should have first adopted a strong resolution signalling its serious intention to institute measures to impose sanctions on the Taliban, if certain actions were not taken in respect to its "support" for terrorism.

The people of Afghanistan, among the world's poorest, were the tragic victims of more than a decade of bitter conflict and natural disasters, he said. The sanctions imposed on the Taliban would most certainly affect the people in a punitive way, since the Taliban were effectively in control in most parts of the country and administered virtually every aspect of life in the parts of Afghanistan under their control. For those reasons, the Malaysian delegation would vote in favour of the draft resolution with a heavy heart. He appealed to the Taliban to comply with the Council's requirements so as to spare the hapless people of Afghanistan from further suffering and misery. He appealed to the Council to ensure that, in implementing the text, the welfare of the people of Afghanistan was taken to heart.

RASHID AL-DOSARI (Bahrain) said the existence of a few terrorists on Afghan territory was the responsibility of all Afghan factions. If the terrorists were disabled, then law would prevail in that country and Afghanistan would regain its status in the international community.

The Afghan factions were also responsible for the internal situation in Afghanistan and its repercussions in the country, he said. Moreover, those States that provided arms to the Afghan factions were also responsible for fuelling the Afghan war. Those States should have convinced the Afghan factions to disarm and return to a dialogue to settle their problems. He noted the deterioration of the humanitarian situation in the country, which had been exacerbated by natural disasters. For that reason, he had been apprehensive about the possible negative repercussions of the resolution and had worked with other delegations to make sure that they would not happen.

Action on Draft Resolution

The Council then unanimously adopted resolution 1267 (1999).

SHEN GUOFANG (China) endorsed the views of the representative of Malaysia. China believed that sanctions would exacerbate the suffering of the people of Afghanistan. Sanctions must be used only as a last resort, and should be clearly targeted. China was against all forms of terrorism. Based on that position, it had participated in the negotiations and requested that the text be limited to the issue of combating international terrorism. It noted the text's reference to the Council's commitment to the sovereignty, independence, territorial integrity and national unity of Afghanistan, and its respect for Afghanistan's cultural and historical heritage. Further, China noted that the sanctions would take effect only 30 days from today and would be ceased immediately upon fulfilment of the stated requirement.

ANDRAS VAMOS-GOLDMAN (Canada) said his delegation supported the resolution. It was appropriate and necessary that the Council take action against terrorism. He hoped the text would assist in the process of bringing to justice those responsible for the 1998 bombings in Kenya and the United Republic of Tanzania. The Taliban's flouting of human rights and humanitarian principles, which had given rise to so much insecurity in the region, merited further action.

✳ ✳ ✳

SCENARIOS COVERING PROHIBITED ACTS OF SEXUAL EXPLOITATION AND SEXUAL ABUSE FOR THE VARIOUS CATEGORIES OF UNITED NATIONS PERSONNEL

The following scenarios demonstrate examples of prohibited acts under the current standards of conduct expected of all categories of U.N. personnel (civilian, civilian police, military observers and military members of national contingents) as set out in the U.N. Staff Rules and Regulations and/or the DPKO Disciplinary Directives (including the Ten Rules: Code of Personal Conduct for Blue Helmets). These acts also specifically violate standards listed in: ST/SGB/2003/13 on Special Measures for Protection from Sexual Exploitation and Sexual Abuse; and ST/SGB/1999/13 on Observance by United Nations Forces of International Humanitarian Law. N.B. Allegations and reports of sexual harassment are covered by separate procedures described in ST/SGB/253 and ST/AI/379 (as may be amended).

The acts described below constitute misconduct and could lead to the appropriate disciplinary and administrative measures, such as summary dismissal or recommendation to repatriate. More information on determining the relevant procedures to be followed when alleged acts of misconduct occur should be obtained from the relevant Department/Agency Headquarters.

Example of Prohibited Act	Why It Constitutes Misconduct
Betty is a 16 year old girl living in a small village. Betty has four younger brothers and sisters. Her parents do not have very much money and find it very difficult to provide the costs for education,	Under section 3.2 (b) of the Secretary-General's Bulletin ST/SGB/2003/13, Johnson is prohibited from sexual activity with anyone under 18, regardless of the local age of consent. This encounter also

Example of Prohibited Act	Why It Constitutes Misconduct
clothing and food for all of the children. There had even been some discussion about Betty dropping out of school to assist her mother in working at the market. However, all the problems have been solved as Betty has started a sexual relationship with Johnson, a senior UNHCR officer. He has promised to pay for her school fees and help to pay for her brothers and sisters to continue with their education. Betty's parents are very relieved that this opportunity has come and encourage Betty to maintain the relationship. It has really helped the family and now all the children can continue in school.	constitutes sexual exploitation as defined in section 3.2 (c) of ST/SGB/2003/13: Johnson has abused a position of differential power for sexual purposes, by exchanging money for sexual access.
Carlos, a military commander posted in the southern district, has helped set up a boys' soccer club in the town where his national contingent is deployed. Carlos enjoys the soccer games, but he particularly enjoys the access the club gives him to local adolescents. He gives presents (magazines, candy, sodas, pens) to various boys in exchange for sexual acts. He thinks there's nothing wrong with this, since the	Carlos' acts are in violation of the Ten Rules: Code of Personal Conduct for Blue Helmets and ST/SGB/1999/13 on Observance by U.N. Forces of International Humanitarian Law. He has abused a position of differential power for sexual purposes, by exchanging money and goods for sexual favours. Such acts constitute serious misconduct. In addition, Carlos is in breach of the same policy for per-

Example of Prohibited Act	Why It Constitutes Misconduct
boys like the presents he gives them.	forming sexual acts with children (anyone under 18, regardless of the local age of consent).
Joey is a locally-hired driver for a U.N. agency, who transports relief items from the warehouse to the refugee camp where the items are distributed. On one of his trips he recognized a 15-year old refugee girl walking on the side of the road and gave her a lift back to the camp. Since then, to impress her and win her over, he frequently offers to drive her wherever she is going and sometimes gives her small items from the relief packages in his truck, which he thinks she and her family could use. The last time he drove her home she asked him inside her house to meet her family. The family was pleased that she had made friends with a U.N. worker. Joey really likes the girl and wants to start a sexual relationship with her. He knows her family will approve.	Under section 3.2 (b) of the Secretary-General's Bulletin ST/SGB/2003/13, Joey is prohibited from sexual activity with anyone under 18, regardless of the local age of consent. Moreover, the rules also strongly discourage sexual relationships between U.N. staff and beneficiaries of assistance, since they are based on inherently unequal power dynamics and undermine the credibility and integrity of the work of the U.N. (see section 3.2 (d) of ST/SGB/2003/13).
Marie is a 30-year-old refugee whose desperate circumstances have forced her into prostitution. On Saturday night she was picked	The exchange of money for sexual services violates the standards of conduct expected of any category of U.N. personnel. In this case, (in-

Example of Prohibited Act	Why It Constitutes Misconduct
up by John, a UNICEF staff member in a U.N. car, as he was driving back home after dinner. John took her home and paid her for sex. As prostitution is not illegal in the country where he is posted, he figured he was doing nothing wrong.	volving a civilian staff member) the act violates section 3.2 (c) of the Secretary-General's Bulletin ST/SGB/2003/13.
Josie is an adolescent refugee girl in one of the camps. Pieter, one of the food distribution staff, who works for WFP, has offered to give her a little extra during the distribution if she will be his "special friend". She agrees willingly. Both of them agree that they should start a sexual relationship and neither one of them think that anything is wrong. Josie hopes that the relationship will be a passport to a new life in another country, and Pieter does nothing to discourage these hopes.	Pieter's relationship with Josie constitutes sexual exploitation: exchange of goods for sex or sexual favours is explicitly prohibited under section 3.2 (c) of ST/SGB/2003/13. This includes any exchange of assistance that is due to beneficiaries of assistance. Moreover (and irrespective of the local age of consent) if Josie is under 18, Pieter is in violation of section 3.2 (b) of ST/SGB/2003/13.
Darlene is a CIVPOL. She's always on the lookout for good business opportunities since she has to support her family back home. She's asked by another CIVPOL, Stanislas, to contribute some of her MSA towards renovating a bar in the	Darlene and Stanislas are aiding sexual exploitation. This violates the Ten Rules: Code of Personal Conduct for Peacekeepers. The peacekeepers, UNMOs and CIVPOLs who frequent the bar are engaged in sexual exploita-

Example of Prohibited Act	Why It Constitutes Misconduct
town, in return for a cut of the bar's profits. Darlene soon finds she's getting a steady income from the bar, and gives more money to hire more staff, including security, and so on. She herself doesn't go to the bar, but she knows that there is a lot of prostitution going on there and that several peacekeepers and CIVPOLs use the bar often. However, she doesn't think that concerns her, since she isn't directly involved in those issues. She's just glad of the extra money.	tion. For these categories of personnel, using a prostitute violates the Ten Rules: Code of Personal Conduct for Blue Helmets and the ST/SGB/1999/13 On Observance by U.N. Forces of International Humanitarian Law.
Sven is a Military Observer. He has developed a close relationship with his landlady, Amanna, who also does his cleaning. They eat meals together and talk in broken English. Amanna's family (her husband and three young children) was killed in the violence that engulfed the country five years ago, so she is very lonely and enjoys the opportunity to talk. One night Sven returns from a reception for the Force Commander who has been visiting the district where he is deployed. Sven is drunk. He has not had sex for eight months. He	Sven has breached the Ten Rules: Code of Personal Conduct for Peacekeepers, by using his differential position of power to coerce Amanna into having sex with him.

Example of Prohibited Act	Why It Constitutes Misconduct
presses Amanna to come to his bedroom, urging her to make love with him. Amanna looks extremely embarrassed, and tries to leave the room. Sven's sure she likes him, but is just being shy. Then he changes tactics, and tells her he will have to think of leaving her house and finding a new home if she won't come to bed with him. Amanna is horrified at the prospect of losing her only source of income, so she complies with his demands. After all the violence she has seen, she has come to expect this kind of behaviour from men, but she had thought that Sven would be different. She was wrong about that.	

Produced by the Inter-Agency Standing Committee Task Force on Protection from Sexual Exploitation and Abuse

Acknowledgment: A number of the scenarios above have been adapted from materials contained in the Facilitator's Guide: *Understanding Humanitarian Aid Worker Responsibilities: Sexual Exploitation and Abuse Prevention,* produced by the Coordination Committee for the Prevention of Sexual Exploitation and Abuse in Sierra Leone.

U.N. peacekeepers perpetuated horrific sex scandals, such as bribing little girls with bananas and milk in exchange for sexual relations. In this nearly comical document, the U.N. earnestly explains to employees that using U.N. cars to pick up prostitutes and giving little boys candy in exchange for sex (just to cite two examples) is wrong.

NOTES

Introduction

Chapter 1: Welcome to U.N. World

9   "was failing": *Counter-Terrorism Committee Report*, U.N. Security Council, January 13, 2004.

10 "to the gathering": U.N. Al Qaeda Committee report, August 27, 2004.

11 "was stopped": ibid.

11 "what this means": ibid.

11 "difficult to believe": ibid.

11 "much staffing": U.N. Foundation Web site (UNFoundation.org).

13 "impugn a cause with which they agree?": Ambassador Nicholas Rostow, comments, Security Council, U.N. headquarters, July 20, 2005.

13 "under occupation to liberate themselves": Ambassador Fayssal Mekdad comments, Security Council, U.N. headquarters, July 20, 2005.

15 "freedom fighters": Yassar Arafat, General Assembly speech, November 13, 1974.

15 "massacre": Nasser Al-Kidwa, CNN interview, April 18, 2002.

16 "money in Syria,": Rowan Scarborough, *The Washington Times*, July 6, 2005.

16 "implement the resolution": Annan press encounter, New York, at Manager of the Year Award Presentation, March 8, 2005.

17 "North America, and Asia": "Patterns of Global Terrorism," U.S. Department of State report, 2004.

17 "one of the truck bombs": *USA v. Omar Ahmad Ali Abdul Rahman, et al.*, conversations, May 23, 1993.

18 "hypocrisy at the U.N.": author interview with Ambassador Daniel Gillerman, May 2005.

19 "one hundred Bin Ladens": video from Steve Emerson and Rita Katz, The Investigative Project, April 28, 2001.

19 "negative message": author interview with a diplomatic source.

19 "different reasons": author interview with a diplomatic source.

20 "have nuclear weapons": John Bolton, Hudson Institute, August 17, 2004.

20 "lying in front of everyone": Christopher Dickey, "Iran's Nuclear Lies," *Newsweek*, July 11, 2005.

20 "threat of the Security Council": *New York Post*, August 29, 2005.

21 "absurd anti-American conspiracy theories": "An Alliance on Iran," *Washington Post* editorial, September 27, 2005.

21 "has pointedly noted": Joel Brinkley, "Half a Step Forward to Rein in Iran," *New York Times*, September 27, 2005.

22 "at the broader picture": Annan statement at news conference, U.N. headquarters, September 12, 2005.

22 "to develop a nuclear bomb": author interview with Alireza Jafarzadeh, December 8, 2005.

22   "St. Paul, Minnesota": Executive Summary of the *Report of the Commission to Assess the Ballistic Missile Threat to the United States*, July 15, 1998.

22   "Madison, Wisconsin": ibid.

22   "by 2015": Senate International Foreign Relations Committee report, June 2005.

23   "compared to [the U.N.]": author interview with source.

24   "has been accomplished": David Sanger, "Month of Talks Fails to Bolster Nuclear Treaty," *New York Times*, May 28, 2005.

24   "several books on that": ibid.

24   "fiasco": *Disamament Times*, May 2005, page 7.

25   "left in the world . . . the United States": John Bolton, comments to Global Structures Convocation, February 3, 1994.

25   "passing year": author interview with a diplomatic source.

26   "bloodthirsty fiendish bloodsucker": James S. Robbins, "where's Boltonz," *National Review*, August 13, 2003.

26   "that I don't live up to my press clippings!": author interview with Ambassador John Bolton, September 29, 2005.

27   "dealing with the program of aggressive communist states" author interview with source.

28   "several different peacekeeping missions": U.N. report, 2005, March 24, 2005.

28   "zero-tolerance": *Washington Post*, November 27, 2004.

Chapter 2: The U.N. Press Corps Cover-up

33   "twenty-seven solo press conferences": U.N.org/news/statements.

33   "President Bush's seventeen": WhiteHouse.org/news/pressbriefings.

33   "be ineffective": United Nations Correspondents Dinner Program, December 3, 2004, page 7.

34   "problem areas of the U.N.": author interview with a U.N. source.

34   "head of the World Bank": reporter's question to Annan at news conference, U.N. headquarters, March 21, 2005.

34   "and in the end, nothing": author conversation, September 2005.

35   "sympathetic press corps": author interview with Ian Williams, April 2005.

35   "are in love with it": author interview with Cliff Kincaid, May 2005.

36   "which promote the U.N.?": AIM survey.

36   "She told me": author interview with Linda Fasulo, August 2005.

37   "Jim Wurst told AIM": Wurst, letter to Accuracy in Media, February 2005.

38   "about the Soros deal": Malloch Brown, U.N. News Conference, June 21, 2005.

39   "Stockholm syndrome": author interview with John Batchelor, June 2005.

40   "allegations of irregularities": *New York Times*, editorial, April, 28, 2005.

40   "not 'exonerated'": Paul Volcker, Fox News interview, April 26, 2005.

40   "covering the institution": author interview with an unnamed source.

41   "not covered by American rules.": author interview with Richard Wald, May 2005.

Chapter 3: The Pinstripe Posse and the Sultan of Sutton Place

47   "in unpaid parking tickets": interview with author, September 30, 2005; source with New York City Mayor's Office.

48   "approximately $20,644": Independent Inquiry Committee into the United Nations Oil for Food Program, September 7, 2005.

49   "don't want to go back to their home country": author interview with a diplomatic U.N. source.

49   "40 people out of 23,000" U.N. Office of the Spokesman.

50   "wife and kids": author interview.

50   "U.N. organization much good": author interview.

50   "unhappy life": author interview.

52   "forty-five thousand worldwide": U.N. Office of the Spokesman, September 2005.

52   "you're in": author interview with a U.N. staff source.

53   "covering up": author interview with a U.N. staff source.

53   "hurt America? No!": author interview with a U.N. diplomatic source.

54   "job placement bureau": congressional task force on the United Nations report, June 2005.

54   "Shakespeare wince": London *Sunday Times*, June 19, 2005.

55   "(the U.N. official) gets a kickback": author interview with a diplomatic source.

58   "and other supplies": Princeton University Library, Department of Rare Books and Special Collections AFDF no. 026.

58   "$4,800,000": City of New York, Department of Buildings, Property Profile Overview.

60   "or anything else like that": statement from Kofi Annan to author, May 3, 2005.

Chapter 4: The International Anthem: Blame America!

60   "of anti-Americanism at the U.N.": author interview with a U.N. diplomatic source.

61   "let's have lunch!": author interview with a U.N. diplomatic source.

61   "green card for their sons!": author interview with a U.N. diplomatic source.

62   "widespread anti-Americanism": author interview with a U.N. diplomatic source.

62   "by giving aid": author interview with a U.N. diplomatic source.

63   "you are cured": author interview with a U.N. staff source.

64   "its really sickening": author interview with a U.N. staff source.

64   "against the United States": author interview with a diplomatic source.

64   "with a superpower": author interview.

64   "payback time for the U.S.": author interview with a U.N. diplomatic source.

65   "was problem number one": Michael Soussan, congressional testimony, House International Relations Committee, April 28, 2004.

66   "the weakest sanctions regime": author interview with Michael Scharf.

66   "all over again": author interview with a U.N. diplomatic source.

66   "hostility or problems": author interview with A. Peter Burleigh, March 2005.

67   "of what happens with the U.S.": author interview with Ambassador Daniel Gillerman, May 2005.

67   "deal for your country": author interview with a diplomatic source.

67   "I'm still disappointed": author interview with a diplomatic source.

68   "and dealt with by us": author interview with A. Peter Burleigh, March 2005.

68   "how could she?": CBS News interview with Christiane Amanpour, March 16, 2003.

69   "where their veto position is important": Charles Duelfer congressional testimony, Senate Subcommittee on Investigations, November 15, 2004.

69   "international covenants": interview with Bloomberg News, November 7, 2002.

69   "a backyard": The New York Times, November 21, 2003.

69   "the multilateral system": Annan media statement, June 7, 2005.

70   "this territory": author interview with A. Peter Burleigh, March 2005.

70   "so many U.N. activities": ibid.

70   "left to follow": author interview with a U.N. diplomatic source.

71   "already have the answer": Daily Telegraph, September 9, 2005.

72   "happy to see Saddam Hussein's regime fall": Dominique De Villepin media statement, July 2003.

72   "consideration is lacking": author interview with a U.N. diplomatic source.

72   "kill it anyway?": author interview with a U.N. diplomatic source.

73   "they grow to resent it": author interview with Charles Hill, April 2005.

75   "misinformed, misunderstood, and misrepresented": congressional testimony, House International Relations Committee, March 15, 2005.

76 "toward the U.S.": ibid.

76 "let alone police itself ": ibid.

77 "the world against the United States!": author interview with John Ensign, June 2005.

79 "talent and qualities": Annan news conference statement, April 15, 2005.

79 "peace and security": Annan statement, U.N. Security Council, March 24, 1999.

80 "so I think we are doing the right thing": *NewsHour with Jim Lehrer*, March 24, 1999.

80 "pummeled for it": author interview with Charles Hill, April 2005.

81 "can be exceptions made for the others": author interview with A. Peter Burleigh, March 2005.

81 "vocally obstructed the invasion of Iraq": *National Post*, November 22, 2004.

82 "most sinister forces": Freedom Alliance News, FreedomAlliance.org, November 25, 2003.

83 "we can't be bothered": Ambassador Danforth, U.N. remarks, November 23, 2004.

85 "heal the wounds as we speak": Fox News interview by the author, December 21, 2003.

86 "interest of other nations and their peoples.": Annan response at U.N. news conference, March 21, 2005.

Chapter 5: Helping the Enemy

88 "to $22 billion": Senate Permanent Subcommittee on Investigations estimate, November 15, 2004.

89 "do what they want with it": author interview with a U.N. diplomatic source.

89 "seventy-eight separate presidential palace compounds": U.S. Department of State report, "Saddam Hussein's Iraq," September 1999.

90 "Oil for Palaces Program": transcripts, Senate Committee on Homeland Security and Government Affairs, November 15, 2005.

90 "corruption covered up by U.N. officials": House Subcommittee on Oversight and Investigations, March 17, 2005.

91 "borne of indifference": House International Relations Committee hearing, March 15, 2005.

91 "harm our own interests": ibid.

91 "dual use goods programs": *CIA Iraq Survey Group Report: Regime Strategic Intent*, September 30, 2004.

93 "conventional weapons in this case": Associated Press, October 7, 2004.

93   "$1.8": Independent Inquiry Committee estimation into the U.N. Oil for Food program, September 7, 2005.

94   "valuable work that so many people do at the United Nations": Annan response to questions posed by author, May 3, 2005.

95   "twenty-eight of them": U.N. Security Council membership lists, 1994–2003.

96   "suppliers of humanitarian items": congressional hearing, House Subcommittee on National Security, Emerging Threats, and International Relations, October 5, 2004.

97   "military purposes": ibid.

97   "or territorial integrity of Iraq": U.N. Security Council resolution 986, April 14, 1995.

97   "outside the control of the U.N.": *CIA Iraq Survey Group Report*, September 30, 2004.

97   "I seen my opportunities and I took 'em": William L. Riordon, "A Series of Very Plain Talks on Very Practical Politics," *Plunkitt of Tammany Hall* (New York: Signey Classic New American Library, 1963).

98   "five hundred thousand children": UNICEF media release, March 2003.

98   "distributed properly": "Saddam 10 Years Later," U.S. Department of State, January 21, 2001.

98   "the Iraqi people are starving": ibid.

99   "amplified that impact": *CIA Iraq Survey Group Final Report*, September 30, 2004.

99   "throng of professional mourners": ibid.

100   "this propaganda war": Michael Soussan, testimony, House International Relations Committee, April 22, 2004.

100   "world opinion about who is to blame": (London) *Times*, March 5, 2002.

100   "five thousand children dying each month": President Bill Clinton, Pacifica radio, November 14, 2000.

101   "killed by sanctions": Campaign against Iraq Sanctions report, March 1999, scn.org.

101   "phone system was modernized": U.N. Office of Iraq Program report, November 21, 2003.

101   "sense of complacency": Annan statement to Security Council, September 2001.

102   "given for free": U.N. news conference, October 19, 2000.

102   "take back those words": Madeleine Albright, *Madam Secretary: A Memoir* (New York: Hyperion, 2003), p. 275.

103   "We have provided food": CNN, February 18, 1998.

103   "all kinds of people around the world": author interview with Charles Hill, April 2005.

103   "lock in the Security Council": *Iraq Survey Group Final Report*, September 30, 2004.

104   "as it wanted": Security Council resolution 1284, December 17, 1999.

105   "driving everybody crazy": author interview with Charles Hill, April 2005.

105   "squandering Iraqi money": Benon Sevan statement to Security Council, July 12, 2001.

105   "assigned two": U.S. Government Accounting Office report on Oil for Food, April 7, 2004.

106   "responsibility and accountability": testimony before House Subcommittee on National Security, Emerging Threats, and International Relations, April 21, 2004.

106   "on the ground": U.N. Foundation Oil for Food facts, UNFoundation.org.

106   "were compromised": author interview with Entifadh Qanbar, March 2005.

107   "collaborate with the Mukhabarat": The Middle East Media Research Institute, March 9, 2005. Testimony by Nimrod Raphacli, before the House International Relations Committee.

107   "bad things could happen": Independent Inquiry Committee into the United Nations Oil for Food Program, September 7, 2005.

108   "old style mafia management": Rehan Mullick testimony, House International Relations Subcommittee on Permanent Investigation, March 17, 2005, and author's interview with Mullick, March 17, 2005.

108   "Security Council documents": House Subcommittee on National Security, Emerging Threats, and International Relations, April 12, 2005.

109   "to help those people": House International Relations Subcommittee on Permanent Investigations hearing, March 17, 2005.

109   "of the Security Council": Rolf Ekeus, interview with Yale University United Nations Oral History Project, April 28, 2000.

109   "operating in Iraq": author interview with Hans Blix, May 2003.

110   "how much the Iraqis knew": Yale University United Nations Oral History Project, April 28, 2000.

110   "related development": *CIA Iraq Survey Group Final Report*, September 30, 2004.

110   "Dr. Blix": Office of the Spokesman for the U.N. Secretary-General.

Chapter 6: Allies or All Lies?

113   "hands against our soldiers": House Subcommittee on National Security, Emerging Threats, and International Relations, October 5, 2004.

113   "in denied revenue": *FrontPage Magazine*, April 10, 2003.

113   "at least $1.1 billion": Fox News, April 27, 2003.

113   "$125 billion total": CIA, *World Fact Book*, August 2007.

113   "neighboring Arab countries": "Club de Paris: Iraq List of Debt Treatments," Parisclub.org.

113   "6 percent each": CIA, *World Fact Book*.

114   "over $2.6 billion": Independent inquiry committee into the Oil for Food program, interim report, February 3, 2005.

114   "coalition of the venal": House Subcommittee on National Security, Emerging Threats, and International Relations, October 5, 2004.

114   "the U.N. is supporting": ibid.

115   "I totally agree, sir": ibid.

115   "strategic purchasing": author interview with a U.N. diplomatic source.

115   "commercial and political interests": author interview.

116   "aligned against us": author interview with John Loftus, July 2005.

116   "same points as the French": U.S. Department of State declassified cables from the U.S. U.N. mission to the Secretary of State, Washington, D.C., no date.

116   "for their support": House International Relations Committee, February 9, 2005.

116   "Saddam Bribery System": Senate Permanent Subcommittee on Investigations, interview and report, May 17, 2005.

116   "around the world": ibid.

117   "compensation for support": ibid.

117   "buying influence": ibid.

117   "France, and China": ibid.

117   "stop payment": U.S. Department of State, declassified cables from the U.S. Mission to the United Nations to Secretary of State, Washington, D.C., no date.

117   "U.N. Official Number 1": U.S. Department of Justice, Southern District of New York indictments, April 14, 2005.

117   "tarnish its work.": *Financial Times*, letter to the editor, 2005.

118   "answer is that is nobody": testimony, Senate Permanent Subcommittee on Investigations, May 17, 2005.

119   "buy influence": Senate Permanent Subcommittee on Investigations, *Oil for Food Report*, May 12, 2005.

120   "within the Security Council": CIA *Iraq Survey Group Final Report*, March 2005.

120   "will be solved very soon": Senate Permanent Subcommittee on Investigations, *Oil for Food Report*, May 12, 2005.

120   "another one million as 'Megawatti' ": *The Guardian*, May 29, 2005.

121   "from Saddam": *U.S.A. v. Samir A. Vincent*, January 18, 2005.

121   "was a United Nations official": ibid.

122   "wring the towel dry": U.S. Attorney David Kelley, news conference, January 18, 2005.

123   "in other United Nations programs": Independent Inquiry Committee into the United Nations Oil for Food Program, September 7, 2005.

123   "United Nations Federal Credit Union at the New York headquarters": ibid.

124   "before the war": France media statement, Oil for Food InfoFrance, December 8, 2004.

124   "as a whole": Foreign French Ministry statement, May 17, 2005.

124   "transparent investigation": Chinese Foreign Ministry, Xinhua News Agency, statement, December 7, 2004.

125   "national interest": author interview with unnamed U.S. Department of State source.

Chapter 7: The French Connection

127   "carcasses of dictatorships": author interview with John Loftus, July 2005.

128   "why we are against the war": statement by Jean-David Levitte, October 7, 2004.

129   "before the war is even less clear": Steve Coll, *Washington Post*, November 3, 2003.

129   "actively with the United Nations": statement by Levitte, Embassy of France, November 10, 2003.

130   "dealing with France": internal Iraqi documents of Iraqi intelligence source released by House Committee on Energy and Commerce, June 21, 2005.

130   "Iraqi and Arab issues": ibid.

130   "Vladimir Putin": ibid.

130   "Chirac's election campaign": ibid.

130   "too offensive": BBC, January 23, 2003.

131   "lift sanctions": internal Iraqi documents released by House Committee on Energy and Commerce, June 21, 2005.

131   "scam unfold": Representative Joe Barton, statement, May 16, 2005.

132   "every break in the book": author interview with a congressional source.

133   "to a higher level": internal Iraqi documents released by House Committee on Energy and Commerce, June 21, 2005.

133   "given priority": *Jerusalem Post*, December 1996.

134   "but not me": Chirac interview, *CBS News*, March 19, 2003.

134   "played a role": Yale University United Nations Oral History Project.

135   " 'back you with support,' and they did": ibid.

135   "of U.N. weapons inspectors": Peter Van Walsum, "U.N. Security Council: From the Cold War to the 21st Century," Carnegie Council Panel Discussion, New York: Merrill House.

136   "stop threatening American pilots": U.S. Department of State briefing, April 7, 2000.

136   "avoiding U.N. sanctions": *CIA Iraq Survey Group Final Report*, March 2005.

137   "didn't want to come out": ibid.

137   "after 1993": France Oil for Food statement, 2005.

139   "national economic objectives": Schweich testimony, House Committee on Energy and Commerce, April 12, 2005.

139   "with U.N. resolutions": French presidential statement, July 10, 2001.

139   "because of oil": Levitte, embassy of France statement, May 22, 2003.

140   "misleading the public": Levitte, embassy of France statement, May 15, 2003.

140   "and ally of the U.S.": Levitte, embassy of France statement, April 7, 2004.

140   "Frankly, I don't know": *Los Angeles Times*, April 7, 2004.

141   "regime and its cronies": Ambassador Cunningham Security Council minutes, of debate on Security Council Resolution 1284, U.S. Nations Mission.

141   "elite and military": ibid.

141   "humanitarian situation in Iraq": Security Council minutes, U.S. Department of State cables released by House Committee on Energy and Commerce, June 21, 2005.

141   "illicit oil charges": ibid.

142   "numerous humanitarian concerns": ibid.

142   "deal with the issue": Security Council minutes, U.S. Department of State report, March 17, 2000.

142   "The committee decided to keep the issue of oil smuggling under review.": ibid.

143   "July 13, 2000, meeting of the 661 Committee.": Ambassador Patrick F. Kennedy, congressional testimony, House Subcommittee on National Security, Emerging Threats, and International Relations, October 5, 2004.

143   "with the Russians": Rolf Ekeus interview, Yale University United Nations Oral History Project, April 18, 2001.

143   "very little else": Richard Perle, interview with Tony Snow, transcript, *Fox News Sunday*, January 26, 2003.

144   "on a pig and danced it out there": author interview with a diplomatic source.

144   "the market and squeeze the United States": author interview with diplomatic source.

144   "may be the answer why": congressional hearing, Subcommittee on National Security, Emerging Threats, and International Relations, October 5, 2004.

Chapter 8: The Russians Are Coming

146   "The Russian vote was for sale": author interview with a U.N. diplomatic source.

146   "which was the money": ibid.

147   "the financial arrangements": ibid.

147   "you pay to play": ibid.

147   "get this money back": Sergey Lavrov interview, Yale University United Nations Oral History Project, April 18, 2001.

147   "$8 billion in debt": Robyn Dixon, *Los Angeles Times*, March 14, 2003.

147   "to sustain his regime": *CIA Iraq Survey Group Final Report*, March 2005.

147   "crimes against the international community": testimony, House International Relations Committee, November 18, 2004.

148   "removal of sanctions": *CIA Iraq Survey Group Final Report*, March 2005.

148   "on the Security Council": Scott Peterson, *Christian Science Monitor*, August 20, 2002.

149   "and diplomatic support": Peter Barker, *Washington Post*, August 17, 2002.

149   "relations between the two countries": Naji Sabri, BBC, August 17, 2002.

149   "payments would be untraceable": *CIA Iraq Survey Group Final Report*, March 2005.

149   "$4 million in cash": U.S. Department of Treasury, *Terrorist Financing and Financial Crimes Report*.

149   "one month into the war": *CIA Iraq Survey Group Final Report*, March 2005.

150   "for immediate sale": ibid.

150   "the cover of Oil for Food contacts": ibid.

150   "selling such a weapon to Iraq": Robert Little, *Baltimore Sun*, April 10, 2003.

150   "and assorted agricultural equipment": *CIA Iraq Survey Group Final Report*, March 2005.

151   "impossible for us at the U.N.": author interview with a U.S. diplomatic source.

151   "to get their votes": ibid.

151   "There was substantial proof ": congressional testimony, Subcommittee on National Security, Emerging Threats, and International Relations, April 12, 2005.

152   "We have informed the U.N. Secretary-General of this": *Iraq Watch*, Iraqwatch.org, November 14, 2000.

152   "Oil for Food Program": *CIA Iraq Survey Group Final Report*, March 2005.

152   "within the Oil for Food deal": *People's Daily* (Bejing), November 26, 2001.

152   "looking after itself ": Justin Blum and Colum Lynch, *Washington Post*, May 16, 2005.

153   "most odious and fantastic personalities of our time": congressional testimony, House International Relations Committee, November 17, 2004.

153   "with radioactive waste": ibid.

153   "during Desert Storm": Indiana University, CS.Indiana.Edu, 1996.

153   "in Iraqi oil transactions": NewsfromRussia.com, May 19, 2005.

153   "not a drop": BBC, May 16, 2005.

154   "did receive the oil allocations": Permanent Senate Permanent Subcommittee on Investigations report, May 12, 2005.

154   "the whole point": ibid.

154   "the Iraqi embassy": ibid.

154   "son of Russian ambassador in Baghdad": oil allocation list, House Committee on International Affairs, September 2004.

154   "of the Russian Parliament (Duma) supported Iraq's position": *CIA Iraq Survey Group Final Report*, March 2005.

155   "the Russians were looking for that": author interview with a U.N. diplomatic source.

155   "and slice the pie!": author interview with a U.N. diplomatic source.

Chapter 9: Chinese Takeout

156   "contracts in Iraq": Security Council statement, June 26, 2001.

157   "as France and Russia": author interview with John Loftus, July 2005.

157   "to the Iraqi regime": *CIA Iraq Survey Group Final Report*, March 2005.

158   "Security Council resolutions on sanctions": Chinese Embassy statement, Associated Press, November 26, 2002.

158   "good track record in the United Nations": embassy of the People's Republic of China statement, June 3, 2001.

158   "trade cooperation with Iraq": *Iraq Watch*, November 28, 2000.

158 "strengthen its cooperation with the U.N.": *CIA Iraq Survey Group Final Report*, March 2005.

159 "China was the second largest": CIA, *World Fact Book*.

159 "bring America down one notch": author interview with a U.N. diplomatic source.

159 "judge the matter on its own merits": People's Republic of China Embassy statement, March 6, 2003.

160 "to help Iraq": *Wall Street Journal*, November 9, 2004.

160 "Annan: No comment.": response to questions from author to Secretary-General Kofi Annan, May 3, 2005.

Chapter 10: U.N.-Civil Servant

162 "a good boss who worked incredibly hard": author interview with a U.N. source, April 2004.

162 "to being killed": author discussion with Benon Sevan, September 2003.

163 "Mr. Sivan—U.N.": *Al-Mada* newspaper January 25, 2004.

163 "spelled right!": author discussion with a U.N. source, January 2004.

163 "[Mr. Armando Carlos]": Senate Permanent Subcommittee on Investigations report, February 15, 2005.

164 "politically favorable to Iraq": United Nations Independent Inquiry Committee report.

164 "man of influence": ibid.

164 "solicited an oil voucher": ibid.

164 "to help a friend": ibid.

165 "or employees there": ibid.

165 "never made recommendations to anybody": ibid.

165 "far too long": Security Council minutes. Benon Sevan, United Nations Independent Inquiry Committee report, February 9, 2005, p. 133.

165 "contracts put on hold": U.N. Security Council, September 4, 1998.

166 "1.8 million": Independent Inquiry Committee report into the United Nations Oil for Food program.

166 "complained": ibid.

167 "it hurts the Iraqi people": Benon Sevan to the Security Council, August 26, 1999.

167 "at this very difficult period": Benon Sevan to Security Council, September 21, 2000.

168 "according to U.N. investigators": Independent Inquiry Committee report into United Nations Oil for Food program.

168 "satanic lackeys": Iraqwatch.org via Iraqi News Agency, November 16, 2002.

168   "international unanimity": ibid.

168   "$1,500,310": Independent Inquiry Committee report into United Nations Oil for Food program.

169   "I will talk to the panel, not to you!": Fox News transcript, May 10, 2004.

169   "I might have": Independent Inquiry Committee report interview with Benon Sevan, issued February 3, 2005.

169   "at that meeting": ibid.

169   "the organization": Judith Miller and Warren Hoge, *The New York Times,* June 2, 2004.

169   "defamation": author-viewed e-mail to Sevan friend.

169   "blown up": ibid.

170   "'formal' interview": Independent Inquiry Committee report into United Nations Oil for Food program.

171   "Mr. Sevan's written request": ibid.

171   "solicited and received": ibid.

171   "conflict of interest": ibid.

171   "ethically improper": ibid.

171   "to the Committee": ibid.

171   "criminal prosecution can proceed": Senator Norm Coleman statement, media release, February 3, 2005.

172   "Zeytountsian.": Sevan, U.N. financial disclosure form, Independent Inquiry Committee report into United Nations Oil for Food program.

172   "cash income": ibid.

172   "purchased by Mr. Sevan": ibid.

173   "in New York": ibid.

173   "$160,000": ibid.

173   "guided their actions": Senator Norm Coleman statement, Senate Permanent Subcommittee on Investigations, February 15, 2004.

173   "never took a penny": Eric Lewis media statement, February 7, 2005.

174   "familiar with the finances": ibid.

174   "international fraud cases": Lewis biography from the law firm Baach, Robinson & Lewis, PLLC.

174   "dates of the Sevans' cash deposits": Independent Inquiry Committee into the United Nations Oil for Food program, September 7, 2005.

174   "Optima credit card": ibid.

174   "elevator shaft and died": U.N. discussion between author and a U.N. diplomatic source.

175   "in this direction": Representative Henry Hyde, chairman, House International Relations Committee statement, February 4, 2005.

176   "about Mr. Sevan": U.N. statement by Mark Malloch Brown, February 3, 2005.

177   "anybody buys that": Burton statement, House International Relations Committee hearings, May 19, 2005.

177   "than the best, and we clearly aren't": ibid.

177   "small, sad part": Malloch Brown media statement, February 4, 2005.

178   "insult to injury": Colum Lynch, *Washington Post*, March 28, 2005.

178   "exceptional": Eckhard, U.N. media statement, March 22, 2005.

178   "we bobbed": Malloch Brown media statement, March 29, 2005.

179   "eroded the program": Richard Williamson testimony, House International Relations Committee, March 17, 2005.

179   "mandate established by the Security Council": Lewis media statement, February 7, 2005.

Chapter 11: $400,000 in a Desk Drawer

180   "no smoking gun": Paul Volcker interview with Judith Miller, *New York Times*, January 19, 2005.

181   "adequate oversight": Senator Norm Coleman media statement, January 10, 2005.

181   "to release these documents": Annan media statement, January 10, 2005.

182   "audited to death": Fred Eckhard media statement, January 10, 2005.

185   "spent its money in Iraq": fifty-eight internal U.N. audits released through the Independent Inquiry Committee Investigation of the Oil for Food Program, January 9, 2005.

185   "as much as 35 percent": U.S. Department of Defense Contract Audit Agency report, April 7, 2004.

185   "were never examined": Shays media statement, January 10, 2005.

185   "the Iraqi people": U.S. Department of Defense Contract Audit Agency report, April 7, 2004.

186   "strictest administrative standards": Sevan statement, Office of Oil for Food Program, May 31, 2004.

Chapter 12: How the U.N. Funds Terrorism

188   "his span of knowledge": interview with Miri Avitan, Jerusalem, April 2005.

190   "smiling . . . Yasser Arafat": House International Relations Committee report, March 3, 2005.

190   "January 22, 2002": Israeli Defense Forces report on Palestinian Terrorism, February 25, 2004.

191   "her son and so many others": interview by Aaron Klein with Shoshi Cohen, April 2004.

192 "excluding 9/11": U.S. Department of State, Patterns of Global Terrorism report, April 2004.

192 "fourteen-year-old schoolgirls": Terror Victims Association, Eretz Yisroelorg, April 27, 1997.

193 "April 2002": Israeli Ministry of Foreign Affairs, Israeli Defense Forces Military Intelligence report, September 2002.

193 "March 2004": statement of Lisa Klinghoffer, ADL, March 10, 2004.

193 "Saddam Hussein regime": Israeli Foreign Ministry, September, 2002.

194 "children without mercy": Israeli Defense Force, Palestinian Support for Iraq and Saddam Hussein report, September 2003.

195 "instead of $10,000": Deroy Murdock, *Hussein and Terror.com: Saddam Hussein's Philanthropy of Terror*. Palo Alto, CA: Hoover Institution, Stanford University Press, September 22, 2004.

195 "not in secret": Aziz interview with MBC network September 14, 2002.

196 "proceeds helped accomplish": Israeli Foreign Ministry report, September 2002.

196 "suffering Iraqi people": Israeli Defense Force report, "Iraq's Involvement in Palestinian Terrorist Activity against Israel," January 2003.

196 "was murdered": Con Coughlin, *The* (London) *Daily Telegraph*, August 25, 2002.

197 "who injured me": interview with Aaron Klein, *World News Daily*, April 2004.

197 "Hussein Grant": Israeli Defense Force report, April 2004.

198 "the aggression against Iraq": International Communist Seminar agenda, May 2, 1999.

198 "It's all about money": author interview with Charles Viccia, June 2004.

199 "six different targets": *Ballistic, Cruise Missile and Missile Defense Systems*, Center for Nonproliferation Studies report, September 2005, Cns.Miss.Edu. analysis of s-300pmu.

200 "in Washington, D.C.": U.S. Department of the Treasury, Office of Public Affairs, Terrorist Financing and Financial Crimes report, April 4, 2004.

200 "$43.5 million": ibid.

200 "Al Wasel and Babel General Trading Company": ibid.

200 "real owners of the company": U.N. *List of Entities Established Pursuant to Security Council Resolution 1483 (2003)*, report, June 2, 2004.

202 "underwrite their tyranny,": Zarate statement, U.S. Department of the Treasury, April 15, 2004.

202 "most wanted Iraqis": Fox News, September 23, 2004.

203 "Oil for Food business altogether": Claudia Rosett, Foundation for the Defense Democracies, April 28, 2004.

203 "to Hussein": congressional testimony, House International Relations Committee, November 17, 2004.
204 "outside of Iraq": testimony of Juan Carlos Zarate, Senate Permanent Subcommittee on Investigations, November 15, 2004.

Chapter 13: Humanitarian Error

207 "from the Americas": U.N. Department of Public Information Statement.
207 "Sierra Leone": statement by Edward Mortimer, U.N. Director of Communications, to author, March 2005.
208 "with HIV/AIDS": Senate Permanent Subcommittee on Investigations report, November 15, 2004.
208 "quipped Senator Coleman": Senate Permanent Subcommitte on Investigations hearing, November 12, 2004.
209 "wasn't fit for humans": Hankes-Drielsma, congressional testimony, House Subcommittee on National Security, Emerging Threats and International Relations, April 21, 2004.
209 "without fear or favor": Baach, Robinson & Lewis, statement, August 4, 2005.
209 "to that contracted": Benon Sevan statement to U.N. Security Council, November 19, 2002.
210 "December 1998": Cotecna media release.
211 "involved in mine": Annan statement, November 29, 2004, at U.N. Headquarters.
211 "Cotecna's owners": Independent Inquiry Committee Interim Report, March 29, 2005.
211 "Cotecna was bidding": ibid.
211 "hidden payments": Cotecna response, March 30, 2005.
212 "a great relief": Annan statement to the media, March 29, 2005.
212 "did not exonerate Kofi Anan": Paul Volcker statement to author, Fox News, April 26, 2005.
212 "I would not have used that word.": ibid.
212 "resigned in protest": Benny Avni, New York Sun, April 22, 2005.
212 "back up the assertion": Independent Inquiry Committee Interim Report, March 29, 2005.
212 "being 'manipulated' ": Benny Avni, New York Sun, April 13, 2005.
212 "to pressure them": ibid.
213 "the Hilton hotel": Independent Inquiry Committee Second Interim report, March 29, 2005.
213 "they discussed": ibid.
213 "Secretary-General's residence": ibid.

213   "U.N. Deal": Andrew Alderson, *Sunday Telegraph*, January 24, 1999.
213   "with the contract": Independent Inquiry Committee Second Interim Report, March 29, 2005.
214   "my dear chap": Annan news conference, U.N. headquarters, September 12, 2005.
215   "but only 986": ibid.
215   "quality of the goods": Vernon Kulyk testimony, Senate Permanent Subcommittee on Investigations, February 15, 2005.
216   "in the bar": Arthur Ventham, testimony, Senate Permanent Subcommittee on Investigations, February 15, 2005.
217   "for it is not given": Patriotic Union of Kurdistan letter, House International Relations Committee, April 28, 2004.
217   "overruled": Howar Ziad letter, ibid.
218   "catastrophic consequences": Yadger Heshmet letter, September 3, 2001.
218   "the average Iraqi": Benon Sevan statement to Security Council, United Nations, November 19, 2003.
218   "bold-faced lies": Michael Soussan testimony, House International Relations Committee, April 28, 2004.
219   "Iraqi information ministry": U.N.org Office of Iraq Program, U.N.org\depts\up.
219   "750,000 television sets": ibid.
221   "a peace pipe, yes": Annan interview, United Nations Oral History Project, Yale University, May 10, 2000.
222   "He's a man I can do business with": Annan media statement, February 24, 1998.

Chapter 14: More Money, Please

224   "want it to do": Malloch Brown testimony, House International Relations Committee, May 19, 2005.
225   "$3.7 billion": U.N.org About U.N.
225   "specifically the Security Council": UNUSA.org
226   "U.N.'s operating budget": U.N.org
228   "Enlarger Fiefdom": author interview with Representative Thaddeus McCotter, July 2005.
228   "occurring at the U.N.": Thaddeus McCotter testimony, House International Relations Committee, May 19, 2005.
228   "information and communications": U.N. Millennium Development Goals, U.N.org Millenniumgoals/background.
230   "auditing, monitoring, and evaluation": American Interests and U.N. Reform: Tasks Force on the United Nations, June 15, 2005.

231 "*The New York Times* reported": Warren Hoge, *New York Times*, January 2, 2005.

232 "fools and liars": Jeffrey Sachs, Project Syndicate Columns, Project-Syndicate.org.

232 "in Maine": Benny Avni, *New York Sun*, May 5, 2005.

233 "grand bargain": Malloch Brown testimony, House International Relations Committee, May 19, 2005.

233 "money and power grab": author interview with Melanie Morgan, June 2005.

234 "with the American people": author interview with Howard Kaloogian, July 2005.

234 "contribute more toward them?": author interview with Representative Thaddeus McCotter, July 2005.

235 "check writing exercise": Andrew Natsios U.N. media statement, May 27, 2005.

235 "of any nation": author interview with Dr. Carol Adelman, July 2005.

235 "nation of all": Brad Knickerbocker, *Christian Science Monitor*, December 29, 1999.

235 "stingy": Jan Egeland comment to media, U.N. headquarters, December 27, 2004.

236 "for all people": Malloch Brown testimony, House International Relations Committee, May 19, 2005.

236 "of human rights": Tariq Aziz comments, U.N. Millennium Declaration Summit, September 4, 2002.

236 "out to carry": Tom Lantos testimony, House International Relations Committee, March 15, 2005.

237 "lacking is the will": Annan speech, U.N., September 6, 2000.

237 "quite the opposite": author interview with Representative Thaddeus McCotter, July 2005.

237 "U.N. would actually do that": author interview with Howard Kaloogian, July 2005.

238 "pours more money into Africa": author interview with Carol Adelman, July 2005.

238 "failed the poor": David Brooks, *The New York Times*, June 28, 2005.

238 "Clinton": U.S. Mission to the United Nations, September 8, 2005.

239 "neediest segment of the world population": author interview with William Orme, July 2005.

239 "in development funds": U.N.org UNDP report.

239 " 'to the developing world": author interview with Carol Adelman, July 2005.

239 "we are skeptical of government": author interview with a U.N. diplomatic source.

240 "held against us?": author interview with Representative Thaddeus McCotter, July 2005.

240 "will receive billions of dollars": Andrew Natsios media statement at U.N., May 27, 2005.

240 "for their own development": U.N.org Millennium Goals report.

241 "is all wrong": author interview with Howard Kaloogian, July 2005.

241 "that runs it": Thaddeus McCotter congressional testimony, House International Relations Committee, March 15, 2005.

241 "of the developing countries": author interview with Carol Adelman, July 2005.

242 "poverty by half ": author interview with Ann-Louise Colgan, July 2005.

243 "lawn furniture": Madeleine Albright address, Yale University, *Yale Daily News*, April 17, 1996.

244 "surrender of sovereignty": Edwin Meese article, HumanEventson line.com, April 25, 2005.

245 "use of and access": Frank Gaffney, Jr., congressional testimony, House International Relations Committee, May 12, 2004.

245 "freedoms and oversight": William H. Taft testimony, Senate Committee on Foreign Relations, October 21, 2003.

246 "participating states": HeritageFoundation.com.

246 "intelligence activities": Michael Mullen testimony, Senate Committee on Foreign Relations, October 21, 2003.

INDEX